Praise for *When We Walk By*

"A compelling story of rediscovering our own humanity—and a road-map for how we can make large-scale changes that improve everyone's way of life. Read this book to understand how being connected can save us all."

—ANDREW YANG, entrepreneur and former 2020 presidential candidate

"Forgotten humanity and failed systems are the headlines. People experiencing homelessness are humans like you and me, deserving of the same respect and dignity. By focusing on ways to reduce stigma and to repair flawed systems, the authors conclude with a call to action that begins with each of us looking inward. It's a must-read!"

—ELLEN BASSUK, MD, founder of C4 Innovations and the National Center on Family Homelessness and associate professor of psychiatry at Harvard Medical School

"Homelessness makes people sick. Solutions must address resource and relational needs, not just medical ones. The authors' work is a master-class in meeting folks where they are, listening first, and designing and delivering services informed by the experiences of our unhoused neighbors."

—DR. MICHAEL K. HOLE, professor, entrepreneur, and "street doctor" serving families experiencing homelessness as an assistant professor of pediatrics in the Department of Population Health at Dell Medical School and the Department of Public Policy at the LBJ School of Public Affairs, University of Texas at Austin

"Kevin F. Adler walks with our homeless neighbors, never by them, and his heart is as big as the sky. He's devoted his life to helping those among us who are most in need by connecting, nurturing, caring, and putting his words into action with innovative programs like Miracle Messages. Listen to this man's wisdom. We are all the better for it."

—KEVIN FAGAN, *San Francisco Chronicle* staff writer

"This heart-opening book will expand your empathy and understanding of this human rights crisis right in our own backyard and show you how to help your unhoused neighbors—and how they may be able to help you."

—JUSTIN BALDONI, actor and filmmaker

"I am often asked 'what can I do to help?' by people who are stably housed. I will now point them to this book as a great starting point. Kevin writes that our unhoused neighbors are people to love, not problems to solve. If we all start from this place of understanding, we can make much faster progress reducing the unnecessary suffering of so many of our unhoused brothers and sisters."

—MARK DONOVAN, founder of Denver Basic Income Project

"This book proves that there are wonderful, smart people all around wanting to help provide solutions, resources, and tools to help end homelessness. If we think more outside the box and lead with humanity, we can end homelessness within this generation. I strongly believe that."

—JENNIFER SPEIGHT, actor and voice-over artist with years of lived experience of homelessness

"*When We Walk By* reminds us of our shared humanity, our shared needs, and how we should promote a political economy of sharing, especially with our neighbors who have little or nothing. Read this, heed the call. No more just walking by!"

—DENNIS CULHANE, Dana and Andrew Stone Professor of Social Policy at the School of Social Policy & Practice, University of Pennsylvania

"I will always be grateful to Miracle Friends. At first, I was thankful to have Jen's company and friendship. She helped strengthen me mentally and emotionally so that I was able to feel hopeful again. Then the kindness and financial support from the Miracle Money program allowed me to take action and turn my hopes into reality."

—RAY, person who formerly experienced homelessness

"In a book that explores our national failures and points to common-sense fixes, the authors challenge us to see the humanity of our neighbors and care more deeply about the societal failures that lead to too many people ending up on the streets when alternative, safer options exist. This book should guide policymakers, and quickly, as they seek a cure to what ails our nation."

—TONY MESSENGER, Pulitzer Prize–winning journalist and author of *Profit and Punishment*

"*When We Walk By* exposes the truth about the level of compassion fade in our societies today. Adler and Burnes lay bare a stellar opportunity for the reader to connect to those who are abandoned and displaced on our streets. They illuminate a system broken beyond repair and provide the hope that is required for all of us to shift gears, from the ground up, to solve one of the most distressing problems of our times . . . if only we cared. A remarkable read."

—HEATHER HAY, senior consultant at Foundations for Social Change, creators of the New Leaf Project

"Through eye-opening analysis, remarkable stories, and practical and innovative solutions, this book offers citizens and their elected officials alike a clear window into understanding homelessness as one of the most intersectional issues of our time, and then doing something about it. Readers of this book will no longer 'walk by' feeling helpless."

—MICHAEL D. TUBBS, youngest mayor of any major city in American history (Stockton, California), special advisor for economic mobility for California Governor Gavin Newsom, author of *The Deeper the Roots*, and founder of Mayors for a Guaranteed Income

"The authors of *When We Walk By* argue that despite a growing visible homelessness crisis in the United States, individuals experiencing homelessness are often treated as invisible. Their insightful analysis of what's needed to address this crisis begins with reminding us that social connection is a key element of human survival that often gets overlooked day to day. This book offers a fresh, integrated perspective about the importance of a human response to a complex social problem."

—BENJAMIN HENWOOD, PhD, LCSW, professor at the USC Suzanne Dworak-Peck School of Social Work and coauthor of *Housing First*

"An up-close and personal look at how and why we discriminate against those without stable housing through the concept of relational poverty. . . . Unforgettable personal stories from our homeless neighbors drive home the consequences when we choose to 'walk by.' However, if we push back against misinformation and fight for housing as a human right, we'll embrace the truth that homelessness is solvable and that no one should have to experience it alone."

—ELIZABETH SOFTKY, person who formerly experienced homelessness and Lived Experience Advocate for Miracle Messages

"The homelessness crisis is a symptom of structural inequalities rooted in dehumanization. The authors brilliantly examine our inequitable systems through the lens of healing our humanity and solving the problem at its root. A must-read for us all!"

—TRISTIA BAUMAN, senior attorney at The National Homelessness Law Center

"Infused with generations of academic research and lifetimes of lived experience, the book offers a passionate take on a critical social issue that is uniquely human, heartbreaking, redeeming and, ultimately, a call to action to solve homelessness with clear steps for individuals and policymakers alike."

—PAUL MUNIZ, Senior Vice President of Community Engagement at the Family Resource Network

"Unlike many writers on the topic, Adler and Burnes turn their insightful lens on the 'housed,' challenging us to see the humanity of 'the unhoused.' Yes, they argue, we must change the systems that drive homelessness—including the lack of affordable housing, health care, living-wage jobs, and an unfair criminal legal system. But we must also affirm the humanity of people experiencing homelessness—and, in doing so, our own."

—MARIA FOSCARINIS, former president and CEO of
the National Homelessness Law Center

"Having dealt with similar issues for a family member, I have seen first-hand the individualized and systemic challenges Kevin F. Adler and his coauthors describe that face those experiencing homelessness. For all those attempting to directly address these challenges and for all concerned about the hundreds of thousands of Americans who are unhoused, this book is highly moving and profoundly enlightening."

—DR. GLORIA DUFFY, president of the Commonwealth
Club of California, member of the Congressional
Commission on the Strategic Posture of the United
States, former chair of the Civilian R&D Foundation/
US National Science Foundation, and former US deputy
assistant secretary of defense

When We Walk By

When We Walk By

FORGOTTEN HUMANITY,

BROKEN SYSTEMS, AND THE ROLE

WE CAN EACH PLAY IN ENDING

HOMELESSNESS IN AMERICA

Kevin F. Adler and Donald W. Burnes

WITH AMANDA BANH AND ANDRIJANA BILBIJA

North Atlantic Books

Traditional land of the Ohlone people

Berkeley, California

Published by
North Atlantic Books
Berkeley, California
Traditional land of the Ohlone people

Cover photo © J. Anthony via Stocksy
Cover design by Amanda Weiss
Book design by Happenstance Type-O-Rama

Printed in Canada

When We Walk By: Forgotten Humanity, Broken Systems, and the Role We Can Each Play in Ending Homelessness in America is sponsored and published by North Atlantic Books, an educational nonprofit based in Berkeley, CA (traditional land of the Ohlone people), that collaborates with partners to develop cross-cultural perspectives; nurture holistic views of art, science, the humanities, and healing; and seed personal and global transformation by publishing work on the relationship of body, spirit, and nature.

North Atlantic Books's publications are distributed to the US trade and internationally by Penguin Random House Publisher Services. For further information, visit our website at www.northatlanticbooks.com.

Library of Congress Cataloging-in-Publication Data
Names: Adler, Kevin F., author. | Burnes, Donald W., author.
Title: When we walk by : forgotten humanity, broken systems, and the role we can each play in ending homelessness in America / Kevin F. Adler and Donald W. Burnes, with Amanda Banh and Andrijana Bilbija.
Description: Berkeley, California : North Atlantic Books, [2023] | Includes bibliographical references and index. | Summary: "A guide to understanding housing instability, supporting our unhoused neighbors, and reclaiming our humanity"-- Provided by publisher.
Identifiers: LCCN 2023017244 (print) | LCCN 2023017245 (ebook) | ISBN 9781623178840 (trade paperback) | ISBN 9781623178857 (ebook)
Subjects: LCSH: Homelessness--United States. | Housing policy--United States.
Classification: LCC HV4505 .A355 2023 (print) | LCC HV4505 (ebook) | DDC 362.5/92--dc23/eng/20230627
LC record available at https://lccn.loc.gov/2023017244
LC ebook record available at https://lccn.loc.gov/2023017245

1 2 3 4 5 6 7 8 9 MARQUIS 27 26 25 24 23

This book includes recycled material and material from well-managed forests. North Atlantic Books is committed to the protection of our environment. We print on recycled paper whenever possible and partner with printers who strive to use environmentally responsible practices.

Dedicated to Mark Steven Adler, Kevin's beloved uncle, who managed to send a birthday card nearly every year of his 30-plus years living on and off the streets in Santa Cruz, California.

This book was published within a week of November 1, 2023, on what would have been his 70th birthday. It is for you, Mark, and for the 582,462 other uncles, aunts, mothers, fathers, sisters, brothers, sons, daughters, friends, and neighbors experiencing homelessness each night in the United States.

May we each take time to hear your stories and act, before it's too late.

Contents

Preface

If we have no peace, it is because we have forgotten that we belong to each other—that man, that woman, that child is my brother or my sister.

—MOTHER TERESA

EVERYONE IS SOMEONE'S SOMEBODY. And Mark was my uncle: the most family-oriented member of my extended family, the uncle who shared my love of super burritos, was easy to talk to, remembered every birthday, and always sent a card. The year before he died, Mark mailed me an eagle bandana for my birthday along with his go-to staple of a Hallmark card for a "beloved nephew," always with just his first name carefully added in block letters.

Mark also suffered from schizophrenia and lived on-and-off the streets for over 30 years, bouncing between transitional housing, shelters, and the streets of Santa Cruz, California. He would disappear for months at a time, only to reemerge in the form of a collect call from a payphone. If I happened to pick up the call, he would ask me how my brother and I were doing, and then ask to speak to my dad, usually followed by a request for 20 or 50 dollars. If we were in touch during the holidays, Mark would come over for Thanksgiving or Christmas dinner as the guest of honor. Toward the end of the meal, bellies full and satisfied, we would all talk about our desire to spend more time together as a family.

But that rarely happened before Mark would disappear again.

One day, during my sophomore year of college, my dad called me crying. He said he had some bad news: Mark had passed away. His body was found alone in the room of a transitional housing facility where he had been staying. He was 50 years old.

We held a small funeral for Mark in Santa Cruz, not far from the streets where he often slept. The memorial service was the only time I ever saw my grandpa cry. He slowly stepped up to the pulpit, stood with my grandma at his side, and spoke a few words about his late son. He asked the officiant to play "Danny Boy." As the Irish ballad began, my grandpa—a deeply reserved World War II veteran who rarely showed any emotion—wept.

A few years went by. I headed to the University of Cambridge for graduate school. At some point, I took a six-month leave of absence to return home to be by my mom's side in the intensive care unit, as she battled stage four breast cancer. She was the strongest and kindest person I ever knew. After she passed away, I returned to Cambridge to finish my master's degree in sociology, and then moved back to Livermore, California, to get my abandoned childhood home ready for rental.

After eight emotionally grueling months of sorting through my mom's belongings, meeting with contractors, and spending a lot of time alone, I was exhausted. So once the house was successfully cleaned, cleared, and rented out, I went backpacking in Southeast Asia, lived in Oaxaca for a year on a Rotary scholarship, and began turning my dissertation into my first book, which was published in 2015 as *Natural Disasters as a Catalyst for Social Capital*.

Finally, I moved to Silicon Valley to pursue my dreams as a social entrepreneur, and I dove headfirst into the education technology space, co-founding two startups. I believed in the work my team and I were doing, but I also began to feel a growing tension between my own lofty ideals of trying to make the world a better place and my sense of disconnect from the people I wanted to serve. With a hunger to be hands-on at this formative early stage of my career, it felt a bit discombobulating to spend much of my day tinkering with buttons and dropdowns on a website and trying to network with wealthy investors and midlevel software engineers, all while walking by people who were living and dying on the streets in front of me, en route to my office, apartment, and social events.

Most of the time, I would just walk by. But occasionally, I would stop, or at least slow down for a moment and look up. On these occasions, I might mutter a quick "hello" or awkward "sorry." If I was trying to be especially considerate, I might offer a fleeting half-smile or nod. I was not exactly comfortable interacting with my neighbors experiencing homelessness in this season of my life. Still, my thoughts would often remain with the person as my body continued forward. In my mind's eye, I would look closer than I allowed myself to look moments ago. I would try to see their faces, glance into their eyes, and imagine that they too were someone's somebody: someone's father, mother, brother, sister, son, daughter—or maybe even some kid's beloved uncle.

Back then, nearly a decade ago, when I took the time to see people experiencing homelessness at all, I would see them as *them*, not really part of *us*. *They* were problems to be solved, not people to be loved. If I thought much about *them*, I would usually feel sad, then guilty, then frustrated. *How did they get like this? What could I do? Why was there seemingly no progress being made, despite tens of millions of dollars being spent every single year by the local government? And why did I feel so helpless? Did others know what to do?* I would consider these questions for a few moments, and then move on to my next meeting or dinner or whatever.

That began to change in November 2013. After spending Thanksgiving with my relatives near Santa Cruz, my dad and I decided to stop by Mark's gravesite on our way home. It was the first time we visited since Mark's funeral eight years earlier. We found his small marker, and sat down together amid the rolling green lawns.

Sitting there with my dad, I began to wonder more about the part of Mark's life that I never saw as a kid. Where did he usually end up after my dad dropped him off at the Greyhound bus station in Livermore, or drove him back to Santa Cruz? How did he spend his time? Did he panhandle? Did he work? Did he have enough food and water? Was he ever arrested? Did he have a caseworker? Did he self-medicate? What sorts of things did he think about? And every few years, when he would go off his medications for schizophrenia and disappear for months at a time, did he know that his family dearly missed him?

Sitting at the gravesite, surrounded by thousands of other markers, I began to ask my dad some of these questions. What resulted was a powerful father-son conversation on the life, death, and legacy of my beloved uncle, his younger brother. Toward the end of the conversation, I finally asked a question that had been lingering on my mind: "Dad, why did you feel it was important to have a gravestone marker for Uncle Mark? We haven't exactly been frequent visitors here." He responded, "I guess I just felt that it was fitting for my brother to finally have a permanent place to rest, just for himself. Mark spent most of his life on the streets. But now in death he has what he never had in life."

I was moved by what my dad said, as well as the poignant notion of a permanent plot of land for a man whose life was characterized by impermanence. But I also reflected on how little the marker actually told us (or anyone else who might walk by) about who my uncle was and what he meant to our family. The simple marker only offered his name, birth and death dates, and a dash in between. All the memories, emotions, setbacks, and dreams were enclosed within that dash.

After an hour or so, we got into the car to head home. I pulled out my phone, opened up Facebook, and began to scroll absentmindedly. My dad started the car and drove out of the cemetery. A few quiet moments passed. Then I stopped scrolling and looked up. I was struck by a mini-realization: I could learn more about my random acquaintances by scrolling for a few minutes on social media than I could learn about my late uncle by sitting for hours at his gravesite.

I wondered if there might be a better way to tell the story of my uncle—and of people like my uncle, still living on the streets—than an unadorned grave marker or obituary. These musings were on my mind a few weeks later when, sitting in church, the senior pastor invited our congregation to sit with the question "Who is Jesus?" and respond through some kind of artform or creative outlet. I thought back to the profound conversation I had with my dad at my uncle's grave and the reflective car ride home. On that Sunday morning, a simple question came around to my heart, and has been hanging out there ever since: *How would Jesus use a smartphone?*

In other words, how might we use modern storytelling tools like smartphones, social media, and wearable cameras in more humanizing ways, especially for people who are on the margins of our communities? Fewer selfies and cat videos—as delightful as they can be—and more understanding, bridge-building, empathy, solidarity, and immersive storytelling.

I felt inspired, so I collected a couple of donated wearable cameras from friends (including one whose partner worked at GoPro) and created a storytelling side project that I named Homeless GoPro.[1] The premise was simple: invite individuals experiencing homelessness to capture a glimpse of their world for an hour or two by wearing a camera with a chest mount and narrating their experience. The prompt I shared with each participant was straightforward enough: "What do you wish other people knew about you? Share what you see and what's on your mind."

I met the first "homeless autobiographer" through a mutual friend who introduced us via text. We arranged to meet at a street corner in the Castro District of San Francisco. It was broad daylight. I was surprised by how anxious I felt. As I walked the final few blocks to meet Adam, I instinctively slipped my hand into my pocket and gripped my car key between my thumb and forefinger. Even with a beloved uncle who lived on the streets for 30 years, this is where my journey walking alongside our unhoused neighbors started: with a makeshift weapon in my hand.

Over the course of the next 12 months, 24 courageous homeless autobiographers recorded dozens of hours of footage using the wearable cameras.[2] I watched all of it. The more I saw and the more people experiencing homelessness I spoke with, the wider array of emotions

I began to experience: from narrowly fearful, sad, and cautious, to utterly shocked, heartbroken, and connected.

In rediscovering the humanity of our neighbors experiencing homelessness, I connected more deeply with my own. In watching and hearing their stories of resilience, suffering, and hope, two patterns stood out.

The first pattern was that every child who walked by an individual experiencing homelessness never seemed to just walk by. They would stop, point, stare, tug, and ask their mom or dad, "Why is that man on the streets?" Most of the time, the parent would scold or shield their child, simultaneously reprimanding them for being rude while dragging them away. But occasionally I would see the parent slow down with their child, encouraging their questions, and even following their child's lead in approaching the neighbor experiencing homelessness.

Watching video clips of children reacting to the sight of unhoused neighbors made me wonder if we might have known something intuitively as kids that we seem to have forgotten as adults: people experiencing homelessness are, first and foremost, people, and it is confusing and wrong that anyone should experience homelessness. And watching the disparate responses of their parents made me wonder if, 20 years from now, one set of those children would grow to become more trusting, openhearted, compassionate adults.

The second pattern that emerged was that, at some point during a recording session, each homeless autobiographer would mention someone else: a parent, sibling, child, romantic partner, favorite teacher, mentor, cousin, or friend. Usually they expressed a mix of joy and sadness in recalling their loved one, who was now almost always distant, separated, or deceased.

In one video clip, Adam, the first homeless autobiographer who I became friends with and who generously wore the camera on multiple occasions, described the impact of relational brokenness and isolation in especially succinct, unforgettable terms:

"I never realized I was homeless when I lost my housing, only when I lost my family and friends."

These words were my epiphany. I have repeated them hundreds of times since, as they eventually inspired me to leave my job and start working full-time with people experiencing homelessness, tackling what I have come to call *relational poverty* as an overlooked form of poverty on the streets. Adam's vulnerable words intuitively made sense to me—that there is a connection between homelessness and relationships. But it raised as many questions as insights:

Why was no one talking about this possible link between homelessness and relationships? How common was relational brokenness and isolation on the streets? How many individuals experiencing homelessness are disconnected from their families and friends? Is it by choice? Would some of them want to reconnect with their loved ones if given the chance, or at least try? And if so, why weren't they already reconnected? What stood in their way?

I decided to find out.

This book is the byproduct of my decade-long journey exploring these questions and many others that followed. This is the book I wish I had when I first started this work, and perhaps more importantly, what I wish others might understand about homelessness in the United States.

In some ways, I feel as ill-equipped to write this book today as I would have nearly 10 years ago. There is still so much I do not personally understand about homelessness, and I do not have any lived experience of homelessness myself, a privilege for which I am eternally grateful. But I have formed many meaningful friendships with my neighbors experiencing homelessness, which emerged from hundreds of conversations and thousands of interactions over a decade.

Most of these relationships have come through my role as the founder and CEO of Miracle Messages, an award-winning non-profit organization I started in December 2014 and continue to help lead. Miracle Messages helps people experiencing homelessness rebuild their social support systems and financial security, primarily through family reunifications, a phone buddy program, and basic income pilots. To date, we have reunited over 800 families, trained and matched over 300 individuals experiencing homelessness with caring volunteers around the world for weekly phone calls and text messages, and created one of the first basic income pilots for individuals experiencing homelessness in the United States; its small proof of concept resulted in an astonishing 66% of unhoused participants securing housing as a result of receiving $500 a month payments for six months. I will share more of the founding story and work of Miracle Messages throughout this book.

My esteemed coauthors each have their own journeys.

When Donald W. Burnes, PhD, first agreed to coauthor this book with me, I pumped my fists for joy. Don is a national thought leader on homelessness, with 35 years of deep expertise. He is the coauthor of three other books on this topic, the founder of the Center on Housing and Homelessness Research (formerly the Burnes Center) at the University of Denver Graduate School of Social Work, the cofounder of the Burnes Institute for Poverty Research at the Colorado Center on Law and Policy, and the former head of an inner-city agency in Washington, DC, that provided essential services for people living in extreme poverty and those experiencing homelessness. But Don is not a mere academic, policy wonk, or former program director. Our shared humanity is his passion. Don is a deep thinker who endeavors to see each person experiencing homelessness as someone's somebody, each with their own unique and profound story to tell. I have met few people in my life who possess equal parts bona fides *and* humility like Don, and I am much the better for our friendship.

But if this book were just left to Don and me, we might still be waxing poetic without ever sharing our ideas with the world through these pages. From the nearly two dozen talented student interns who helped shape this book over the past four years, Amanda Banh and Andrijana Bilbija stood out. We met Amanda and Andrijana while they were both undergraduates at Princeton University, Don's alma mater. They joined us for a summer as student researchers and thought partners, and never left—mostly because we would not let them. Amanda and Andrijana each brought tremendous commitment, passion, and brilliance to this book, and we are grateful for them as contributing authors.

As coauthors, the four of us have had many rich conversations in developing and writing this book. We now invite you into the conversation with us, and truly hope you will extend it to *your* neighbors, housed and unhoused alike—for every relationship begins with a conversation.

Kevin F. Adler
May 2023

Introduction

Housed People

Imagine you are sitting in a lecture hall with a hundred other people. The speaker opens the session by asking two simple questions: "First, raise your hand if you care about the issue of homelessness." Likely, because you are reading this book, your hand flies up into the air. You look around; aside from a couple of people who are distracted by their phones or dozing off, every other hand is up, which is no big surprise. Then the speaker asks a second question: "Now raise your hand if you know someone who is currently experiencing homelessness—perhaps a friend, a family member, a neighbor, or yourself." Maybe your hand goes up once again. Or maybe, like the vast majority of people in the room, your hand remains quietly in your lap. You look around again: aside from a couple of tentative hands in the air, very few people seem to know a single person who is actually experiencing homelessness. The speaker looks around as well, but does not seem surprised: they have given this talk before.

While many of us care about the issue of homelessness, surprisingly few of us know our unhoused neighbors. This leads to a disconnect—even if unintended—between "us" and "them."

According to the 2022 Annual Homelessness Assessment Report to Congress by the United States Department of Housing and Urban Development (HUD), on a single night in late January 2022, there were 582,462 people experiencing homelessness around the country,

348,630 of whom were sheltered and 233,832 of whom were unsheltered. Of those in shelters, approximately 59% were individuals and
41% were in families. Of those who were unsheltered, roughly 92%
were individuals and 8% were in families.[1] For the third straight year,
unsheltered individuals (216,146) outnumbered sheltered individuals
(204,774).

As large as these figures may seem, they are woeful undercounts.
The HUD total estimate of 582,462 people experiencing homelessness
in the US only includes people who are in shelters, transitional housing
(housing that has a specific deadline for termination, often 24 months,
and usually involving intensive social services), or who can be visibly
counted on the streets *on any given night*, as measured by the annual
Point-in-Time (PIT) counts that occur throughout the US in January.[2] It
does not include those who are living with others because of economic
hardship or housing loss, or people who are living out of sight of PIT
count canvassers, including in vehicles, abandoned buildings, tunnels,
and elsewhere not meant for human habitation.

Over the course of a year, the actual number of adults who experience homelessness in the United States is estimated to be closer to
2.5 million to 3 million people,[3] or approximately five times the HUD
number.[4] In addition, there are an estimated 1.1 million public school
children who are considered unhoused based on the US Department
of Education's broader definition of homelessness (2020–2021 school
year),[5] which includes school-age children who are doubled up or tripled up with friends or relatives.[6] Another 1 million children under six
years old are in these cramped combined households, along with their
roughly 1 million parents.

Adding all these numbers together, and using the Department of
Education's broader definition of homelessness that includes people
who are couchsurfing or otherwise doubled up or tripled up with loved
ones, the actual total number of people who experience homelessness
at some point over the course of the year is likely closer to 6 million
people, or roughly 1.8% of the total population in the United States.

Many marginalized groups are disproportionately driven into homelessness, and greatly overrepresented within these figures. For example,

despite constituting approximately 12% of the general population in the United States, African Americans make up 37% of all people experiencing homelessness, and 50% of people experiencing homelessness as members of families with children.[7] Hispanic people make up 19% of the general population but 24% of all people experiencing homelessness. Native Americans compose roughly 2.9% of the general population but 3.4% of the unhoused population. Lesbian, gay, bisexual, transgender, queer, and/or questioning (LGBTQ+) youth make up an estimated 9% of the youth across the country but a whopping 40% of all of the unattached, unhoused youth nationwide.[8] Other groups overrepresented among the homeless population in the United States include people with disabilities, immigrants, and veterans.

As some of these figures indicate, racism and discrimination are very much embedded into our country's homelessness problem and relate to many of the topics we will cover in the following pages: depleted social networks and social capital, stigma and otherizing, paternalism, discrimination within the housing sector, health disparities, inadequate opportunities for youth, and much more. According to a recent report from Supporting Partnerships for Anti-Racist Communities (SPARC), there are deep racial disparities in homelessness and its related systems (e.g., the legal system, the criminal justice system, child welfare, education, health care), particularly for Black and Indigenous residents. "Homelessness is not colorblind. People of color are far more likely to experience homelessness," said Jeff Olivet, the executive director of the US Interagency Council on Homelessness and lead author of the SPARC report.[9] Groups who have been greatly discriminated against are far more likely to be at risk of homelessness and housing insecurity.[10]

The experience of homelessness is as diverse and multifaceted as the aforementioned homeless population figures might indicate. Bridging the mental gap between "us" and "them" requires better understanding who "they" are.

People fall into homelessness for countless different reasons, including eviction; domestic violence; employment wages not being enough to cover daily living expenses; medical emergencies; undiagnosed, misdiagnosed, and/or untreated illnesses; clerical errors;

unemployment and layoffs; divorce and separation; the death of a loved one; intra-family disputes over housing; LGBTQ+ youth escaping an unsafe home environment; aging out of foster care; racism and discrimination; long-standing trauma; natural disasters; and bad luck; to name just a few. In other words, the vast majority of individuals experiencing homelessness are unrecognizable from the average securely housed person in the United States, who is living paycheck to paycheck, is unable to save much money, probably works hard but is not perfect, and is only one emergency away from potentially not being able to pay the rent.[11] "They" are us.

Yet when we think about homelessness, we tend to imagine the searing, highly upsetting sight of unsheltered street homelessness that many of us frequently encounter, rather than the highly relatable faces of family members, friends, and classmates who we may be walking by, or even the many beloved celebrities who have experienced homelessness, including Halle Berry, Drew Carey, Jim Carrey, Kelly Clarkson, Daniel Craig, Kelsey Grammer, Steve Harvey, Jewel, Steve Jobs, David Letterman, Tyler Perry, Chris Pratt, William Shatner, Martin Sheen, Hilary Swank, and Shania Twain.[12] It is tempting to assume that all people experiencing homelessness are the same as those who we can visibly see, thus creating a large homogenous group called "the homeless." Consequently, according to one major survey of thousands of adults in the US, 85% of people erroneously cite drug and alcohol use as a major cause of homelessness, while 67% of people incorrectly cite mental illness and related mental disorders as major factors.[13]

Have you ever been referred to as a "housed person"? Probably not. Such a label would be ridiculous, as no one thinks about housed people as a single, unified group. In many ways, "homeless person" is a similarly unhelpful identity. We have defined an incredibly varied group of people by their lack of one physical need: stable housing. When we offhandedly use empty terms like "the homeless," all differences, context, patterns, and stories get washed away and replaced with a singular, monolithic image that is neither positive nor representative.

When we define an entire group of people by their lack of stable housing, we have little reason to get to know our neighbors experiencing homelessness as actual human beings. This is a tragedy, as most of us want to help address homelessness and care strongly about this issue. According to a 1,000-person national opinion poll, 82% of Americans believe that the country should be doing more to prevent homelessness.[14] And 74% of Americans—including 88% of Democrats, 62% of independents, and 65% of Republicans—support policies that expand investments in housing development programs to build more affordable housing units for low-income people.[15]

Even so, the overall number of people experiencing homelessness does not appreciably decline year-to-year. We have a nationwide deficit of seven million affordable housing units and overwhelmingly agree that more should be done to help,[16] yet we protest new affordable housing projects in our own neighborhoods. This disconnect illustrates one of the central arguments we will be making in this book: we say that we care, but our actions and systems say otherwise.

As coauthors, we believe that the United States is still a long way off from addressing homelessness adequately because of two major factors. First is the crisis in our service systems that prevent us from providing the affordable housing and other life-sustaining services that so many Americans desperately need. Second is the crisis in our shared humanity, how we have lost sight of the fact that people experiencing homelessness are our fellow human beings, just like us; we regard our unhoused neighbors as problems to be solved, rather than as people to be loved.

While this book is about homelessness, it is really about us "housed" people, too: how our daily actions unwittingly reinforce the divide between "us" and "them," where we need to shift our focus, and what we can each do to address the crises in our service systems and in our hearts.

Broken Systems

Homelessness may be the most intersectional issue in the United States. From sky-high health care costs to housing unaffordability, from severe income inequality to our mental health crisis, from how we neglect youth to how we lock up adults, from the consequences of racism and discrimination to the brokenness of our immigration system, home-lessness intersects with seemingly all structural problems in the US.[17] At some level, all roads lead to homelessness. As one individual experiencing homelessness lamented, "I feel like I didn't fail. The system failed me."

As such, there is no silver bullet for ending homelessness, and no way to eliminate it entirely. While it is possible to ensure that homelessness is rare, brief, and nonrecurring—as we will discuss in Part III of this book—there will always be someone temporarily without housing.

Although the literature about homelessness is growing rapidly, few if any books have tried to pull together all the system threads into one place to highlight homelessness as the intersectional issue that it is. We have not attempted to paint a complete picture of the flaws of any single system; the literature is replete with such analyses, which we reference throughout this book. Instead, we try to move beyond an issue vacuum to explore the impact of many broken systems together, from affordable housing to health care to criminal justice and more—for this is the world that our neighbors experiencing homelessness actually live in.

> "On the streets, we're thinking about surviving. We're thinking about tomorrow. We're not thinking about next year. We'll have a meal today, but we really don't know the situation tomorrow." —Ray

> "We were like family so to speak. It was me and so many other people who were homeless. We camped out. We made little tents, little set-ups under the bridge. We didn't leave. I felt like part of a family. I didn't have anyone else at that time." —Linda

> "What is the hardest thing about being homeless? Dealing with people's prejudice. Perception. That to me is the hardest. [. . .] I think people treat me fair if they don't know that I'm homeless." —Ronnie

> "In an open shelter, everybody is at risk. There's a lot of violence against women, untreated mental illness. It's a rare night

when the paramedics don't show up to haul people in and out. People are always coming and going. The system, they're supposed to help you find housing, good luck with that. In our shelter, there were only two people who cared enough to help people find housing." —Elizabeth

"No one was listening to me. Certain things are so normalized—I didn't realize that it was not okay. In a way, I felt like an anomaly. I experienced symptoms that were dismissed due to me being an unwed, single Black mother living under the poverty line in Washington DC. That's exactly how it was dismissed, every single time. I can't explain it. They thought I was crazy." —Jennifer

"Shame. I didn't want to tell anyone I had fallen into addiction. How could this guy who has this beautiful wife, two kids, and made a life for himself fall so hard? I couldn't bring myself to tell anybody. We have to be honest about what's really happening. When you're living with the daily trauma of being unhoused—and it's trauma—it's really easy to turn around and start self-medicating." —Tom

"I just wish people knew that I was so much more of a threat to myself than I would ever be to them." —Joseph

"All the time, people would tell me: 'Get a job.' I just cried, I just cried. A couple of times, I would actually sit there and say: 'You know what? I do have a job. We're just down on our luck right now. Not all homeless people are homeless because of choice.' They would just walk away." —Lainie

"I had bumps on the bottom of my feet from athlete's foot. They were yellow, and that really scared me. I couldn't go to the hospital because I didn't have insurance at the time. I was washing my feet in the McDonald's toilet. And even now, I'm working but I've been wearing the same pair of pants for the last six months." —Gabe

"To my baby Makayla [. . .] I love you. I miss you. I've never stopped loving you." —Timothy

"My niece and nephew, Josh and Rachel — tell 'em I intend to come home and see them sometime, if I can." —Jeffrey

"My group foster home parent would give us a hundred dollar bill and would say, 'If you run away with this money, I will find you.' They would threaten you. The hard thing was that we were so lacking of parents that even if they just offered a little bit of attention, it would seem grandiose. But, boy, we were left alone." —Rand

* * *

Ray, Linda, Ronnie, Elizabeth, Jennifer, Tom, Joseph, Lainie and her son Gabe, Timothy, Jeffrey, and Rand are twelve people who currently or formerly experienced homelessness, whose stories will be featured throughout this book. Each background is unique: Ray is a traveling salesman and an immigrant from the Philippines. Linda is a loving mom of three. Ronnie dedicated his life to running and making art. Elizabeth is a former schoolteacher and nonprofit leader. Jennifer is a community organizer and after-school instructor. Tom is a speaker and homeless advocate. Joseph lives with schizophrenia. Gabe holds the dream of becoming a chef, while his beloved mom, Lainie, hopes to open a food truck (together with Gabe, of course). Timothy's dream was to reconnect with his only daughter. Jeffrey wrote letters from time to time to his family. Rand is a social worker. Collectively, these twelve distinct voices tell a unified story of broken systems and forgotten humanity. Their words reveal how easy it is for someone to fall into homelessness in the United States, and how difficult it is to overcome it.

Homelessness is a housing issue, as we will see in Elizabeth's experience of losing her home of 14 years and ending up in a dangerous congregate shelter. Homelessness is an income inequality issue, as we will see in Gabe and Lainie through their many years of working full-time without ever being able to get back on their feet, a reality shared by millions of low wage earners in America. Homelessness is a health issue, as we will see in Jennifer's and Tom's stories, a result of gaping flaws in our physical, mental, and behavioral health care systems that plague so many of our communities. Homelessness is a criminal justice issue, as we will see in the relational brokenness that accompanied Timothy's many years behind bars followed by his perpetual loss of freedom to find decent housing and work with his felony record. Homelessness is a family welfare issue, as we will see in Rand's story, all too often a consequence of divorce, child abuse, and neglect in the foster care system. And homelessness is a basic humanity issue, as we will see in countless stories through this book, including the persistent stigma and shame that Ray feels, Linda's belief that her struggles are hers to shoulder alone, the relational poverty and isolation that Jeffrey and many others describe. Together, these stories convey the intersectionality of homelessness and, therefore, the inherent need for a wide range of solutions and interventions.

Forgotten Humanity

As we traverse city streets, stop at traffic lights, walk down suburban sidewalks, and hike along rural roads or mountain paths, we walk by our unhoused neighbors, usually ignoring their plight and the factors that may have led to their circumstances. For many of us, "walking by" is all we know how to do, believing the problem is far too big to address, and being unsure of what to say to our neighbors experiencing homelessness. Sam Tsemberis, the originator of the Housing First model in the United States, said, "we have to shut down a piece of our own humanity to be able to walk past another human being that is in such a difficult situation."[18] A recent study by Chris Herring suggests that "as public perception of the homeless community shifted toward criminalization, 911 calls related to homelessness skyrocketed, resulting in a 72% increase in police interactions with members of the homeless community." More policing did not result in favorable outcomes or solutions, but rather, criminalizing homelessness and poverty "dispossess[es] the poor of property, create[s] barriers to services and jobs, and increase[s] vulnerability to violence and crime." Herring continues, *"This can lead to a cycle in which housing secure people are contributing to reduced security for people experiencing homelessness and a system that criminalizes poverty"* (emphasis in the original).[19] When we walk by, we effectively accept the status quo and sentiment that nothing can be done to help our neighbors experiencing homelessness. This hurts everyone, housed and unhoused alike.

Instead of providing affordable housing units, developing forward-thinking homeless navigation centers to coordinate care, integrating individuals with mental health issues into our communities, ensuring immediate access to medical care as needed, hiring returning citizens with felony records, or simply getting to know our unhoused neighbors as neighbors, we instead respond with fear, confusion, and avoidance. Local residents protest "not in my backyard," politicians cower, and the news media perpetuates the uniform imagery of "the homeless." Not surprisingly, the lived experience of our neighbors experiencing homelessness tends to be marked by extreme stigma and shame, exclusion, paternalism, rote stereotypes of "lazy, crazy, addicts, and rejects," and a pernicious hyper-individualism that looks at hardship and suffering solely through the lens of individual attributes and choices—"they" must deserve it.

Perhaps most consequential of all, we barely know each other as fellow human beings. Aside from stable housing, the most significant resource our neighbors experiencing homelessness lack is nurturing relationships, which most of us likely take for granted.[20] Consider for a moment who you would call if you had a crisis at two o'clock in the morning. Most of us have an established network of support we can call on, day or night, no matter the crisis. Even a few trusted people on standby is far better than nothing. But many individuals experiencing homelessness are deeply isolated and do not have these support networks, sometimes because they have never had them, sometimes because bridges have been burned by one side or the other (or both), and sometimes because the networks they rely on are simply unable to provide them with the support they need, often because they too have extremely limited resources.

There is an important distinction between being alone and experiencing what we call relational poverty. Most of us want to be alone from time to time, even from our closest friends. This is different from not having nurturing relationships with others, and not being able to build them: because of how our society treats people experiencing homelessness, the relational poverty they experience is often of *our* making. We have cut them off, so to speak.[21] We neglect, stigmatize, otherize, and criminalize them—we do this as individuals, and our cities do this for us at scale. To be sure, we are rarely aware of any of this. We are socialized from a young age to walk by people experiencing homelessness because "there's nothing we can do."[22] This is disastrous for our neighbors experiencing homelessness, as social connection is critical in helping those without homes regain greater self-sufficiency and in preventing tens of millions of at-risk Americans from falling over the edge into homelessness—the "proto-homeless," as Jennifer Wolch and Michael Dear refer to in *Malign Neglect: Homelessness in an American City.*[23]

When We Walk By adds a new dimension—the power of relationships and our shared humanity—to the issue of homelessness. In this book, we examine the key systemic failures that cause homelessness, but we also focus considerable attention on how the rest of us who are housed perceive and treat those experiencing homelessness. We argue that, to have a fighting chance to end homelessness in our lifetimes, we must humanize our way of thinking about and feeling toward our neighbors experiencing homelessness, recognizing that they, like us, are human beings. And we must go further, and embrace our unhoused neighbors as people to be loved, not problems to be solved. This all may sound rather sweet and obvious at first, but it is critical. Hearts and minds are as important to change as service systems and local ordinances; indeed, changes to one are not possible or sustainable without changes to the other.

The Power of Connection

The COVID-19 pandemic was the first time that many of us felt what it is like to be completely disconnected from our communities. This

painful but temporary period of isolation dramatically affected our
mental health and well-being. This is how many of our neighbors experiencing homelessness live every day. As one individual experiencing
homelessness memorably put it in the early months of the pandemic:
"You don't need to teach me about social distancing. That's my life
already."

Because of the need for social distancing, many large shelters were
forced to either close or dramatically reduce their numbers. At the
same time, because of the pandemic, hotel bookings were way down.
For once, the forces of supply and demand converged in favor of individuals experiencing homelessness, and thousands of hotel and motel
rooms were bought or leased to house people who had been forced
out of congregate shelters. For example, in Portland, Oregon, the city
spent $65 million to buy 20 underutilized motels to house 2,000 people
experiencing homelessness.[24]

This approach provided temporary housing, but it didn't address
the issues of social isolation, loneliness, and anxiety. While sheltering alone in confined motels or hotels, cut off from friends and social
support, people experiencing homelessness suddenly found themselves
even more isolated than before, exacerbating their sense of separate-
ness. The issue of relational poverty among individuals experiencing
homelessness became even more pronounced during this time. As one
senior official at a treatment center put it, "I can't tell you how upsetting it is to go into some guy's room and find him either staring into
space or having committed suicide."[25]

The elevated levels of loneliness, disconnection, and despair that
we all felt to varying degrees during the pandemic also created new
opportunities for collaboration and innovation where it has long been
needed—what was invisible to most quickly became evident to all.

Kevin and his team at Miracle Messages were able to collaborate
with the City and County of San Francisco to implement Miracle Messages' new phone buddy program into the local shelter-in-place hotels
in May 2020. In an effort to reduce isolation among people experiencing homelessness in a time of government-mandated separation, and to
support understaffed and overwhelmed service providers, the Miracle

Friends phone buddy program matched a few dozen unhoused participants with caring volunteers for weekly calls and texts, supported by
mentors, regular trainings, and case workers at partner sites as needed.

Today, Miracle Friends has grown to over 300 indispensable virtual
friendships, with committed volunteers throughout the US and globally befriending individuals experiencing homelessness through at least
20–30 minutes a week of phone calls and text exchanges, with tremendous benefits described by both the unhoused and housed friends alike.
Miracle Friends continues to grow and welcome unhoused participants
and new volunteers from anywhere in the world, and will be described
in greater detail in chapter 13.

Less than six months into the Miracle Friends phone buddy program,
with friendships built and trust established, volunteers began reporting
in their call logs how a relatively small amount of money could make
a profound difference for their unhoused friends in helping them meet
their basic needs, including food security, transportation, hygiene, health
care, and housing. So the Miracle Messages team decided to launch one
of the first basic income programs for people experiencing homelessness
in the United States. In a very small pilot, Miracle Money provided $500
a month for six months for unhoused participants who were active in
the Miracle Friends program and nominated by their phone buddies.
The initial fundraising goal of $15,000 was met in less than 24 hours by
scores of enthusiastic donors via a Facebook fundraiser. Within weeks,
a total of $50,000 was raised, which enabled Miracle Messages to select
14 participants from dozens of worthy nominations for the inaugural
Miracle Money pilot in the San Francisco Bay Area.

Remarkably, 66% of the participants who were experiencing
homelessness immediately prior to Miracle Money (six of nine)
were able to secure stable housing as a result of their $500 a month
direct cash transfer. As Kevin remarked at the time: "They spent the
money better than we could have spent it for them. These results
[. . .] are a testament to the ingenuity of our unhoused neighbors and
friends. When we invest in our unhoused neighbors, offering even
modest financial resources and supportive relationships, problems
get solved and people get housed."[26] Additional insights and stories

from Miracle Money and other basic income pilots for people experiencing homelessness will be shared in chapter 4 on paternalism, and throughout this book.

How This Book Is Organized

When We Walk By recasts homelessness in the United States as a byproduct of twin crises that are quietly ravaging our cities, towns, and rural areas: our basic humanity has failed, and our service systems have failed, to devastating effect. In revealing the role each of us plays in perpetuating (and ending) homelessness in America, and in emphasizing the intersectionality between homelessness and many broken systems, this book aims to increase understanding of why we have made so little progress in addressing this ongoing national tragedy.

This book is neither an academic analysis nor an activist manifesto. Rather, *When We Walk By* offers an intimate look at how and why we unwittingly treat those without stable housing as problems to be solved rather than people to be loved, and how our systems have failed to provide Americans with their basic needs. Unforgettable personal stories from neighbors experiencing homelessness make visible what is all too often invisible, showing what happens when we choose to walk by.

In Part I we examine our failed humanity through the lens of *relational poverty*—a deadly, often-overlooked form of poverty that is especially pervasive among people experiencing homelessness, leading to nearly unimaginable levels of social isolation, stigma, and shame. As a nation, we see people experiencing homelessness as "them," rather than as part of "us." We tend to ignore, exclude, distrust, judge, and criminalize them, and view them as unworthy and incompetent. The result? We don't know who "they" are, and this leads us to feel perpetually helpless and frustrated on this issue, and cynical that any real progress can be made.

In Part II we debunk the myth that homelessness is the result of bad individual choices or personal attributes. We examine the multitude of failed systems that result in millions of Americans experiencing homelessness and housing insecurity each year, a disproportionate number of whom are people of color. Failures include a nationwide shortage of affordable housing, wage stagnation and income inequality, a prohibitively expensive and complex health care system, inadequate education and foster care systems, a dearth of mental and behavioral health facilities and treatment options, an inhumane criminal justice system, racism and discrimination, and a lack of attention to strategies to prevent homelessness to begin with, all of which have an inordinately harmful impact on Black people, Hispanic people, Indigenous peoples, LGBTQ+, and other minority groups and marginalized people in the United States.

Fixing broken systems will not happen without healing our humanity, and vice versa, as the twin crises of broken systems and forgotten humanity are deeply intertwined. As such, in Part III we look at some of the most promising policies and programs for tackling homelessness, and we offer tangible ways people can come together to help house their unhoused neighbors and build transformative relationships. Examples include providing greater financial security for people experiencing homelessness through direct cash transfers and basic income pilots, forming genuine friendships through phone buddy programs or by volunteering at local service providers, using person-first language ("people experiencing homelessness" versus "the homeless") to help shatter harmful stereotypes, and fighting for more hospitable and inclusive communities that are safer for all people. We provide a set of recommended actions that you, our reader, can meaningfully engage in on an individual level to help in the fight to end homelessness.

Despite its raw depiction of discomfiting realities, *When We Walk By* is ultimately an optimistic book, illustrating how the problem of homelessness is mostly solvable, and how each of us can make a profound difference in the lives of our unhoused neighbors. We close with a vision for America in which homelessness truly becomes rare, brief, and nonrecurring, in which no one experiences homelessness alone, and in which no one feels helpless about this issue.

PART I.

HUMANITY

1

Relational Poverty

We think sometimes that poverty is only being hungry, naked, and homeless. The poverty of being unwanted, unloved, and uncared for is the greatest poverty.

—MOTHER TERESA

I never realized I was homeless when I lost my housing, only when I lost my family and friends.

—ADAM

ON A CHILLY DECEMBER EVENING in downtown San Francisco, Kevin took a walk down Market Street, offering warm tea and hot biscuits, and asking a simple question to his neighbors living on the streets: "Do you have any family or friends you would like to record a message to for the holidays?"

That's how Kevin met Jeffrey. A middle-aged man with a scraggly beard, protruding blue eyes, and a hangdog look, Jeffrey was sitting by himself outside the Old Navy flagship store on Market at 4th Street. Initially Kevin walked by Jeffrey, presuming that he would not want to interact. His appearance was disheveled, he was mumbling to himself, and a partially consumed alcoholic beverage rested by his side.

Kevin took a few steps further, then did an about-face, reminding himself that he had committed to try to engage everybody on his
walk that day who he believed might be experiencing homelessness.
He approached Jeffrey, who glanced up but barely acknowledged his
presence. He tried to exchange pleasantries—"Hello," "How are you
doing?" "What's your name?"—but his efforts were met with single-
word responses and apparent disinterest.

Getting ready to leave, Kevin went ahead and asked, "Jeffrey, are
there any family members or other loved ones that you would like to
try to reconnect with?"

For the first time in their interaction, Jeffrey turned and looked
Kevin right in the eyes. "My dad, Harold. My niece and nephew, Josh
and Rachel. My sister, Jennifer. I haven't seen them in a while."

Taken aback, Kevin asked if he would like to record a video message
to his family for the holidays. Jeffrey said yes, and recorded these short,
powerful words: "I intend to come home and see you again someday, if
I can," with his voice breaking slightly on the word "someday."

Kevin asked Jeffrey about his hometown, the spelling of names, and
any addresses where he once resided that he could remember. Jeffrey
said that he had corresponded with his family through letters at times
over the years but had been out of touch "for a while" and did not
know how to reach them anymore, and vice versa. Kevin asked if he
could share Jeffrey's video message online, in the hope of finding his
loved ones. Jeffrey said yes. "And how will I find you again, in case I
am able to find your family?" Kevin asked.

Jeffrey paused for a moment, then replied, "I'm around here,
usually."

A week later, Kevin was able to find a Facebook group connected
to Jeffrey's hometown. He wrote a short note to the group administra-
tors, who subsequently posted the video. Within one hour, hundreds
of people liked and shared the post. Messages began to stream in from
former classmates and neighbors who wanted to help: "I went to high
school with Jeffrey and work in construction. Does he need a job?" "I
work at the Congressman's office. Does he need health care?" "Is there
a way I can donate to him to help him get back on his feet?"

The story made the local news as the leading story in Jeffrey's small hometown in North Central Pennsylvania. Over the following weeks, $5,000 was raised by former classmates, neighbors, and friends, to try to bring Jeffrey home and get him the support he would need for his severe alcoholism and untreated mental health issues.

Within 20 minutes of Kevin's initial Facebook post, Jeffrey's sister Jennifer was tagged in the comments. She sent Kevin the following message:

> Hello. I am Jeffrey's sister, Jennifer. I contacted the [redacted] Police Department with my contact info, and would like to pass it along to you with the message to him if he wants to come home I will find a way to make it happen. My home phone is [redacted], my cell is [redacted] and my email address is [redacted]. My address is [redacted]. I have not been able to locate him for at least 13 or 14 years, despite having attempted to track him over the internet many times. I am beyond shocked, and have no words. I wasn't even aware he knew the names of my children. Any help you can give will be deeply appreciated, and if you have any questions please contact me using any of the ways I've given you.

Kevin and Jennifer spoke the next day, on Christmas. She told Kevin that Jeffrey had been a missing person for 12 years. Jennifer recorded a short video message to her brother, introducing her two children, and issuing a heartfelt promise: "I've been talking to many people trying to do what I can to get you home, and the help that you need once you're here. My holiday message to you is this: if you don't give up, I won't either."

A few weeks later, Jeffrey and Jennifer were able to reconnect on a phone call. A few months after that, Jennifer traveled by train across the country to reunite with her brother. It was the first time they had seen each other in over 22 years.

It turns out that Jeffrey wasn't the only one. Since December 2014, when Kevin first met Jeffrey and helped him reconnect with his loved ones, over 800 individuals experiencing homelessness across the United States have been able to reunite with their family and friends through

Miracle Messages, the nonprofit organization Kevin founded, which helps people experiencing homelessness rebuild their social support systems and financial security.

Linda returned home to live with her daughter in Wisconsin after 28 years. Isaac reunited with his elderly mom and siblings in Texas after nearly 40 years. David was picked up by his brothers and taken back home to New York after more than 10 years missing on the streets in Florida. In each case, addressing relational poverty was the critical first step toward addressing homelessness.

No One Should Go Through Homelessness Alone

Though we often think of poverty as a lack of financial resources, what Jeffrey experienced before reconnecting with his sister was *relational* poverty, or a profound lack of nurturing relationships combined with stigma (and often shame) that makes fostering social ties incredibly difficult. Relational poverty often exacerbates financial poverty, and even causes homelessness. Relational poverty *is* poverty.

While it is easy to recognize a lack of income, shelter, sanitation, clothes, or food, there is often no obvious way to tell when someone lacks supportive relationships, and the resource advantages that accompany them. But as many as one in three people experiencing homelessness have lost their social support systems.[1]

Aside from the lack of stable housing, relational poverty may be the most universal characteristic of people experiencing homelessness. In fact, relational poverty can turn housing insecurity into homelessness. As Gregg Colburn and Clayton Page Aldern have indicated in their recent book, "homelessness risk is far greater for people with limited support from a community, low self-esteem, and a lack of belonging."[2]

Unfortunately, relational poverty is often overlooked by many of the organizations that supply housing and other services to the unhoused. Research has shown that strong relationships are linked to better physical and mental health for people experiencing homelessness, as well as a lower likelihood of victimization.[3] Yet service providers often regard efforts to rebuild relationships and provide social connections not as a necessity but as a "nice to have" for their unhoused clients—a damaging example of the paternalism that is so rife in the service sector, as we will discuss in chapter 4.

People experiencing homelessness generally see the importance of relationships very differently, as Jeffrey and over 3,000 other unhoused clients have demonstrated over the past nine years by recording messages to their loved ones through Miracle Messages. Although the external indicator of homelessness is a lack of stable housing, the lived experience is often one of extreme isolation, disconnection, broken or nonexistent social support, stigmatization, and shame.

The opposite is often true, too; relationships and connections significantly help people pull themselves *out* of homelessness. In fact, according to data from the City and County of San Francisco's Department of Homelessness and Supportive Housing, between March 2015 and February 2019, over 60% of successful shelter exits in the city occurred through family or friend reunification.[4] That's double the percentage of successful shelter exits that resulted from moving into permanent housing (30%) and six times the percentage from moving into temporary placements (10%).

Homelessness is a housing problem, but it is not only a housing problem. Relational poverty is a major driver of homelessness, and supportive relationships are a vital part of the solution to ending homelessness. This is why Housing First is not Housing Only: indeed, one of the five core principles of the Housing First strategy is social and community integration. As Canada's largest national research institute devoted to homelessness describes it, "If people are housed and become or remain socially isolated, the stability of their housing may be compromised."[5]

Our neighbors experiencing homelessness and housing insecurity need networks of support and nurturing, dependable relationships, just like the rest of us who are stably housed. Community and connection are essential, not a nice to have. As human beings, we need more than just a physical home: we need a *social home* as well.

This perspective is a broad shift away from the sociology of homelessness over the past 40 years, which has concentrated on housing and labor markets, and more like the social network approach to understanding homelessness that can be glimpsed as early as the work of Nels Anderson 100 years ago in his analysis of Chicago's skid row.[6] With homelessness on the rise and frustrations boiling over, we believe that now is a critical time to return to this framework.

Or in the words of Ray, an individual experiencing homelessness who participated in Miracle Messages' phone buddy program, and who was placed in a hotel room through Project Roomkey during the COVID-19 pandemic (and whose story is featured in chapter 2):

> "One of the things about being homeless, you would think that getting a roof over your head would be the solution; you would think giving someone a hotel room would be the first step to getting out of homelessness, but that really wasn't the case for me. It was nice, don't get me wrong, but I didn't know what else to do. I would sit there all day, and it was just like sitting out on the streets all day. You don't have any source of support other than a roof over your head. Although I felt safer, although I felt okay in terms of getting fed, I always had this knowledge, this fear, that this security was temporary. Having a social network, having family, that is really, ultimately, what one who is unhoused needs: to get to a point where you don't have to walk the streets alone anymore."

Social Capital:
We Need Connections to Survive

Social capital is critical for our economic well-being

Why exactly are our relationships so important for our well-being? According to Harvard political scientist Robert Putnam, author of the landmark book *Bowling Alone*, strong social networks encourage norms of reciprocity and mutual support, build trust and cooperation, and provide a sense of belonging and purpose.[7] In other words, strong social networks and positive social norms give us resource advantages, which is called *social capital*, and is just as critical as financial capital for our security and well-being.

In fact, social capital can be converted into economic capital.[8] When you have resource advantages from social networks and norms, tangible benefits result. For example, if your paycheck doesn't stretch to the end of the month, you can turn to your support networks to borrow money. Or if your child is sick and needs to stay home from daycare, you can find someone in your trusted community to provide temporary childcare so you can still go to work and get paid. And if you no longer feel safe at home with your partner's recent volatility and drinking problem getting worse, but you can't afford an extended stay in a hotel room or Airbnb, you can call a few close friends to stay with and help you navigate next steps.

Millions of housed individuals and families are right now living on the brink of financial disaster, and we as coauthors believe that the only thing keeping them from homelessness is the support of their networks. One out of every two Americans is a paycheck away from not being able to pay rent[9]—given this harrowing statistic, it is rather astonishing that "only" 6 million Americans experience homelessness each year. Why aren't tens of millions of us homeless?[10]

Friends, family members, teachers, classmates, neighbors, coworkers, and significant others, as well as our congregations, clubs, and community organizations, are making up the precarious difference between housing and homelessness for at least half of us. When we're in need, we receive essential financial support, emotional support, and other types of assistance from our relationships and communities. Most of us depend on social capital to get by, though clearly not all groups have access to social capital rich networks and resources, which is often another consequence of racism and discrimination deeply embedded into many social capital-rich institutions in our society: it's hard to form similarly resource-rich networks when some groups face much higher barriers in attending elite universities, embarking on lucrative careers, being selected for competitive jobs and promotions, socializing in exclusive clubs, and so on.

Even so, people are resilient. Strong social networks need not only consist of deep bonds between kin and friends. Matthew Desmond, author of *Evicted*, detailed in an ethnographic study that the urban poor rely on "disposable" ties with acquaintances, which tend to be weak, brittle, and short lasting, to avoid homelessness upon eviction.[11] Those lacking both kinship-level and disposable ties are most vulnerable to homelessness. In other words, having *weak ties* with acquaintances who can offer support in times of need is just as important as our strong ties with family members when considering the elements that make up a strong social network.[12]

And social capital doesn't just keep us from teetering over the edge—it also helps us climb the economic ladder. A recent study by Raj Chetty, a Harvard economist, and his colleagues highlights the importance of social capital for economic mobility. Based on tens of millions of data points, their research suggests that low-income children are more likely to attend college and make more money as adults if they have social contacts with children and adults who mostly come from the upper half of the socioeconomic distribution.[13] The strength of these weak ties represents a type of bridging social capital,[14] and, remarkably, it was found to be even more influential than zip code in predicting economic mobility. "Growing up in a community connected across class lines improves kids' outcomes and gives them a better shot at rising out of poverty," explains Chetty.[15]

Social capital is critical for our physical and mental health

Just as financial poverty has a broad impact on those whom it affects, the dearth of social capital—which we have named relational poverty—has its own wide-ranging repercussions. In the 1980s, study after study found that, even controlling for an array of factors like gender, age, exercising, and eating well, those who were socially isolated were significantly more likely to die earlier than their socially connected peers.

Psychologist Julianne Holt-Lunstad confirmed these findings in 2015 in a meta-analysis that found that experiences of social isolation, loneliness, or living alone were associated with a 26%–32% increased likelihood of early mortality. Prolonged isolation is estimated to decrease a person's lifespan by 15 years, equivalent to smoking 15 cigarettes a day.[16] Relational poverty is a deadly form of poverty, with associated health risks comparable to those of financial poverty.

The rate of homelessness among older adults is on the rise—half of single homeless adults are over 50 years old—and older adults are especially susceptible to relational poverty.[17] A 2020 report from the National Academies of Sciences, Engineering, and Medicine found that a third of adults aged 45 and older feel lonely, while nearly a quarter of adults aged 65 and older are socially isolated.[18] Older adults are more likely to live alone, lose family or friends, have chronic illnesses, and be hearing impaired, all factors that increase their risk for loneliness and social isolation.

Loneliness and social isolation lead to not only a shorter life but a lower quality of life. Among older adults, loneliness and social isolation are associated with higher rates of depression, anxiety, and suicide, as well as a 50% increased risk of dementia, a 29% increased risk of heart disease, and a 32% increased risk of stroke.[19] Similar to a long commute or a demanding job, loneliness acts as a physical stressor on the body, leading to elevated cortisol levels and high levels of inflammation.[20] Like chronic stress, chronic loneliness is the deadliest of its kind. The longer a person stays homeless, the more likely they are to be chronically lonely.

Why Do So Many People Experiencing Homelessness Suffer from Relational Poverty?

Gaining meaningful social capital takes time, opportunities, energy, a sense of belonging, and digital access that people experiencing homelessness typically do not have.

One primary way people create relationships is through their workplaces or in locations where communities gather, like churches, libraries, coffee shops, or bars. Many people without homes lack the opportunities to place themselves consistently in circumstances that allow for the buildup of social capital, and the stigma associated with homelessness can keep unhoused people out of environments where they may otherwise have been able to make safe and healthy social connections. In a society that shuns "the homeless," it is far less likely you will get invited to that house party or networking event if you are "a homeless neighbor" instead of just "a neighbor." In a vicious downward cycle, financial poverty results in greater relational poverty, which results in greater financial poverty, and so on.

The collective social neglect and poor treatment of people experiencing homelessness only worsen their ability to foster otherwise pivotal social connections—serving only to keep them homeless longer. Having been neglected or rejected for a host of reasons by family, friends, and systems, many people experiencing homelessness are generally leery of trusting anyone, including other unhoused people and even themselves. Once they're disconnected from their previous networks, separation grows, and the general level of distrust magnifies. It is little wonder that some people who are chronically homeless have been isolated and disconnected for decades—Miracle Messages routinely facilitates reunions over 30 years in the making. Jeffrey had been a missing person for over 12 years and disconnected for 22 years, living in isolation on the streets. Among the scores of people from Jeffrey's hometown who reached out to see how they could help after his story went viral was someone in San Francisco who knew Jeffrey's family and happened to live just four blocks away from where Jeffrey often stayed on the streets. So close that he likely passed by Jeffrey each week, yet still a world away.

In addition, the experience of battling poverty, trauma, and isolation for years (or even decades) leads to reactive attachment disorders, which makes it exceedingly difficult to create healthy relationships and maintain networks of support. For many people experiencing homelessness, these traumas begin early in life in the form of adverse childhood experiences (ACEs), which include experiences like parental separation, abuse, and household mental illness. As homelessness advocate Matthieu Lambert explains, "When life has taught you—through abuse or neglect by those who are meant to care for you the most—that people cannot be trusted and everyone always leaves, you naturally have a tendency to protect yourself by not letting anyone get close and actively pushing away those who try."[21]

Some might argue that people living in tent encampments and shelters are not relationally impoverished, as they connect with other people experiencing homelessness who are in a similar predicament. Though this certainly happens and provides some reprieve to the negative effects of relational poverty, it doesn't address the abject lack of resources, or *flexible capital*, available in those networks to buffer against the descent into chronic homelessness.

Jeff Olivet, Marc Dones, and their colleagues in the Supporting Partnerships for Anti-Racist Communities (SPARC) team named this "network impoverishment."[22] After speaking with 148 African Americans experiencing homelessness, they found that a unique pattern emerged: "People are not unwilling to double up, take people in, or live in another person's home—but they do not have the capacity to accommodate the additional consumption of resources (e.g., food and household goods). That in turn, strains relationships [. . .] the network itself functions in an impoverished state."[23]

Although this small sample of African Americans who were experiencing homelessness had social networks, members of their network were unable to provide much financial assistance because they themselves were extremely poor. Network impoverishment is more prevalent among people of color, who are also disproportionately likely to experience homelessness. This may explain an unusual finding: compared to their white counterparts, people of color enter homelessness with higher incomes and lower rates of mental illness, drug addiction, and health issues.[24] Because white families, even those in poverty, have more flexible capital in their networks, the theory is that more negative life events are required to trigger the experience of homelessness for white individuals than for African American individuals.

* * *

As we have tried to describe in this chapter, relational poverty is prevalent among those experiencing homelessness, is extremely difficult to overcome, and can be as devastating as financial poverty.

To be sure, histories of abuse and neglect and ongoing trauma and danger keep many people experiencing homelessness from choosing to reconnect with their would-be support networks, and for good reason. Sometimes family is part of the problem, not part of the solution. As Kevin and his team at Miracle Messages share with each unhoused client who is on the fence about reconnecting, as well as the approximately one-in-five loved ones who decline to reconnect, "You know your relationships better than we do."

But the fact remains that there are countless people experiencing homelessness who are interested in trying to reconnect with their loved ones. And there are likely tens of thousands of families looking for missing relatives who may be homeless.[25] Miracle Messages has organically received hundreds of "find them" case submissions from families desperately looking for their missing loved one, without ever advertising the service. The next time you visit a shelter, take a look at the bulletin board as you walk in: there is a good chance you will see a missing person flyer, with a plea to "call mom" or "please come home."

So if both people experiencing homelessness and their family members and loved ones often want to reconnect, why are they not already connected?

Digital literacy and access barriers play a role in keeping people disconnected. Phones frequently get lost, stolen, or broken; vital contact information for loved ones like phone numbers gets erased or lost with each new device; the free "Obamaphones" usually require proof of enrollment in a public benefit program, and there are limits to the number of free phones available to each individual;[26] the cost of monthly talk, text, and data plans can be prohibitive; finding a safe, reliable place to charge a device is difficult; learning how to use each new device is challenging; forgetting passwords and login information for email addresses, social media, and other important mobile apps is common, as is getting locked out after multiple failed login attempts; visual and auditory impairments make navigating unfamiliar devices in noisy environments especially challenging; even just having regular access to the internet is hard. Bo, an individual experiencing homelessness in Austin, Texas, whom Kevin helped reconnect with his sister after six years apart, viscerally described what he does to maintain internet access and download emails: "I sleep outside of Google to use the Wi-Fi."[27]

Bureaucratic barriers also play a role. Under the Health Insurance Portability and Accountability Act (HIPAA), shelters cannot openly confirm or deny whether someone is residing there.[28] This makes sense on the surface, as disclosing a vulnerable person's whereabouts to the wrong person would endanger them and violate their right to keep private the fact that they are experiencing homelessness as protected health information. However, common sense often goes out the window in fear of violating HIPAA (and getting sued); as such, even checking in with an unhoused guest to see if they would like to reconnect with an inquiring loved one is rare. As a result, family members and friends looking for their missing loved one who may be experiencing homelessness are left to wander the streets, ask around, and post missing person flyers at shelters.

But for most people experiencing homelessness who want to reconnect with their loved ones but have not done so, the reason for the disconnection is far deeper than a misplaced phone number or overly restrictive shelter. The separation has much more to do with emotional barriers: the fear of rejection, self-loathing and self-rejection, not wanting to be a burden, feeling worthless. In other words, *shame* (and its corollary, *stigma*) is one of the primary drivers of relational poverty among our neighbors experiencing homelessness, and is the topic of the next chapter.

KEY TAKEAWAYS

Relational poverty—a profound lack of nurturing relationships combined with stigma (and often, shame) that makes fostering social ties incredibly difficult—is a deadly form of poverty common among people experiencing homelessness, with associated health risks like those of material poverty, including increased risks of early death, poor mental health, dementia, and cardiovascular disease.

Relationships buffer tens of millions of unhoused Americans from the descent into homelessness, help facilitate the exit of homelessness, are a source of financial capital, facilitate economic mobility, and are primary concerns in the lives of individuals experiencing homelessness. And yet, the lens of relationships is often cast aside when considering solutions to homelessness.

Being without a home—which leads to a loss of opportunity, increased bureaucratic and access barriers, competing priorities, reactive attachment disorders, and experiences of shame and stigma—strains the creation of healthy relationships and the buildup of social capital over time.

Relational poverty can come in the form of network impoverishment: the experience of having social networks that lack resources, or flexible capital, to provide the necessary support to avoid or exit homelessness.

2

Stigma, Stereotypes, and Shame

IF YOU MET RAY, you would probably first be struck by his unhesitating kindness, quick smile, and genuine humility. But beyond his geniality, Ray's most remarkable characteristic might be the quiet resilience that has defined his life. Ray is a father, a hardworking middle-aged man who was raised in the Philippines among three brothers in a home bounded by equal parts strictness and love. By his own admission, Ray lived a "pretty normal" life, until one fateful day, when Ray suddenly found himself on the floor of Oakland International Airport, his knees having given way due to excruciating pain. Unbeknownst to Ray at the time, the shortness of breath, fatigue, and difficulty walking that he had experienced months prior to his homebound flight to Oakland were the early manifestations of a condition that would come to touch every aspect of his life.

When Ray was 42 years old, he was diagnosed with pulmonary congestive heart failure. He was prescribed medication, and shortly after being discharged from the hospital, he returned to work. Ray would often travel to three different cities a month, closing business deals day in and day out. Ray recognized that his fast-paced lifestyle was probably incompatible with his diagnosis, but he soldiered on, as he had a family to support, rent to pay, a daughter in high school, and no other choice. Less than a year after he fell to the ground at Oakland Airport, Ray once more felt very ill, and was again admitted to the hospital for congestive heart failure. This time, Ray was not so lucky: he had a stroke, and could no longer continue to work.

"It just started going downhill from there. It was hard to recover from it. I had to spend time in the hospital. I couldn't spend time at work. I was suffering. My personal life was one where I lived in isolation, trying to avoid being embarrassed because, first of all, I wasn't able to take care of my health. Secondly, I'm not able to hold down my life like I'm expected to."

Unable to make his way up a set of stairs, much less hustle through meandering airport terminals en route to his next client meeting, Ray was laid off from his job in sales. He began living off his savings, which he quickly depleted. Unable to pay rent, Ray relinquished his keys to his landlord within months of his stroke. For the next few years, Ray was sick, tired, isolated, and without a home.

Because he was living alone in California, away from his teenage daughter and recently separated from his wife, no one knew the extent of Ray's illness or housing predicament. Phone calls and visits from friends and family were masked with downplayed symptoms, concerns of loved ones brushed off with his steadfast determination to hide any sign of weakness. Ray was the type of person people depended on; he was never the dependent. He told others he was fine. Everyone believed it, except himself.

"I took on an attitude that 'I can handle this on my own.' I didn't want to show that I needed help. As family and friends came and visited, I really played it down, and I don't think anyone really got the full scope of what situation I was in until way later in life. Not many people, even today, know what I went through."

As his symptoms worsened, Ray gradually distanced himself from his social circle, carefully crafting a facade of happiness to mask the overwhelming isolation, sadness, depression, and loneliness he harbored from within. His scant remaining savings went to hotel rooms, followed by late-night bus rides to keep warm during the winter, followed by pretending to be a university student so he could stay at the library through the evening. For over a year, Ray walked the streets of San Francisco, immersed in physical pain and a deep-set loneliness that was supplemented by a sharp sense of fear and distrust of the unknown. During Ray's experience with homelessness, he spoke to no one; he reached out to nobody. He was embarrassed by his situation. He didn't feel that he could be good company. He gave up, and blamed himself for what happened to him—his health and his homelessness. He had no one to tell him otherwise. What followed was a downward spiral of negative thoughts, self-loathing, and deteriorated coping mechanisms that left Ray feeling stuck, afraid, deservedly poor, and alone.

"I remember thinking to myself: 'I have no idea what I'm doing.' I walked the streets and stayed away from people. There was a lot of not knowing, a lot of fear, a lot of embarrassment, a lot of loneliness, a lot of depression—all of that combined. I didn't feel like I could be good company to people. I didn't want to share what I was going through. The best way to say it was: I just gave up."

Lazy, Crazy, Addicts, Rejects

"I didn't want to be a burden to anyone."

—RAY

Ray's fear, not of his congestive heart failure, but of the perception of who he believed he had become—a sick, worthless man without a home, finding refuge on buses and in public libraries—illustrates the stigmatization facing America's unhoused. Stigma is a social phenomenon that consists of labeling, stereotyping, separation, status loss, and discrimination.[1] People without homes are labeled "the homeless," whose mere presence in society is at odds with what we deem as acceptable. Negative stereotypes emerge on who "they" are, which further separate "us" from "them." And as an undesirable "other," disregard becomes normalized, discrimination becomes justified, and Ray withdraws from other people out of fear of being "a burden."

Erving Goffman, one of the most influential American sociologists of the 20th century, characterizes stigma as "an attribute that is deeply discrediting" in which the person stigmatized is "reduced in our minds from a whole and usual person to a tainted, discounted one."[2] In other words, the stigmatized individual is considered to be less than human.

Another sociologist, Arlie Russell Hochschild, more recently described stigma as an "empathy wall" that presents "an obstacle to deep understanding of another person, one that can make us feel indifferent or even hostile to those [. . .] in different circumstances."[3] For Hochschild, understanding how this empathy wall makes people feel who are on the wrong side of it is vital. "To understand their emotions, I had to imagine myself into their shoes. To do this, I came upon their 'deep story,' a narrative as *felt*" (emphasis in the original).[4] As Hochschild suggests, stigma stands in the way of our having a more humane and compassionate understanding of people experiencing homelessness.

People experiencing homelessness tend to feel shame for their situation in part because we fail to connect with them as fellow human beings. In this chapter, we highlight some of the words and thoughts that the majority of us securely housed people may unknowingly use to create and perpetuate stigma and stereotypes of "the homeless." We also attempt to understand how this makes our neighbors experiencing homelessness feel by listening to their stories, as we believe personal storytelling is one of the most effective ways to overcome the empathy wall.

Stigma erases the multiplicity of titles every human being holds. Unwittingly, many of us perceive people experiencing homelessness as less than human. We define "the homeless" as a monolith, grouped by their lack of one physical need. As coauthors we believe that, 50 years from now, we will look back on how our society refers to "the homeless" as shockingly antiquated, offensive, and meaningless, similar to how LGBTQ+ individuals were once unthinkingly lumped together as "the homosexuals."[5] Yet for now, the coarse concept of "the homeless" persists. In reducing their individual humanity and context, we fill in the gap with negative stereotypes—lazy, crazy, addicts, rejects—which are reinforced by our perceptions of a subsection of people experiencing homelessness who are highly visible on the streets. And we conclude that homelessness must be a choice of the individuals who are experiencing homelessness, as if being without stable housing were a lifestyle choice akin to attending folk concerts or surfing at dawn.

We are guilty of *confirmation bias*. Based on very limited direct experience or narrow perceptions, we assume that all people experiencing homelessness are exactly the same. For most of us stably housed people, the only direct contact we have with "the homeless" fits our stereotypes: the abject suffering, rampant drug use, public defecation, and severe, alarming untreated mental illness we encounter on the streets; the individuals, mostly single men, we see panhandling with cardboard signs at intersections and outside shops; people sleeping or passed out on sidewalks, in alleys, or in doorways; people in tattered clothes pushing shopping carts filled with all their worldly possessions. We extrapolate from these narrow but searing experiences to the whole and grossly overgeneralize who "the homeless" are and what we assume they need. Yet less than 40% of all people experiencing homelessness, using the narrow HUD definition, are unsheltered living on the streets.[6] That means at least three out of every five people experiencing homelessness are totally imperceptible as what most of us think of when we think of "the homeless."

In reality, a substantial majority of those without housing do not have a severe mental illness and are not addicted to alcohol or drugs. According to a 2022 medically reviewed paper from the American Addictions Center, "Most research shows that around 1/3 of people who are homeless have problems with alcohol and/or drugs,"[7] and "according to the Substance Use and Mental Health Services Administration,

20 to 25% of the homeless population in the United States suffers from some form of severe mental illness."[8] And for those with such problems and unimaginable circumstances, we need empathy, not disdain—if for no other reason than there are tens of millions of "housed people" in the US who struggle with addiction and mental illness, although they are much more likely to have access to quality treatment options and care.

We are also guilty of *attribution bias*, or the tendency to perceive individual behaviors as though they are immutable personal characteristics, and overlook the circumstances in which they appear.[9] We assume the guy speeding on the highway is an impulsive, unsafe driver, but we rationalize our own speeding as resulting from being tired, hungry, or late for an important meeting. When we listen to Ray's story, it is clear that there was nothing Ray personally did to deserve homelessness. He became homeless due to very unfortunate circumstances involving a health crisis, job loss, self-imposed social isolation, and refusing to ask for help. However, public perceptions of the causes of homelessness tend to center around perceived character flaws rather than circumstances. According to Dr. Romeo Vitelli, a Canadian psychologist, from a review of social media, many Americans think that people experiencing homelessness are "dirty/unhygienic; socially deviant; potentially violent or sexual predators; threatening, violent, and/or engage in criminal behavior; deserve to be homeless; and are lazy."[10]

These biases are not created in a silo. In fact, they are ingrained in our society in ways we may not even notice. For example, an analysis of the 40 most watched television shows between 2017 and 2018, including *Roseanne*, *American Housewife*, and *Grey's Anatomy*, revealed that, when people experiencing homelessness were featured, nearly half lacked speaking parts and 80% were only featured for one episode.[11] Their stories were usually told by others and portrayed their homelessness as a result of personal failures. Even on television, people experiencing homelessness lack dignity and nuance, their only identity being the sad, poor, down-on-his-luck single man.

When a person experiencing homelessness is portrayed in a dignified or more complex way (e.g., *The Pursuit of Happyness*), their journey from rags to riches[12] usually morphs into a type of *inspiration porn*, meant to make those with secure housing feel better about themselves: for evidently if a person experiencing homelessness just works hard enough, they will be fine. In the United States, we tend to glorify and praise those who "pull themselves up by their bootstraps" and out of poverty, which—laudable as those stories may be—reinforces the individual responsibility narrative for those who remain in poverty.

Homeless nonprofits can perpetuate these stereotypes of homelessness as well. Well-meaning fundraisers urge their audiences to "help the homeless" by cherry-picking photos of people experiencing homelessness in the most decrepit and helpless of circumstances, which reinforces negative stereotypes. Fundraising tactics that visually depict the lives of a relatively small subsection of people experiencing homelessness may appeal to donors precisely because they match previously held perceptions of people experiencing homelessness. "The public must be given what they want, that is, images of charitable beneficiaries that fit comfortably with widely held stereotypes about 'victims' and that prompt the largest amount of donations" conclude researchers studying public perceptions of people experiencing homelessness.[13] This is another example of how the stories we share—whether on television, social media, or even from local nonprofits—can perpetuate stigma and exaggerate harmful stereotypes.

Language and labels play a powerful role in influencing the public perception of people experiencing homelessness. Using person-first language is dignifying, as we might describe a person with disabilities rather than a disabled person, or a returning citizen rather than a felon or ex-convict. As coauthors, we recognize that fluidity of communication is also important, and that reiterating the identifier "person experiencing homelessness" over and over again can be a mouthful. We find that "unhoused neighbors" or something of that sort usually works. At a basic level, we generally try to avoid language that absentmindedly clumps all people experiencing homelessness into "the homeless." Such commonplace descriptors reduce a diverse, complex swath of our population to an identity rooted in their lack of one physical need, and are often used in derisive, dehumanizing ways. Though the significance of using person-first terms may seem slight or even pedantic at first, the repercussions are real: people who are dehumanized in our society are more likely to be excluded, demeaned, criminalized, loathed, attacked, and ignored.

The Impact of Stigma

An unhoused blogger recently offered some practical if depressing advice for others experiencing homelessness to conceal their housing status: "Holding down a job may require that you camouflage your homelessness, though, depending on what kind of work you do. If you are a white collar worker or a service industry worker, you must keep your secret hidden [. . .] Get a mailbox at a UPS store or similar establishment, and use that as your home address [. . .] Keep clean, wear a smile, and market the skills you have. You can add finishing touches to your look by keeping a nice haircut, and getting a manicure at your nearest nail salon."[14]

This "others-aware" homeless blogger is all too familiar with how the general public stigmatizes people experiencing homelessness, and the repercussions it can have on employment. This is an example of *stigma consciousness*, where a person is acutely aware of the stigma they face and the associated stereotypes and expectations others typically hold against them.[15] In turn, this stigma consciousness compels a person to conceal some aspect of their behavior or identity, as an effort to preemptively avoid social rejection, job loss, or other negative outcomes.

Just as Ray questioned his own self-worth upon losing his job and housing, those experiencing stigma consciousness have an incessant inner dialogue revolving around the fear of rejection and the desire to avoid feeling judged by others. This perpetual state of fear and anxiety leads to a multitude of negative outcomes for the stigma-conscious individual, including strained social interactions, self-isolation and smaller social networks, lower self-esteem, depressive symptoms, unemployment and income loss, and an overall lower quality of life.[16] Constantly having to devote cognitive resources to adjusting for a devalued and stigmatized identity is not easy—after a while, it can really wear a person down.

Stigma consciousness further separates "them" from "us" and can create very different sets of opportunities in life without directly invoking any discriminatory policies, norms, or behaviors. For example, the significant amount of time the homeless blogger spent trying to conceal his identity took away from time where he could otherwise be preparing for interviews or strengthening his professional skills. Compared to someone who didn't have to conceal their identity, such time-consuming mental finessing put him at a disadvantage in getting a job and keeping it. Viewing and treating others differently—the simple act of separation and devaluation—lead to major differences in the quality of life between the stigmatized and the nonstigmatized. Stigma consciousness among people experiencing homelessness is further exacerbated for individuals who are members of groups that already face harmful stereotypes based on their race, sexual orientation, country of origin, or religion, as but a few examples.[17]

Sometimes people experiencing homelessness perpetuate their stigmatized identities themselves, in order to receive necessary goods and services. Research from Emily Meanwell at Indiana University indicates that people experiencing homelessness engage in the mental gymnastics of trying to present themselves as needy enough to receive services and not self-sufficient whilst also demonstrating that they are morally worthy of help. According to Meanwell, they "profane" themselves and their past according to the dictates of shelter providers and the stereotypes of who "deserves" care and prioritization.[18] In doing so, our unhoused neighbors are often forced to degrade themselves. Furthermore, as Isabel Wilkerson noted in *Caste*, stigmatized individuals often create further stratifications within their own group, as no one wants to be on the very bottom rung of society.[19] Perhaps this is why many people experiencing homelessness refuse to identify themselves as "homeless," preferring terms like "unhoused," "houseless," or "homefree" to distinguish themselves closer to "us," as opposed to one of "those people." This stigmatization and the need to conceal or alter one's identity, sometimes at the expense of others in the group, are even more pronounced for African Americans, Hispanic people, Native Americans, other people of color, and LGBTQ+ individuals. This is the essence of code switching, having to adjust one's identity to be more acceptable to others. As Michelle Obama memorably wrote in her memoir, *Becoming*, "You have to be twice as good to get half as far."[20]

Even long after the cause of a person's stigma is relieved—when they are no longer experiencing homelessness—the effects of being stigmatized can linger, causing the person to modulate their behaviors and conceal part of their identity in fear of being stigmatized once again. For example, a few times a year on average, Kevin will receive a random direct message from another friend who reaches out to share why his work at Miracle Messages resonates for them: that they, too, once experienced homelessness. Regardless of whether the friend's circumstance was spending a few months in a shelter while being raised by a single parent, struggling to make ends meet as an aspiring actor or entrepreneur, or fleeing domestic violence, almost all these messages include the request "please do not share this with anyone else."

From senior executives at Fortune 500 companies to high-profile founders of successful startups, many individuals who have experienced homelessness at some point in their lives remain in the closet, so to speak, fearful that revealing their story would result in negative professional and social repercussions. It's understandable; even decades later, few experiences are as shocking and stigmatizing as homelessness.

Being stigmatized also strains a person's social networks. The stigma associated with being unhoused keeps people out of spaces they would otherwise be able to occupy to build social capital. Instead of going to a church to join a community, people who are unhoused go to church to receive assistance. Ray went to libraries for quiet refuge from the streets, not for book clubs or author readings where he would socialize with others. Through constant labeling as a "charity project," never an equal, those experiencing homelessness are rejected from spaces and the embedded potential relationships nested therein.

We believe it is incumbent upon those of us who are securely housed—including those of us who were once homeless—to help right these wrongs and reduce the stigma our unhoused neighbors face every day. We suggest approaches for replacing stigma with respect in chapter 13.

"I Can't . . . I *Feel* Dirty"

During Miracle Messages outreach events, Kevin routinely meets people experiencing homelessness who are interested in reconnecting with their loved ones and begin the process but change their mind right before recording a message. In the past, Kevin usually assumed that the person needed more time to think about it or perhaps got cold feet, and would move on without too much further consideration of it. Until one day, when an especially earnest person experiencing homelessness abruptly changed their mind about trying to reconnect with their family and offered the following explanation: "I can't . . . I *feel* dirty."

As Kevin began asking more follow-up questions to would-be clients who had changed their minds about reconnecting, patterns began to emerge. It turned out that an internalized sense of shame and worthlessness was the primary apparent reason why some individuals experiencing homelessness had a last-minute change of heart about reconnecting with their loved ones through Miracle Messages. This is a type of uncleanliness that is felt, that cannot be easily washed off.[21] Many of our neighbors experiencing homelessness feel deeply ashamed of their situations, and do not want to be a burden for the people they love most. They choose to stay disconnected not in spite of their love for their families and friends, but because of it. For them, as heartbreaking as this is, distance is an act of love.

While Ray was experiencing homelessness, he felt ashamed of his situation. Ray struggled mightily with his identity as *a homeless person* and internalized the stigma it carried. He started to self-identify with the stereotypes that others held about homelessness. Ray wondered if he truly was a failure, and if he was isolated and disconnected from others for good reason—he deserved it. In his words, "I didn't feel like I could be good company to people."

In Don Burnes's previous book, *Journeys out of Homelessness,* a person experiencing homelessness named Barb similarly remarked on the profound shame that accompanies homelessness.

> "My deep, deep shame, and need for hiding [. . .] came from the fact that I was unworthy. I was a 'nothing and a nobody' and didn't deserve to be cared for. I had to hide out so no one else would find that out. [. . .] Many of these societal trappings of acceptability—like having a job, or being able to pay your bills, or having a house, or having a spouse, or having kids, or having friends, or having whatever—are at the root of so much of our shame [. . .] Yet they rob us of our dignity when they are missing, or we lose them."[22]

Like Barb, Ray was kept trapped by his shame. Not seeing his own intrinsic dignity and self-worth, he avoided people and covered up his situation. And not having the type of nurturing relationships and supportive community that we all need, Ray became more and more removed from the reality of his own value as a human being. To paraphrase James Joyce, Ray lived at a little distance from his self-esteem, regarding his own acts with doubtful side-glances.

It would take a special friendship to help Ray see his own dignity again. Fortunately, through the Miracle Friends phone buddy program, Ray was matched with Jen, whom he described as his "guardian angel." Jen supported Ray when he was feeling down, and vice versa. Ray was also selected for Miracle Money, which enabled him to save up enough money to split an apartment with a friend in Kansas, where he now lives and works. At the one-year mark of being stably housed, Ray expressed his gratitude in a heartfelt email: "I will always be grateful to Miracle Friends. At first, I was thankful to have Jen's company and friendship. She helped strengthen me mentally and emotionally so that I was able to feel hopeful again. Then your kindness and the financial support from the Miracle Money program allowed me to take action and turn my hopes into reality. I don't know how else to put it but . . . thank you for giving me life."

This is the difference that love, a few nurturing relationships, and very modest financial resources can make in helping our unhoused neighbors get off the streets and countering the stigma and shame associated with homelessness. We will address solutions like these in more detail in the last two chapters of our book, but for now, it is worth highlighting how imperative it is that we each take the first step, namely, by questioning widely held stereotypes of homelessness. For example, about 45% of unhoused adults are working, but the vast majority of them do not earn enough money to afford rent. For those who do not work, old age or disability or both keeps some from employment, while others are unable to overcome the huge barriers that exist to employment for our unhoused neighbors, a topic we will explore at length in chapter 7.[23] And as previously noted, far less than half of all those experiencing homelessness in the United States can be categorized as unsheltered people. The rest, invisible to most of us, include many who live in shelters or transitional housing like tiny homes. Using facts and figures like these, we can debunk harmful stereotypes of "the homeless."

While data suggest that over 60% of Americans view the causes of homelessness as a variety of personal failings, such as drug use, alcoholism, mental illness, laziness, and bad decisions,[24] it is our goal in this book to prove that the real culprits are systemic in nature: inadequate housing and disastrous housing policies, inadequate wages and poor jobs, health care and child care that are simply too expensive, health insurance that doesn't cover those most in need, an inhumane criminal justice system, transportation systems that do not meet the needs of those who desperately need good, low-cost public transportation, educational systems that fail to provide quality education for all students, and cultural systems that don't help people build or maintain social capital. In addition, profound failures in our basic humanity enable these broken service systems to remain broken: as we saw in the previous chapter, relational poverty isolates many of those experiencing homelessness, depriving them of social capital resources that are so essential for a positive and successful life. And hostile and false stereotypes that view homelessness as a personal failing perpetuate the stigma that our unhoused neighbors live with, which has major implications for their overall health and well-being. But that is not all: negative presumptions about who "they" are and where "they" came from lead to widespread official exclusion of our unhoused neighbors, in a type of cruel modern equivalent of leper colonies—sometimes no more subtle than physically shipping people out to other states or "homeless islands."[25] We will explore this topic in the next chapter.

KEY TAKEAWAYS

Stigma—a social phenomenon that consists of labeling, stereotyping, separation, status loss, and discrimination—is a common experience of individuals experiencing homelessness, both for being without a home and for being members of other marginalized groups (e.g., Black people, Hispanic people, people with disabilities) that are themselves stigmatized.

Stigma is reinforced through various media, including on TV, news, and even through fundraisers that attempt to support individuals experiencing homelessness, along with fallacies in human reasoning, most prominently confirmation bias and attribution bias.

People who are stigmatized develop a stigma consciousness; aware of their stigma and of the low expectations held by others, they expect negative outcomes, such as social rejection, which advances to internalized stigma and then shame—a process that leads to a vicious cycle of strained social interactions, self-isolation, a lower self-esteem, a decreased desire to seek help, and depression.

The lived experiences associated with being physically without a home enforce a sense of shame, such as being unable to bathe properly or apply for a job due to a loss of identification.

We counteract the stigma and stereotypes around homelessness by using person-first language (e.g., "people experiencing home-lessness," not "the homeless"), questioning stereotypes, and offering counter-facts, data, and humanizing stories that reflect the actual state of homelessness.

3

Exclusion

"I did not know that that person, when I was walking by, was [my cousin]."

—EVAN, PARTICIPANT IN THE NEW YORK CITY
RESCUE MISSION EXPERIMENT

The Other

In 2014 the New York CITY Rescue Mission staged a social experiment to see whether five unsuspecting local residents would recognize close members of their very own families who were dressed up to look like individuals experiencing homelessness and living on the streets.[1] Siblings, spouses, parents, and other relatives were disguised under our homogenized image of "the homeless," wearing mismatched sweatshirts and threadbare caps, holding dented cans for spare change, looking generally unkempt, and sitting bundled up on top of cardboard on the streets, in the clear line of sight of their loved ones. They watched silently as their loved ones approached, en route to their homes, workplaces, and next meetings.

Not a single person recognized their own mother, father, wife, or brother. Some of the passing loved ones appeared to slow down for a furtive glance. Others hurried by with averted eyes. Some looked straight ahead. Their reactions (or lack thereof) were captured on hidden camera and are memorable for being so unremarkable: each scene feels utterly casual, expected, and telling.

The roots of such disregard and obliviousness to "the homeless" run surprisingly deep in the human psyche. In 2002 psychologist Susan Fiske and her colleagues developed what they call the *stereotype content model*. In this model, population sectors, such as the middle class, the elderly, addicts, and the wealthy, are categorized along the dimensions of perceived competence and warmth.[2] The model is based on the theory that we evaluate people as either friends or enemies and quickly assess whether they have power or resources.[3] According to their findings, groups stereotyped as low in warmth and high in competence (e.g., the rich) elicited feelings of envy and jealousy, while populations stereotyped as high in warmth and low in competence (e.g., the elderly) tended to incite feelings of pity. On the other hand, populations stereotyped as high in both warmth and competence invoked sentiments of pride and admiration (e.g., the middle class), while populations stereotyped as low in both warmth and competence elicited feelings of contempt and disgust (e.g., the poor).

Fiske and her colleagues found that the population perceived as the lowest in both warmth and competence (the low-low quadrant) was "homeless people." This group engendered the strongest prejudice, inducing feelings of blatant disgust, disrespect, and dislike. To further test these findings, Fiske and her colleague Lasana Harris used functional magnetic resonance imaging (fMRI) on a random sample of participants to evaluate how different parts of the brain, associated with different emotions, became activated or deactivated after being shown pictures of different populations. Groups from all quadrants except the low-low quadrant were found to elicit responses in the medial prefrontal cortex, an area of the brain that is activated in social cognition tasks (e.g., when thinking about or forming impressions of another person) but not in tasks involving nonsocial or object cognition.[4] When participants viewed images of low-low groups, including individuals identified as welfare recipients, people living in poverty, and people experiencing homelessness, their medial prefrontal cortex showed no signs of activation.

In other words, our brains perceive extreme outgroups—including people experiencing homelessness—as nonhuman.

It gets worse. The images of low-low groups *did* elicit responses in the left insula and right amygdala, which are the same areas of the brain that are activated when viewing disgusting objects such as vomit. To summarize these findings: upon viewing images of extreme outgroups, the region of our brain that normally activates when we see a fellow human being is not activated, but the region of our brain that activates when we feel disgusted by the sight of a gross inanimate object is activated. This forms the neurological basis of dehumanization: individuals experiencing homelessness are perceived as less than human, even at the neural level.[5]

The implications from these experiments are astounding. Even if a member of an extreme outgroup like a person experiencing homelessness is not physically excluded from a particular place, our brain cognitively excludes them. This neurological dehumanization results from social divides and the language we have developed that defines "the other," thus fully distinguishing them from us. As we have mentioned previously, we would never refer to people with stable housing as "the housed," but we widely clump those without stable housing into "the homeless."

By dehumanizing our unhoused neighbors, we can feel justified in blaming them for their own misery . . . and ours. According to French philosopher René Girard, every society produces scapegoats: humans compete for the same objects and outcomes, resources are perceived as scarce, and conflict inevitably ensues, which is limited or localized by "uniting against an arbitrary other who is excluded and blamed for all the chaos."[6] The hapless other is targeted by society as "truly guilty or dangerous."[7] Under this framework, we metaphorically walk by our unhoused neighbors (along with literally walking by them) by excluding them as the "arbitrary other," rather than seeing our society's deeply rooted systemic problems reflected in their faces.

. . . But We Are Connected

Notwithstanding our judgmental and exclusionary medial prefrontal cortex and tendency to scapegoat, as humans, we are *much* more connected and similar than we are disconnected and dissimilar. At a genetic level, we are 99.9% identical—any two people on Earth share 999 out of every 1,000 DNA bases. "Within the human population, all genetic variations—the inheritable differences in our physical appearance, health, and personality—add up to just 0.1 percent of about 3 billion bases," describes Jonathan Marks, a biological anthropologist at the University of North Carolina at Charlotte.[8] It seems ludicrous to assume that the 0.1% genetic variation between humans accounts for the extreme variations we see in quality of life, net worth, and housing status. As the aphorism goes, "talent is universal; opportunity is not." Yet we otherize people experiencing homelessness as "the homeless," a semipermanent identifier that would make much more sense if there were a Planet Homelessness from where our unhoused neighbors emigrated.[9]

As humans, we are also deeply connected. In a pioneering study carried out by Microsoft in 2006, researchers evaluated over 30 billion electronic conversations originating from 180 million people from all over the world. The purpose of the study was to determine the veracity of the "small world problem," that is, how many intermediaries it takes us, on average, to be connected to anyone else in the world.[10] Researchers found that only six people lie between us and the entirety of present-day humankind. Five years later in 2011, Facebook analyzed data from its then 721 million users and found that the average distance between users is 4.74, corresponding to 3.74 degrees of separation.[11] Today, with the continued rapid growth of social networks over the past decade worldwide, our degree of separation has decreased from six to less than four, and there is no reason why it will not continue to shrink to even smaller degrees.

Recall from the introduction chapter of this book that HUD conservatively estimates there are 582,462 people experiencing homelessness on any given night in the United States, while the US Education Department numbers indicate that as many as 6 million people nationwide will experience homelessness at some point over the course of the year.[12] Just as we are connected to our family members, friends, coworkers, teachers, and classmates, we are connected to the 582,462 Americans who will experience homelessness tonight, and the 6 million Americans who will experience homelessness at some point this year—for *they* are them. Even three degrees of separation would be the son of your roommate's sister, or the brother of your spouse's favorite coworker—it is that close at a baseline. And given how closeted the experience of homelessness is, your own degree of separation is almost certainly even closer than that, whether you happen to know that your loved one is experiencing homelessness or not.

And yet, in the scores of talks that Kevin has given after founding Miracle Messages, no more than 5%–10% of his audience raises their hands when asked if they know someone who is currently experiencing homelessness, despite nearly 100% of them raising their hands when asked if they care about the issue of homelessness. If we are more connected than ever before, and we say we care about homelessness, why are most of us unable to name a single person we know who is currently experiencing homelessness?[13]

Not in My Backyard

When most of us think about "the homeless," we do not see the loneliness, the isolation, the exhaustion, the lack of agency in deciding even the most basic choices of the day—what to eat, when to eat, when to use the bathroom and bathe, where to sleep, who to interact with, how to feel safe. We do not see the stories of bravery, the fortitude it takes to live in a society where no one seems to acknowledge your presence, let alone your inherent dignity. We are not confronted with the mental and physical resilience that our unhoused neighbors must exert to survive days, weeks, months, years, or even decades of relational poverty and housing insecurity, almost always amid chronic illness, untreated injury, and ongoing trauma. The experience of homelessness is foreign and incomprehensible to most of us, and frankly we prefer to keep it that way.

In our brains, news media, and daily conversations, we form, reinforce, and validate a separate group that we call "the homeless," instead of getting to know the actual people who are experiencing homelessness in our midst—for if we ventured too close, we might recognize ourselves. So for the most part, we live in two separate worlds. No wonder that the participants in the NYC Rescue Mission experiment did not register their family members who were dressed up to look homeless; their family members might as well have been wearing invisibility cloaks or hiding behind bushes.

Where our worlds do intersect, we are left feeling frustrated, disgusted, angry, cynical, and helpless—which often gives way to NIMBYism. NIMBYism, or the "Not in My Back Yard" phenomenon, is typified by residents who oppose new housing developments near their homes, especially affordable and denser housing, homeless shelters, treatment centers, and the like.

At its core, NIMBYism involves a narrowly defined self-interest that excludes people and behaviors that we perceive to be unlike ourselves, such as people experiencing homelessness. NIMBYs who oppose new housing projects in their neighborhoods for people emerging from homelessness cite fears of physical safety, drug paraphernalia, broken bottles, vandalism, and robbery to justify their exclusionary posture, on the assumption that our unhoused neighbors are untrustworthy riff-raff, or that their presence in a neighborhood would be at odds with the local character, which must be defended.[14] Anything that may pose a potential threat to NIMBYs—namely their children, their property values, or their idealized version of where they live— must be stopped. Rampant levels of NIMBYism throughout the country push people experiencing homelessness further to the margins, concentrating them on skid rows and tent islands rather than working to help integrate them into neighborhoods, where we can all thrive. As Chris Herring suggests, the effect of NIMBYism is to exclude and seclude people experiencing homelessness, forcing them away from everyone else and into less desirable, more dangerous spaces.[15]

One of the perpetual fears of NIMBYs is that by providing housing or other facilities for people experiencing homelessness in their neighborhood, crime will increase. Two recent studies in Denver suggest just the opposite. In an evaluation of the tiny home village in the Mile High City, rates of crimes in four major categories declined within a quarter mile of the village, including substantial decreases in robbery and drugs and narcotics.[16] An article in the *Colorado Sun* indicated that, although there was a 14.3% increase in crimes between 2020 and 2021 for the city as a whole, there was actually a 2.8% decrease in crimes in the six neighborhoods where there were sanctioned (or supported) encampments for those experiencing homelessness, known locally as Safe Outdoor Spaces.[17]

But this begs the question: if the fears associated with NIMBYism are mostly boogeymen, then what else might be motivating the contingent of people who want to "safeguard" their communities by closing them off?

Ultimately what underlies NIMBYism is the presumption of intractable differences between "us" and "them," with the most fundamental difference being one of who belongs here and who does not. We might describe this as *placehood*, or who is perceived to have the right to be in a particular area: of course, we are welcome here, but they are not.[18]

But this exclusionary tendency is based on the xenophobic and wildly inaccurate belief that most people experiencing homelessness are not from the area where they are currently homeless. In reality, many of our unhoused neighbors were once our housed neighbors (and family members, friends, and former classmates).[19] A 2019 article by the journalist Inyoung Kang in the *New York Times* entitled "Where Does California's Homeless Population Come From?" illustrates this widespread misconception in the context of Los Angeles County, first by quoting West Coast readers' misguided questions (we've chosen to use readers' first names only), and then by laying out the actual data:

> Christine, a reader from Stockton, wrote: "Where are the homeless people from? If they are transplants, when did they come to California, what brought them here, and how did they end up in their current circumstances?"

Another reader, Jim, from Santa Cruz, wrote that he believed "many, if not most" of the homeless people he saw were not native Californians. He asked: "Why is California bearing the brunt of this national crisis?"

Elizabeth, a reader in Seattle, echoed his sentiments, saying: "Do many homeless or near-homeless move to politically liberal areas, making the assumption that they will receive more assistance?"

The *New York Times* article looks at data from the 2019 homeless count by the Los Angeles Homeless Services Authority, the agency that conducts the largest homeless census count in the country. According to the agency's report, 67.6% of the 58,936 Los Angeles County residents experiencing homelessness had lived in the county for more than 10 years, and 75.2% had lived in the county for more than five years. And 75.5% of respondents said they had lived in Los Angeles County or another county in Southern California prior to becoming homeless, a figure that bumps up to 80% when somewhere else in California is included as an option. In other words, most of the individuals experiencing homelessness that Californians walk by are fellow Californians. As Kang poignantly writes, "Some may have rented an apartment or once owned a home in your neighborhood. Now they sleep in an encampment near the freeway you take to work each morning." Or as Peter Lynn, the former executive director of the Los Angeles Homeless Services Authority put it, "This is a local crisis and a homegrown problem."[20]

Considering all of this, "Not in My Back Yard" is a misnomer; "Already in My Back Yard" (AIMBY) would be more appropriate. Or if we also look at the data about migration to California from other states, which shows that the largest group of transplants are actually college-educated professionals, an even more accurate acronym might be PHITALBTPBYWY: "Probably Here in This Area Long Before That Particular Back Yard Was Yours." It's a mouthful, but something needs to be said to counter the narrative that "the homeless" are mostly out-of-state transplants, which is used by NIMBYs and politicians to justify excluding them. But perhaps Christine, the reader from Stockton and a lifelong Californian, has a healthier suggestion than trying to popularize an unwieldy new acronym: "I hear a lot of people complain that the homeless people are all from 'somewhere else.' I think it might raise empathy and compassion if it turns out that the majority of the people who have been displaced are from the very communities in which they are now trying to survive on the streets."[21]

How Cities Weaponize Design and Policy to Target "the Homeless"

NIMBYism runs far deeper than the occasional angry homeowner protesting a proposed tiny home village or condominium in their neighborhood. Hostile architecture (or hostile design), for example, uses elements of the built environment to purposefully restrict behavior of people experiencing homelessness: armrest dividers on park benches to prevent people from sleeping, water sprinklers that spray intermittently, loudspeakers blaring classical music outside businesses to prevent loitering, sloped windowsills to prevent sitting, jagged boulders under freeway overpasses to prevent camping. These physical manifestations of exclusion have been installed extensively throughout the United States and around the world to prevent people experiencing homelessness from finding a place to sleep, rest, or simply be, and to demoralize, stigmatize, and physically harm them when they have no other options.[22] The message is clear to our neighbors experiencing homelessness: *you are not welcome here.*

Anti-homeless local ordinances are another category of what we would broadly construe as NIMBYism. In a first-of-its-kind report in 2021 on how states regulate acts of survival such as public sleeping and panhandling, the National Homelessness Law Center found that 48 of 50 states and the District of Columbia have laws that criminalize behaviors associated with homelessness. Cities across the country have passed local statutes that prohibit public camping, sitting, loitering, lying down, feeding, asking for charity, vagrancy, and more.[23] "From 2006–2019, the National Homelessness Law Center has tracked these

laws in 187 cities and found that city-wide bans on camping have
increased by 92%, on sitting or lying by 78%, on loitering by 103%,
on panhandling by 103%, and on living in vehicles by 213%,"[24] writes
legal director Eric Tars. It appears that Stanley Mosk, the longest-serving
justice of the California Supreme Court, was prescient when he warned
in a 1995 decision that when courts uphold anti-homelessness laws, they
encourage a "competition among cities to impose comparable restrictions in order to avoid becoming a refuge for homeless persons driven
out by other cities."[25]

Johnny, a 65-year-old man who lived on and off the streets in San
Francisco for many years before getting housed, poignantly described
the impact "quality of life" ordinances had on his quality of life while
living in a tent: "They would take you to jail. When I was homeless,
you couldn't be seen. You had to find a place that hid you from the
public. You had to be up by six in the morning because if not, they
woke you up and took your stuff and they'd say: 'If you want your stuff
back, you have to go 10 miles out of the city.' What they really did was
dumpster it."

Hostile architecture, hostile ordinances, and hostile residents combine
to make existence—let alone integration and connection—exceptionally
hard for our neighbors experiencing homelessness. For many of us, this
hostile architecture and these hostile ordinances may seem invisible or of
little meaning. To those experiencing homelessness, however, they make
a huge difference. When we practice exclusion, we further stigmatize and
demoralize a group of people who are largely from our community, and
who often have no other place to go. We make homelessness an even more
closeted, isolating experience—a scarlet letter "H" for our neighbors.

KEY TAKEAWAYS

We walk by those without homes, even when they are our family,
as illustrated by the New York City Rescue Mission experiment,
an example of how, as a society, people experiencing homelessness are "out of sight, out of mind."

Even if not physically excluded (out of sight, out of mind), our brain excludes "others." Groups rated as low in warmth and competence by the stereotype content model (e.g., "homeless people") don't elicit neural response in the area of the brain implicated in social cognition tasks, indicating that these groups are perceived as objects and less than human.

Fewer than four people lie between us and the entirety of present-day humankind, meaning that we are connected, whether we know it or not, to the hundreds of thousands of Americans who experience homelessness each night; yet few of us can say we are friends with a person currently experiencing homelessness.

The vast majority of people support efforts to address homelessness. But when those efforts require development or change in our own neighborhoods and local communities, many of us may have second thoughts or even push back (the NIMBY phenomenon), leading to further isolation and exclusion of our neighbors experiencing homelessness.

Our neighbors experiencing homelessness are also excluded from our communities through hostile architecture, hostile design, and anti-homeless ordinances, all of which make the experience of homelessness even more dangerous and disconnected.

4

Paternalism

UPON HIS RELEASE FROM SAN Quentin State Prison after a six-year sentence for burglary, Ronnie had nowhere to go and ended up on the streets of San Francisco. Despite all of this, Ronnie managed to keep his addictions and depression at bay for years, and he devoted his life to running, art, and community service.

Ronnie was known by locals as "Ronnie the Runner" or "Ronnie the Artist." In 2014 Ronnie raised over $10,000 for charity by participating in the San Francisco Half Marathon while living on the streets.[1] He was also known for his gripping artwork, which he said was "inspired by the beauty of this city and its diversity, balanced with the struggles of human despair. With my brush, I try to capture these raw emotions in painted images." In 2020 Ronnie's artwork was scheduled to be featured for the first time in a major New York City gallery, as part of the exhibit *Marking Time: Art in the Age of Mass Incarceration*, at MOMA PS1 in Queens. The opening was scheduled to be on September 17—exactly six weeks after Ronnie tragically passed away on the streets at the age of 60.

Kevin first met Ronnie in 2014 as one of the homeless autobiographers who volunteered to wear a camera around their chest for a few hours to narrate some of their experiences on the streets. Kevin also interviewed Ronnie a handful of times over the years, including for a podcast and an "Ask Me Anything" on Reddit. In one of their early conversations, Kevin asked Ronnie whether he had any promising leads for housing on the horizon, or if there was anything he could do to help. Ronnie replied, "Oh, I have housing available to me if I wanted it."

"Really? Then why don't you take it?" Kevin responded. Ronnie looked at Kevin for a moment, apparently surprised by Kevin's surprise. Ronnie took a breath and patiently replied, "Well, it's in a building and area where drugs are present 24/7. If I go to that housing, I'll slip back. I need to be mindful of who I am. I have to be careful. I have addiction issues, and I can't deal with bad areas. I'll be better off if I live under a bridge than going back to my old neighborhood. I have too many good things going for me right now. So I'm just waiting a few more years until I'm eligible for senior housing."

"Has a Homeless Person Ever Refused Food You've Offered Them?"

If someone did not know the circumstances of Ronnie's situation and just heard that a person who was living on the streets of San Francisco had declined free housing that was offered to them, they might be confused, frustrated, or angry. Perhaps they might use the story to affirm a preexisting prejudice,[2] assuming that Ronnie is yet another example of a person experiencing homelessness *choosing* to be homeless. Perhaps they might respond as Tanja did when a person experiencing homelessness refused a meal offer from her young son. She related the story in response to a question posted online, which is quoted as this section's subtitle:

> Months ago 3 of my children, my husband and I were at a taco/Mexican grocery store and a man who seemed *very homeless* sat outside with a sign that said I will work for food, help, please anything will help. So my 9 yr old wanted to help so

badly. We ordered him 2 tacos with rice and beans with a Coke and water bottle. The man seemed irritated and told my son no I only want money. My son still tried to tell him to save it for later and keep it anyway. The homeless man refused which absolutely crushed my son's big heart. *I was so mad I told my son see some people just want drugs.* We then just took the drinks and tacos home. It has been months since, and neither he nor I have given any homeless person anything since. I tend to give out cold water bottles at lights but haven't been lately. [emphasis added][3]

Clearly, Ronnie offered an understandable, even commendable reason for declining housing, as he did not want to jeopardize his ongoing recovery by living in an unsafe environment. And clearly, Tanja and her son did not hear an explanation to their liking for why the "very homeless" man refused their seemingly well-intentioned offer. There could have been many explanations for why the person refused them: perhaps he didn't like tacos, or had an upset stomach, or had just eaten, or had slept poorly and was uncharacteristically rude after a long day, or was a diabetic and had only noticed the sugar-rich Coke, or was preoccupied with finding work or getting a few more dollars for a hotel room for the night, or felt emotionally raw at the sight of a young boy who vaguely reminded him of his own son he hadn't seen in a few years. Perhaps, for some unseen reason, accepting the meal would have done him more harm than good, as accepting the housing would have potentially done to Ronnie. Or perhaps the "very homeless" man just wanted to trick sympathetic parents and their children into giving him money so he could buy drugs, as Tanja suspected. Who knows.

The more important question is not whether a particular individual experiencing homelessness can offer a satisfactory explanation for declining a meal or a housing option, but why we feel entitled to make this assessment in the first place. Would we invite a similar level of interrogation on our decisions of what to eat, where to live, who to date, how to interact with passersby, or how to spend our money?

How would we feel if someone presumed they knew what was best for us and our families, better than we do?

Tanja's reaction—"I was so mad I told my son see some people just want drugs"—provides a clear example of the deeply rooted paternalism and prejudice we exhibit toward our neighbors experiencing homelessness. Often subconsciously, we tend to presume that people experiencing homelessness do not know what is good for themselves and can't take care of themselves—*otherwise why would they be homeless?*—so we must tell them what they need.

Progressive Paternalism and Punitive Paternalism

In an article entitled "Ethical Issues in Geriatric Medicine," Howard M. Fillit defined paternalism as taking actions or making decisions for another person, under the belief that those actions or decisions will benefit the person. "The word is derived from the Latin word for father; the idea is that a paternalist decision is like the decision a good father would make for his child," writes Dr. Fillit.[4] As coauthors, we find this notion of the father making decisions for his child helpful in understanding what we believe are two recurring models in which our society is paternalistic toward "the homeless."

The first model we call *progressive paternalism*, which is characterized by pity and self-righteousness, and in which we try to play the father role as healer, like a doctor with a patient. In this model, we feel sorry for our helpless unhoused neighbors, who are all struggling with severe substance use, untreated mental illness, and/or a lack of opportunities, and we feel a moral duty to fix them.

The second model we call *punitive paternalism*, which is characterized by condemnation and law and order, and in which we play the father role as tough love enforcer, like a judge at a sentencing hearing. In this model, we feel anger toward our misbehaving unhoused neighbors, who are all drug- or alcohol-addicted sinners who make poor decisions, and we have to punish them for their bad behaviors.

Both of these models position us as "saviors," but neither model compels us to take the time to engage with our unhoused neighbors, to listen to their stories and try to understand their challenges, frustrations, and actual needs. The savior complex found in both progressive and punitive paternalism ignores context, and gives us the illusion that we are doing something morally right and for the greater good when we may, in fact, be exacerbating existing problems.

Tanja, in the earlier story in this chapter, is irate at the "very homeless" man's lack of gratitude for her son's offer. Similarly, when we are generous and try to do a good deed for a person experiencing homelessness, we may subconsciously expect to be thanked and praised for our efforts. If you stop at a traffic light, see a person asking for charity, and hand them a dollar bill or a granola bar or a bottle of water, would you feel a tad disappointed if you did not hear "thank you"? As coauthors, we certainly would. But the reality is that one dollar does not go very far toward rent, some people hate granola bars, maybe the person has received six bottles of water in the last hour alone,[5] and like the "very homeless" man Tanja and her son encountered, we have no idea what their situation is.

When we do not take the time to hear the actual stories of our neighbors experiencing homelessness and seek to understand their lived experiences, we are likely giving more for our own sake than for theirs. In his groundbreaking book, *The Book on Ending Homelessness*, Iain De Jong, a policy analyst and industry leader, cites Robert Lupton's famous idea of toxic charity, or the negative effects that modern charity often has upon the very people meant to benefit from it. De Jong writes that "charity can respond to the most immediate needs a person has—such as hunger or shelter—but structurally is not equipped to make the shift from immediate needs to permanent solutions. Consider a natural disaster, such as a hurricane or tornado or earthquake. There can be an outpouring of immediate charity, such as blankets and tents and food and water. But will any of those things put lives back together over the long term? No."[6]

Invisible People, a nonprofit dedicated to shattering stereotypes of homelessness by sharing firsthand stories of the lives of people experiencing homelessness, interviewed Andy, a 21-year old who, due to his father's alcoholism, left home to live on the streets, where he felt safer. Andy described his internal thoughts when well-intentioned passersby presume to know what he needs: "People think that you want food. Yeah, you want food, but you want your own food. They pass you a Burger King. What if you don't want Burger King? [. . .] I could chuck food all day. I need housing. I need a mobile phone. I need essentials. I need a towel; I need a toothbrush; I need toothpaste [. . .] Don't buy a McDonald's. I don't want a McDonald's."[7]

Distrust, but Verify

In 2013 a person experiencing homelessness named Billy Ray Harris returned an engagement ring that was mistakenly dropped in the cup he used to collect spare change. The story made international news, and the grateful owners of the ring created a fundraising page on Harris's behalf. In just a few weeks, over $175,000 was raised to help Harris get back on his feet. Harris was able to use the money to buy a car, put money down on a house, put some in a trust, and get off the streets. In addition, amid the extensive media coverage, Robin Harris, his younger sister, recognized her brother's name in an article and reached out to the local news station that first reported the story. In her words, "I called and I said, 'That's my brother. I've been looking for him for 16 years.'" Shortly thereafter, Harris reunited with his family on the set of the *Today* show.[8]

Harris's good deed was indeed praiseworthy, and the sequence of events that followed the initial news story were widely reported as a near-parable for how doing the right thing can change your life, even if it may seem personally disadvantageous at first.[9]

But taking a step back for a moment, it is worth asking why Harris's selfless act was seen as so remarkable in the first place, enough to merit extensive media coverage and public acclaim. Why is "Homeless Man Returns Expensive Engagement Ring Accidentally Dropped in Change Cup" a front-page, feel-good news story, anyway? If "Homeless Man" were replaced with "Barista" or "Busker," would the story still be noteworthy? Perhaps. What about "Physician Returns Expensive Engagement Ring Accidentally Left Behind by a Patient?" Probably not.

Harris's good deed was notable in the first place because our society does not expect people experiencing homelessness (or people living below the poverty line more generally) to behave in trustworthy, kind, selfless ways. We tend to assume that our paternalism toward our unhoused neighbors is merited because they are irresponsible, dangerous, and untrustworthy. When someone like Harris shows that these stereotypes are wrong, or at least reveals himself to be *one of the good ones*,[10] they may receive front page news coverage and massive support. In the flurry of coverage, only one commentator seemed to provide some nuance to the story: Harris himself, who said, "I am not trying to say that I am no saint, but I am no devil either."[11]

The media itself deserves much deeper scrutiny for how it reinforces harmful stereotypes. For instance, 66% of poor people in the US are white families, but only 17% of the poor people depicted in news and opinion media are white. Conversely, 27% of poor people in the US are Black families, but they represent 59% of the poor people depicted in the media. Whether exalting a single Black man like Harris as one of the good ones while systematically misrepresenting the face of poverty as Black, media portrayals can dangerously distort public perception and validate paternalistic attitudes toward marginalized groups, including people experiencing homelessness.[12]

Harris deserves much credit for pointing out his own flawed humanity in an interview. Even though he was temporarily on the good side of the good-versus-bad media portrayal, he seemed to intuit that the same could not be said for the vast majority of people experiencing homelessness. While Harris may have temporarily earned the public's trust to great acclaim, he did so only because he started from a place of being distrusted as a person experiencing homelessness. Indeed, a prerequisite of paternalism is our assumption that "the homeless" cannot be trusted, built on the premise that "they" are mostly dangerous and unpredictable. Yet data suggest that in most crimes involving a person experiencing homelessness, it is the person experiencing homelessness who is the victim, usually at the hands of a housed assailant.

From the findings in the first national survey on homeless people in the mid-1990s, to local reports from all over the country about homeless people being senselessly murdered and even targeted by serial killers, it's one of the many things that makes homelessness so dangerous for the people experiencing it. While suffering in plain sight, and making many housed people feel uncomfortable, the vast majority of homeless people, including people with mental illness, aren't hurting anyone.[13]

A person experiencing homelessness is less likely to perpetrate a violent crime than a stably housed person and "is in fact more likely to be the victim of a violent crime, especially if they are a woman, teen, or child."[14] In those cases where a person experiencing homelessness is the perpetrator, the victim is typically another person experiencing homelessness.

Another example of how our distrust toward "the homeless" shows up in the world is our suspicion that any money they receive will be spent in a manner we consider unwise, such as purchasing drugs or alcohol. Consequently, we rationalize that giving people experiencing homelessness food or water is better for them. In fact, in studies where the use of such funds has been examined, people experiencing homelessness have overwhelmingly proven to be excellent stewards of their money.

A joint study started in 2018 by Foundations for Social Change, a Vancouver-based charitable organization, and the University of British Columbia, called the New Leaf Project, gave 50 people experiencing homelessness for at least six months a lump sum of $7,500—no strings attached—and followed their progress for the next 12 months.[15] What they found was striking: compared to the control group, those receiving $7,500 both spent 4,396 fewer days homeless and moved into stable housing within an average of three months, compared to five months for the control group. Those receiving the lump sum did not mismanage their money. On average, 52% of the funds were spent on food and rent, 15% on other essential items such as medications and bills, and 16% on clothes and transportation. Nearly 70% of those receiving payments were food secure within one month of receiving their funds, while spending on alcohol, cigarettes, and drugs went down by 39% on average. Participants receiving the lump sum managed to retain on average $1,000 at the 12-month mark. "The direct giving model has been proven to empower recipients to find housing and purchase goods that improve their lives, while restoring dignity, confidence and a sense of well-being," the New Leaf Project final report states.[16]

In December 2020 Miracle Messages launched one of the first basic income pilots for people experiencing homelessness in the United States,[17] and the first to focus on the potentially life-changing impact of social support. In the proof of concept, Miracle Money provided $500 a month for six months to 14 individuals experiencing homelessness or housing insecurity, which was paired with ongoing social support from their Miracle Friend, a phone buddy program by Miracle Messages that matches people experiencing homelessness with caring volunteers from around the world for weekly phone calls and text messages to provide general social support.

Of the nine individuals who were unhoused at the outset of the program, six were able to secure stable housing (66%) within one year of their first payment. Recipients mostly used their funds for food (30.6% of expenditures) and housing (29.9% of expenditures), as well as transportation, savings, storage, child care, medications, debt reduction, unexpected family emergencies, and other essentials. Two recipients got service dogs to help them with their anxiety, one bought clean clothes to wear at their local mosque, and at least two recipients made charitable contributions with their funds. When Kevin asked one of the participants (Elizabeth, featured in chapter 6 on housing) why she had used some of her funds to make a donation to Miracle Messages, she quickly replied, "I didn't do it for you. I did it for myself. So I can once again feel the dignity of being able to support the causes that I believe in."[18]

Programs like Miracle Money and the New Leaf Project challenge the stereotype that giving money to people experiencing homelessness will lead to waste or mismanagement. In the New Leaf Project, those who received the lump sum spent fewer nights in shelters, and consequently saved the shelter system about $405,000 over the year, or approximately $8,100 per person—a net savings of $600 compared to the $7,500 per person that was distributed as a lump sum. "The most efficient way to spend money on the homeless might be to give it to them," as stated in a prescient 2004 article in the *Economist*.[19]

Paternalism as Policy

High levels of distrust for people experiencing homelessness are commonplace beyond just the realm of direct cash payments and engaging people who are panhandling or otherwise living on the streets. Many homeless service providers—from shelters to treatment programs—require their unhoused clients to jump through arduous, often demeaning hoops to qualify. Indeed, the original concept of the "continuum of care" was that a person experiencing homelessness would need to go through a well-defined series of steps of stabilization and abstinence before being offered housing.[20]

Contempt for people experiencing homelessness is part of a wider societal disdain for the poor, and can be seen in social programs at all levels of government. As one example, in 2015 Kansas Governor Sam Brownback signed into law legislation that banned the spending of government assistance on visiting amusement parks or swimming pools, on purchasing lingerie, and on seeing movies. For recipients of Temporary Assistance for Needy Families (TANF)—which many housing insecure families depend upon—daily ATM withdrawals were capped at $25. Asked about the legislation, former Kansas State Senator Michael O'Donnell said, "This is about prosperity. This is about having a great life."[21] The key, Senator O'Donnell said, was getting TANF recipients to behave "more responsibly."

As another example, in 2018 the Trump administration suggested replacing the Supplemental Nutrition Assistance Program (SNAP) with boxes of prepackaged meals. The plan was titled "USDA Restores Original Intent of SNAP: A Second Chance, Not a Way of Life."[22] Former acting White House chief of staff Mick Mulvaney called this a "Blue Apron-type program, where you actually receive the food instead of receiving the cash."[23] The idea of boxes with prepackaged meals in lieu of SNAP benefits advanced the assumption that low-income people lack the capacity to make good nutritional choices simply because they are poor. Rather than trying to expand access to healthy food in poor, disinvested neighborhoods, the Trump administration tried to take away the right of poor people to choose what to eat.

Antagonism toward people living in poverty or experiencing homelessness is not unique to one aporophobic president or paternalistic state lawmakers. A 2020 article by Rahim Kurwa explores the impact of regulations in the Housing Choice Voucher program on Black voucher renters in Antelope Valley, California, located in the northernmost suburb of Los Angeles.[24] The Housing Choice Voucher program is the largest rental assistance policy in the US; individuals considered very low-income are provided with vouchers they can use, upon a landlord's approval, to rent an apartment at market rates. A subsidy is then paid to the landlord by public housing agencies, allowing the individual or family to rent at a lower monthly rate.

The article, published in *Housing Policy Debate*, found that rules in the Housing Choice Voucher program resemble past and present punitive regulations in other housing and safety net programs. Such regulations can create dilemmas for recipients in which they must choose between housing security and supporting family. Two specific rules implemented by the Housing Authority of the County of Los Angeles (HACOLA) control the activity of residents there. The first rule stipulated that tenants must report all changes in family composition to HACOLA, and unauthorized tenants are not permitted to reside in the unit. The second forbids crime or drug-related activity in or around the unit, which includes the activity of tenants' guests, such as if their cousin steps outside to smoke a joint and gets caught. Failure to comply with either rule could result in eviction. This leads to tenants "minimizing contact with family members, not being able to provide care to loved ones, and ceasing activities that build family cohesion."[25]

Compliance with policies was monitored by the police and HACOLA through extensive policing and surveillance of voucher recipients. Interviewees in Kurwa's study revealed feeling highly scrutinized in

their personal lives by the police and HACOLA, as well as minimizing
their family and social relations for fear of eviction. Some interviewees contemplated leaving the program to escape the distress caused by
surveillance. Kurwa concludes that housing voucher regulations, like
crime- and drug-free policies and bans on unauthorized residents, can
incentivize tenants to cut ties with their own families.[26] The effect of
these paternalistic policies, policing, and surveillance is to institutional-
ize relational poverty for poor and vulnerable people.

Serena Rice, a pastor with 20 years of experience in social work,
summed up the state of affairs: "It is still acceptable, even popular, to
ascribe moral weakness to people in poverty rather than to examine the
economic and social structures that hold them there."[27] As a result of
this distrust and disregard for the poor, society circumscribes its assistance and tries to dictate their behavior. Our neighbors experiencing
homelessness are treated no better: they are presumed to be deservedly
poor and reprehensible. *Otherwise, why would they be homeless in the
first place?*

The Impact of Distrust

Such widespread distrust toward "the poor" and "the homeless" would
be downright ridiculous if it were not so cruel and harmful. Gabe and
Lainie, a mother and son experiencing homelessness whose story is featured in chapter 7, recounted the tragic comedy of paternalism from a
recent visit to a food program: "We tried going to Sunnyvale Community Services, but they handed out stuff that we couldn't cook because
we're living in a car. It was tuna fish, peanut butter, and I can't eat
peanut butter or tuna because I'm allergic to nuts and fish."

People experiencing homelessness like Gabe and Lainie face rampant paternalism in the very service systems meant to help them. In
both subtle and blatant ways, the service sector's posture of paternalism toward its unhoused clients is dehumanizing, inefficient, misplaced,
and very costly. As one example, many homeless shelters tend to be

overcrowded, noisy, unsafe, and especially condescending toward their guests. The many rules and regulations—about behavior, about who a guest can bring with them, about shelter hours, about whether pets or partners or belongings are allowed—are all based on the convenience of the shelter providers, not what is best for the guests themselves. People in these settings tend to be treated like cattle; as such, it is no wonder that many people experiencing homelessness decide to live on the streets rather than in shelters.[28]

And when a case worker is able to offer an unhoused client housing outside of a shelter bed, and they choose not to take it (as Ronnie admirably did in declining the housing option that would have been unsafe), they may be refused other options and moved to the back of the waiting list. Ronnie was told he could wait a few years until he would be eligible for senior housing, but was not offered any other adequate housing options in the meantime. Tragically, he died on the streets before he was able to move into stable housing. "I think people treat me fair if they don't know that I am homeless," Ronnie once said.

In a 2013 survey of panhandlers in San Francisco conducted by a local business organization, 94% of respondents reported using the money they received for food.[29] "There's a lot of mythology around giving to panhandlers as 'enabling' homelessness," said Eric Tars, the legal director for the National Homelessness Law Center. "Nobody wants to panhandle, nobody wants to be forced to live on the streets— it's incredibly demeaning, if not outright dangerous. People are only doing it out of pure desperation."[30] But this is not the narrative we usually hear. Instead, our city governments erect signage akin to *don't feed the pigeons* to dissuade people from giving money to people experiencing homelessness. And if we offer food to an unhoused neighbor and they reject it without expressing enough gratitude (or penance), the lesson that we teach our kids is, "See, some people just want drugs."

In the end, our paternalism and overarching distrust toward people experiencing homelessness hurt us, too. When we do not trust the very people we would like to help, we withhold our charity on any terms but our own. And as we witness more people experiencing homelessness, living and dying on the streets, with little to no progress evident despite so much time and money and rhetoric being lobbed at this issue, we are prone to experience *compassion fatigue*, a form of burnout that can affect our physical, emotional, and spiritual well-being. This makes us even less willing to show up for our neighbors experiencing homelessness in all the creative, thoughtful, and impactful ways that we are capable of, let alone as "saviors." With compassion fatigue, we move past paternalism into feeling helpless and even resigned to the massive suffering we see. Deep down we may know that we could do more and connect deeper, but we hold back, not because we do not care, but because we know that we are capable of caring so much but no longer believe that we can make a difference. Instead, we grow wary of being taken advantage of, and become even more protective of our empathy and altruism being exploited.[31] We become more guarded, cynical, distrustful, prejudiced, hostile, and apathetic.

In short, paternalism dehumanizes us all.

KEY TAKEAWAYS

Paternalism—taking actions or making decisions for another person, on the assumption that we know best—often comes in the forms of *progressive paternalism,* which attempts to "fix what's wrong" with a person experiencing homelessness, and *punitive paternalism,* which posits that a person experiencing homelessness, like an unrepentant sinner, behaved badly and needs to be dealt with accordingly so that they find the "right" way.

Paternalism toward "the homeless" is evident in the requirements necessary to qualify for various homeless services, in the fear-based, stereotyped usage restrictions, rules, and regulations associated with federal aid programs, and when housed folks assume the needs of their neighbors experiencing homelessness, expecting a gleeful acceptance of services or help offered. In reality, paternalism strips away self-determination and agency for people experiencing homelessness.

Paternalism is rooted in a type of savior complex, which gives us the illusion that we are doing something morally right when we may really be exacerbating existing problems by perpetuating the belief that those in positions of lower power cannot and should not make decisions for themselves; not trusting people experiencing homelessness to act rationally or use money well, we attempt to control their behavior.

More often than not, our distrust toward people experiencing homelessness is misguided. In most crimes involving a person experiencing homelessness, it is the unhoused person who is the victim. And multiple basic income studies have shown people experiencing homelessness are exceptionally good stewards of their money, which is spent mostly on food, rent, and other essentials.

Disdain and frustration resulting from our paternalism toward "the homeless" lead to hesitancy to help and compassion fatigue—a sense of wanting to help but doubting the real impact of doing so, which results in apathy and inaction and harms us all.

5

Individualism

"WHEN I WENT TO JAIL, I got a letter from her. She found out I was in jail. She said, 'This is your daughter. You have two grandchildren. And we want to bring you home with us. You can have your own room.' She said she'll help and buy me things and I could come live with them. I didn't want to go to them. I didn't want her or my family to see me in the condition that I was in. I didn't want to impose. I didn't think she should have to care for a mother who was lost. She had two children of her own to take care of."

When Linda received the letter in jail from her daughter, it had been 28 years since they had seen each other. Linda was shocked to receive the letter, and didn't quite know what to make of it. In some sense, the letter was from a relative stranger: a mother of two with her own home and family, whom she had not seen in nearly three decades. But in another sense, the letter was from the little girl she loved and missed so dearly, the daughter she taught how to ride a bike without training wheels, the daughter who held tightly to her at the end of a painful court hearing nearly three decades earlier, the daughter who still just wanted her "momma" to come home.

Linda grew up in a big, loving household with three sisters in Milwaukee, Wisconsin. It was a humble beginning filled with mostly happy memories. "My mother did everything she could with us: circus, zoo. She tried her best. She was single. She worked half of my childhood, the other half no."

Inspired by her mother, Linda exuded a strong sense of independence from an early age: working, taking care of herself, and eventually moving to Florida alone by her early 20s. It was there, in Florida, where Linda found a stable job and stable housing, but also where she found herself battling a persistent feeling of chronic loneliness, and soon, against substance use as well. "I felt so lonely. I only had myself. I was using drugs. Right off the bat, I had problems. Drugs, mainly crack cocaine, kept me away from my family."

Linda ended up living beneath a bridge in Florida, a noisy and unsafe location where she was hardly ever able to sleep, where people came from all over the state to purchase drugs at all hours of the day, nonstop. Linda's perpetual drug use led to run-ins with the law and periods of incarceration, bouncing between jails and prisons across the state. It was in one of her jail stays that she received the letter from her daughter, pleading with her to go and live with them, to meet her grandkids, to accept help from her family, and to come home.

As she recalled years later how she felt in reading her daughter's letter, Linda said she felt ashamed, guilty, angry at herself, and very sad. She was ashamed of her drug use, guilty she couldn't take care of herself and her family the way she wanted to, and angry that, even in the midst of reading her daughter's letter from a jail cell, she was still thinking about drugs. And she felt great sadness in thinking about all the memories she missed out on in the 28 years she had been away.

Most of all, Linda said she felt like a failure, a feeling that followed her long after she was released from jail. She blamed herself for everything. She believed she had gravely hurt her family and responded to the pain she felt she caused them by self-medicating through drugs and isolation. Linda believed herself to be undeserving of help and unworthy of her family, including of the tireless love of her daughter, who was 1,289 miles away and still looking for her momma.

Linda never responded to the letter. "At my age, I didn't think she should have to care for me," she said.

The American Dream

These people were not the vagrants and vagabonds, tramps and thieves that the laws had been written to guard against; these were the inheritors of optimistic America, its sons and daughters [. . .] Many of these uprooted persons set out hopefully with the belief that in America all one needed to do when times got rough was to move on [. . .] but the dream was not working.

—JOAN M. CROUSE, *THE HOMELESS TRANSIENT IN THE GREAT DEPRESSION*

When Linda moved to Florida as a young adult, she was hopeful that the American Dream would be hers: a life of opportunity, growth, success, and happiness, only requiring hard work and perseverance. She believed her will and independence would be enough to succeed. She still believed, years later reading the letter from her daughter in jail, that it was her responsibility alone to "get better" and "handle her life." Perhaps Linda was an "inheritor of optimistic America," like many of the "homeless transients" that Crouse described.

At some level, we are all inheritors of optimistic America: we all want to believe that individual hard work and determination can be enough to succeed. We see it in Liz Murray, whose story was told in the Lifetime television film *Homeless to Harvard*: a daughter of drug-addicted parents with AIDS, one of whom also has schizophrenia, becomes homeless, only to defy all odds by finishing high school in two years and earning a scholarship to the Ivy League. Tearjerker stories like *Homeless to Harvard* instill in us a belief that even people experiencing homelessness can overcome the odds and be successful in the Land of Opportunity, just like the rest of us. Best-selling memoirs, feel-good human interest news stories, viral social media posts, and life lessons from our teachers, parents, friends, and colleagues celebrate individual success stories *despite the odds*, reminding us every day that the American Dream is accessible to anyone with the right work ethic and determination—"Attitude Is Everything," as the slogan and accompanying banners at Kevin's elementary school reminded him and his classmates every day.

As such, one of the primary cultural narratives in the United States is that success, like failure, is an individual responsibility. Under this narrative, homelessness is an abject individual failure; there is little regard for how a person experiencing homelessness got to the situation they are in, much less how so many of the rest of us "housed people" rely on our social support systems to get by. "The notion we must do without support is ingrained in our nation's culture," laments *Boot-strapped* author Alissa Quart.[1]

Broken systems—intergenerational socioeconomic immobility, structural racism, housing insecurity, aging out of foster care, and more—are overlooked. If an individual experiencing chronic homelessness manages to beat the odds and turn their life around, then these broken systems are merely the backdrop to their rags-to-riches success story of overcoming great odds as part of their Hero's Journey. Even the conversation topic of how systemic factors determine one's starting point in life and often predict one's life trajectory is considered taboo and pessimistic. Under "pull yourself up by your bootstraps" individualism, which Quart calls "our most toxic myth," we as Americans tend to focus on what an individual did to succeed or fail above all else.

But is that how success (or failure) actually works?

One internationally well-known public figure doesn't think so, despite often being held up as a near-paradigm of individual success in the United States:

> I always tell people that you can call me anything that you want. You can call me Arnold. You can call me Schwarzenegger. You can call me the Austrian oak. You can call me Schwarzy. You can call me Arnie. But don't ever, ever call me a self-made man.

> But this is so important for you to understand. I didn't make it that far on my own. I mean, to accept that credit or that medal, would discount every single person that has helped me get here today, that gave me advice, that made an effort, that lifted me up when I fell. And it gives the wrong impression that we can do it all alone. None of us can. The whole concept of the self-made man or woman is a myth.[2] [. . .]

Like everyone, to get to where I am, I stood on the shoulders of giants. My life was built on a foundation of parents, coaches, and teachers; of kind souls who lent couches or gym back rooms where I could sleep; of mentors who shared wisdom and advice; of idols who motivated me from the pages of magazines (and, as my life grew, from personal interaction). [. . .]

I am not a self-made man. Every time I give a speech at a business conference, or speak to college students, or do a Reddit AMA, someone says it. Governor / Governator / Arnold / Arnie / Schwarzie / Schnitzel (depending on where I am), as a self-made man, what's your blueprint for success? They're always shocked when I thank them for the compliment but say, "I am not a self-made man. I got a lot of help.[3]

The Self-Made (Homeless) Man?

For every one person experiencing homelessness who goes to Harvard, tens of thousands more go to jail.[4] When we consider the likely paths a person experiencing homelessness will follow, we should look at patterns and not just glorify the few individual exceptions to the overall trends. By hyper-focusing on individual choices and personality traits in how we view "the homeless," we sideline the impact of broader socioeconomic trends, government policy, racism and discrimination, and broken systems that limit the opportunities for many in our society.

Rates of homelessness mirror economic and social downturns. Historically homelessness has increased most during economic depressions and social dislocations. In the 1980s a sharp rise in homelessness marked the advent of "modern homelessness" as we know it today. The reasons for this rise were not a sudden new wave of individual failings but large, systemic occurrences: deindustrialization and gentrification of cities, deinstitutionalization of the mentally ill without adequately investing in alternatives, the War on Drugs, mass incarceration, high unemployment, economic inequality, the HIV/AIDS epidemic, a dwindling supply of affordable housing, significant increases in the cost of housing, and deep budget cuts to vital social services.[5] These factors are far more important to understanding the nationwide homelessness crisis we have today than perseverating on whether individuals are responsible and hard working.

According to Leroy Pelton, our whole culture, based on the English legal system, adheres to the maxim that we get what we deserve—what he calls the myth of "just deserts."[6] As an individual, the thinking goes, if I work hard and play by the rules, I deserve a nice home, a loving family, friendly neighbors, a good job, and so on. As philosopher Michael J. Sandel describes in his book *The Tyranny of Merit*, the feeling is that if you work hard enough, you will make it. Under this narrative, if a person ends up experiencing homelessness, it must be because they did not work hard enough or play by the rules, so they are a failure who is a burden to their loved ones and society as a whole. "*I am undeserving*," in the words Linda used to describe herself.

However, as Pelton points out, none of us really deserves our place in life. We are born into a set of circumstances that we don't deserve—what we receive is not based on our own merits or actions. "The community has benefitted most of us far beyond anything we can imagine to have deserved. [. . .] The truth is that most of us have been getting 'something for nothing.'"[7] Pelton argues that the spirit of entitlement encourages us "to belittle and judge others, and begrudge them even governmental attention to their minimal survival needs. We convince ourselves that while we are deserving of everything we get, there are some individuals within our midst who are deserving of nothing at all. [. . .] In reality, a philosophy of desert leads to [. . .] highly subjective determinations that raise questions of individual justice, arbitrary exclusion, and discrimination. Attributions of desert serve as excuses not to house the homeless."[8]

Pelton argues that if an individual's life is to be valued and not violated, that same principle of intrinsic value should be applied to all people. "The reverence for human life, without condition, judgment, or exception, is contrary to the desert conception."[9] Instead of "just deserts," Pelton calls for the principle of life affirmation, to be applied to everyone, including those experiencing homelessness. Basic human needs should be addressed without consideration of deservedness.

The perception of homelessness as a chosen or deserving fate requires a system-blindness that fails to recognize the structural privileges and disadvantages woven into today's economic, political, and social institutions. As we noted earlier, 37% of the homeless population identifies as Black or African American, compared to just 12% of the general population in the United States. The disproportionate over-representation of Black people experiencing homelessness is caused by racism, bias, and discrimination embedded deep in many flawed systems in the United States. A few examples: the imprisonment rate for Black males is 5.8 times higher than that of white males, and imprisonment for Black females was found to be 1.8 times higher than for white females.[10] The median Black family has less than 15% of the wealth of their white counterparts. A 2020 study in Boston showed that white applicants secured a rental viewing 80% of the time, while Black applicants with identical financial credentials got a viewing only 48% of the time.[11] And job applicants with African American–sounding names need to send out about 50% more resumes to get one callback than job applicants with white-sounding names, according to a widely cited article by Marianne Bertrand and Sendhil Mullainathan entitled "Are Emily and Greg More Employable than Lakisha and Jamal? A Field Experiment on Labor Market Discrimination."[12]

When we try to understand homelessness through an individualism-centric lens, believing that everyone can succeed with hard work and determination alone, we ignore the fact that the opportunities and challenges facing Black people (or Indigenous peoples or immigrants or LGBTQ+ or . . .) are not the same as those facing white people. Bertrand and Mullainathan's research on labor market discrimination is just one example of the structural disenfranchisement that has persisted to this day. Similar realities in health care, education, housing, and other systems continue to exist simply due to a person's name or skin color, the intersections of their identity, and the ways in which groups in power respond to those identities.

In this chapter, we do not mean to suggest that individual choices and work ethics are inconsequential, or that all people experiencing homelessness are diligent, hard-working, and upright members of the community, and simply the victims of external circumstances, broken systems, or discrimination. But we believe it is hypocritical for society to "cast the first stone" at our neighbors experiencing homelessness for any poor choices they may have made. Homeless or housed, all of us make mistakes, and none of us are angels or devils, to paraphrase Billy Ray Harris from the previous chapter. As Bryan Stephenson eloquently wrote in *Just Mercy: A Story of Justice and Redemption*, "Each of us is more than the worst thing we've ever done."[13]

But for the vast majority of us, bad life choices do not lead to homelessness. As such, it is far more convenient (and comfortable) for us to question the character and life choices of a person experiencing homelessness than to take the time to understand their story and the broader context at play. Blaming the individual places the onus on them to figure it out, while listening first then recognizing where our shared humanity has fallen short—in the forms of relational poverty, stigma and stereotypes, exclusion, paternalism, and "go it alone" individualism—makes us look in the collective mirror.

Indeed, as we get closer to our neighbors experiencing homelessness as neighbors and loved ones, we will inevitably see homelessness as part of *our* shared responsibility. And we will recall two truths, at odds with America's infatuation with "pull yourself up by your bootstraps" individualism, but applicable to each of us and timelessly phrased by a Bill Withers lyric and a 500-year-old parable: *We all need somebody to lean on*, and *There but for the grace of God go I*.

Or as Linda put it simply, "Some people don't understand, you know, why people get homeless or how they end up homeless. Help, in any kind of way, because today, they may be living on top of the world, but tomorrow you don't know if you're gonna be around. You don't know if you're gonna be in the same position as the person who is homeless."

KEY TAKEAWAYS

Homelessness is incorrectly branded as an individual failing, due to American cultural ideals glorifying individual responsibility in determining life outcomes, but historical trends reveal that homelessness is largely due to systemic forces.

Rags-to-riches stories are inspiring but can lead us to believe similar outcomes are possible for most people in challenging circumstances. They are by far the exception.

The myth of "just deserts," that everyone gets what they deserve, is in part responsible for the belief that individuals experiencing homelessness must have done something bad to "deserve" their circumstances, thus justifying the way we treat them: with contempt, exclusion, and discrimination.

The ideal of "pull yourself up by the bootstraps" rugged individualism fails to account for the structural privilege interwoven in America's systems that makes attaining success and well-being harder for marginalized groups, and that have led to an over-representation of racial and ethnic minorities among people experiencing homelessness.

Rampant hyper-individualism in the US—which presumes that everyone has the ability to succeed based on their hard work and talent alone, regardless of their circumstances—makes exiting (and ending) homelessness an individual responsibility rather than part of our collective duty.

PART II

SYSTEMS

6

Housing

FROM A YOUNG AGE, Elizabeth was instilled with a willful strength and inclination toward serving others. Born in Culver City, California, Elizabeth was the first in her family to attend college, receiving a degree in sociology from UCLA before beginning a nonprofit organization supporting young writers within the local community. Elizabeth also spent 20 years as an educator in Redwood City public schools, worked at local churches, wrote cookbooks, authored a beautiful reflection on Kwanza and her family history in the *Los Angeles Times*,[1] and raised a family of her own. Life wasn't perfect; there were ups and downs, moments of joy, moments of inspiration: stints at graduate school, spontaneous part-time jobs here and there. But Elizabeth lived a life that she described as perfect for her. She was well educated and successful as an advocate, teacher, and nonprofit founder. Elizabeth had her own home, loving children, and a community to look after, and for Elizabeth, that was everything she needed.

Then, on September 26, 2018, Elizabeth was diagnosed with advanced-stage colon cancer. Elizabeth was told that she had about five years left to live, and everything began to change. Elizabeth went in for emergency surgery at Stanford Medical Center, followed by six months of rigorous and routine chemotherapy. Her frail health left her unable to return to her teaching job, where she was eventually laid off. Her modest savings were spent on cancer treatment and rent, and were quickly depleted. Within months of her diagnosis, Elizabeth was taken to court by her landlord, and evicted from her apartment of fourteen years, the beloved home where she lived, prayed, prepared Sunday dinners, raised a family, and felt safe. Six weeks after her court date, and only two hours before she was set to end up "completely on the streets," Elizabeth was notified that a medical bed was available for her at a congregate shelter in South San Francisco. But for the first time in her entire life, Elizabeth was experiencing homelessness.

The precarity of her longtime housing situation shocked Elizabeth, and made her feel sad, angry, and scared. Here today, gone tomorrow. What Elizabeth needed more than anything was a stable, secure place to heal and recover. What she got instead was an open shelter with no privacy; where she, as a woman of color, felt incredibly unsafe and targeted by some of the male residents; where she was unable to access the medical care she desperately required.

"I was still in treatment while I was in the shelter. That was like hell; it was unimaginably horrible. There is nobody in this world who I would wish this upon them: being in a shelter, an open shelter where there's no privacy, and going through chemo. [. . .] Shelters in America are terrible places. They are chaotic, dangerous places. There's a lot of untreated mental illness, which makes living there very difficult. Stalking is very common. By the time I left, there were about 60 to 70 people. People are always coming and going, always coming and going. I was in the shelter for 11 months. It was terrifying. It was physically dangerous. There were fights. There was only peace on holidays, like Easter or Thanksgiving, Christmas. It was just full of hurting people."

With her cancer diagnosis, chemotherapy, and long road to recovery, Elizabeth needed a safe place of her own, a home to rest in her own time. What she got instead was homelessness.

The Need for Affordable Housing

Like the vast majority of the 6 million other Americans who experience homelessness each year, Elizabeth did not choose to experience homelessness, any more than she chose to have cancer. After losing her job, depleting her savings, and being temporarily unable to work, Elizabeth simply could not afford housing.

Affordable housing is essential in the fight to end homelessness. Where housing costs are high, the rate of homelessness tends to be high. Where housing costs are low, the rate of homelessness tends to be low. At some level, homelessness is as simple as that. While there are many factors that contribute to America's homelessness crisis, the availability and affordability of housing are the most significant; *Homelessness Is a Housing Problem* declares the title of a recent book by Gregg Colburn and Clayton Page Aldern. More affordable housing means less homelessness. And in cities where large numbers of residents spend over 32% of their income on rent, there is a rapid rise in homelessness.[2] In many areas of the United States, even small rent increases can place thousands of vulnerable people living paycheck to paycheck at heightened risk of homelessness. And because of the ever-rising cost of building housing, there is a shortage of affordable housing at all levels of the market, including what was once known as starter homes, or "small, no-frills homes that would give a family new to the country or a young couple with student debt a foothold to build equity."[3]

Meanwhile, investment in government-owned public housing has been declining for decades.[4] Today some 880,145 households, or approximately 1.82 million Americans, live in public housing.[5] By comparison, in 1971, over 3 million people lived in public housing.[6] In part due to the passage of the Fair Housing Act of 1968, support for public housing waned under President Nixon, culminating in his moratorium on all federally assisted housing programs in 1973. There has been no significant expansion of public housing since then.[7] In the 1990s the Clinton administration further slashed funding for public housing by $17 billion, a 61% reduction, all while boosting funding for prisons by $19 billion, a 171% increase. In some sense, the construction of prisons became "the nation's main housing program for the urban poor," as Michelle Alexander notes in her landmark book *The New Jim Crow*.[8] President Clinton's policies also made it easier for federally assisted public housing projects to exclude anyone with a criminal record. Many low-income individuals have been shut out of public housing permanently due to low-level drug offenses—one strike and you are out.[9]

As a result of decades of underinvestment, the waiting period for public housing can be measured in decades: a young mother experiencing homelessness who signs up for public housing today could be a grandmother by the time her application is reviewed.[10] Public housing is inaccessible to the vast majority of people experiencing homelessness because it is inaccessible to the vast majority of people.

In the private housing market, there simply aren't enough available and affordable units. The Housing and Community Development Act of 1974 shifted the federal response to the need for affordable housing from public housing to housing vouchers. Today these Housing Choice Vouchers, previously known as Section 8 vouchers, are used by low-income individuals and families to rent from private landlords. These vouchers enable low-income tenants to limit how much rent and utilities they have to pay, generally up to 30% of their adjusted monthly income. If the tenant has no income at all, they owe nothing in rent, the voucher pays it all, up to the voucher limit.

The Housing Choice Voucher program enables landlords to identify the source of an applicant's rent money, leading to widespread preferencing for non-voucher tenants. Many landlords refuse outright to accept vouchers, often out of a mix of bias toward the prospective tenant and fear for the time lag of receiving reimbursement from the federal government.[11]

The change from the public sector's involvement in housing to the use of private-sector housing through the voucher system constituted a significant shift in federal housing policy. However, the shift in policy did not increase the number of units available. The National Low Income Housing Coalition now estimates that, for low-income renters, there is an overall shortfall of 7 million housing units to meet current demand. Renters like Elizabeth are directly affected by this shortfall.

In fact, much of the money spent by the federal government on housing is not directed toward individuals who are extremely low-income, much less those experiencing homelessness. Rather, the federal government spends significantly more on assisting high-income households (making over $100,000) to purchase homes than it spends assisting extremely low-income households to rent homes. A 2012 study by the *Washington Post* found that when looking at total tax expenditures by the government rather than narrowly defined "government benefits," 24% of expenditures went to the top 1% of earners. Only 3% of tax expenditures went to the bottom 20%.[12] (We will return to this topic further in chapter 7, "Work, Wages, and Wealth.")

Barriers to Affordable Housing

When asked to name common misconceptions about people experiencing homelessness that she discovered while staying at the shelter, Elizabeth did not hesitate: "The overwhelming majority of the people at the shelter, they went to work. They get up in the morning, they go to work. They have jobs that even pay well. The problem is they just can't get enough money to get in an apartment or studio, so they rotate between sleeping in cars and staying in the shelter."

People experiencing homelessness face a number of significant barriers to gaining access to affordable housing. One of the main barriers is the high cost of housing compared to the low wages of the many people experiencing homelessness who work. According to the National Low Income Housing Coalition, there is not a single county among the over 3,000 counties in the United States where someone working full-time and earning the federal minimum wage can afford a two-bedroom apartment at the so-called "fair market rent."

The hourly wage that the typical full-time worker in the United States would have to earn in 2022 to afford a "modest and safe" rental home without spending 30% or more of their income on rent and utilities was $21.25 per hour for a one-bedroom apartment and $25.82 per hour for a two-bedroom apartment. The average worker earning the minimum federal hourly wage would need to work approximately 96 hours per week every single week of the year to afford a two-bedroom rental home at the national average fair market rent.[13]

Without housing assistance from the government, a family of four with a poverty-level income of $26,200 could afford a monthly rent of $655 in 2020, based on HUD guidelines that a household should spend no more than 30% of income on housing costs. The average rent of a modest two-bedroom apartment was $1,246 in 2020.[14] The *price gap*—the difference between what a person can afford and how much affordable rental housing costs—is considerably more pronounced in areas with higher costs of living. In Los Angeles the average rent for a roughly 800-square-foot apartment is $2,734, as of July 2022, compared to $1,855 in Sacramento, and $3,340 in San Francisco.[15] For someone like Elizabeth, who lives in an expensive housing market like Silicon Valley and earned modest wages, the price gap was incredibly burdensome. Add in an unexpected medical emergency and sudden job loss, the price gap becomes untenable.

Some 7.6 million extremely low-income renter households spend more than half their income on rent and utilities,[16] which makes affording housing inaccessible without substantial financial subsidies. Yet crucial benefit programs are insufficient and surprisingly hard to access: only about 25% of those who are eligible for federal housing vouchers actually receive them.[17] Don's recent experience in Adams County, Colorado, a Denver suburb, highlights the barriers that people experiencing homelessness face in accessing the benefits they are eligible for. In one recent year, Adams County's housing authority issued 1,400 housing vouchers, mostly to people experiencing homelessness. Sixty percent of the vouchers were returned to the housing authority unused. In some cases, prospective tenants were simply unable to find vacant housing units. In other cases, even when units were available, landlords refused to rent to the individual or family experiencing homelessness because their primary source of rent was the housing voucher.[18] And in all cases, such uncertainty and challenge in finding affordable housing add to the already considerable administrative burden (or "the effort, knowledge, and sheer time it takes for citizens to obtain benefits"[19]) facing our neighbors experiencing homelessness.

This pattern of unused housing vouchers can be seen across the country: 11,000 unused vouchers for veterans across the country;[20] $500,000 of unused voucher money for people in various categories in Vermont.[21] These numbers are shocking, especially when we consider that most vouchers are utilized by existing renters to stay in their current apartments.[22] Because of the nationwide disconnect between the supply of affordable housing and the demand, landlords do not have strong incentives to spruce up or repair properties, lower the rent, or forgive late payments because they know they can find new tenants quickly and easily.

Another significant barrier to housing for many people experiencing homelessness is the threat of evictions. Landlords can count on the eviction court process giving them much more power than the tenants have. As Elizabeth recounted, "They thought they could just put a note in the mail slot and say: 'You gotta get out of here. You have three days.'" In most eviction proceedings, the tenant appears without legal representation, and consequently loses in the hearings over 90% of the time. If the tenant is able to secure adequate legal representation, however, they successfully defeat the eviction almost 90% of the time.[23] For the evicted, not only does having an eviction record make it harder for tenants to rent in the future, but the process of losing a home, possessions, being denied housing assistance, and often being relocated to substandard housing in poor or dangerous neighborhoods all lead to much greater material hardship, homelessness, and physical and mental illness.

Another barrier to affordable housing is racism. Before the 1968 Fair Housing Act, federal housing policy discriminated against people of color through redlining, discriminatory financing, exclusionary zoning, demolishing neighborhoods in favor of highways and other examples of what was called "urban renewal," housing segregation, and property covenants that sought to uphold "desirable characteristics" of a neighborhood by restricting who could live there.[24] According to Ira

Katznelson, a political science professor and author, "The exclusion of Black veterans came through the mechanisms of administration [. . .] the path to job placement, loans, unemployment benefits, and schooling [through the GI Bill] was tied to local VA centers, almost entirely staffed by white employees, or through local banks and public and private educational institutions."[25] A staggering 98% of FHA-insured loans given between 1934 and 1968 went to white Americans.[26]

These discriminatory practices, though illegal today, continue in various forms, including gentrification. Data show that the percentage of African Americans who are homeowners today is essentially the same as it was in 1968: 42% in 1970 and 42%–45% in 2020.[27] Both in formal policies and informal neighborhood practices, discrimination in housing has served to create and maintain segregated communities along racial and class lines. In part because of the paucity of affordable units and the overwhelming demand for housing by low-income households, the types of discrimination so present in our recent past continue in more subtle forms. Landlords have few incentives to fairly and equally consider all prospective tenants, as there is significantly more demand for affordable housing than supply. And many local public housing authorities make it illegal to rent to someone with a felony conviction, which disproportionately hurts African Americans, Native Americans, Hispanics, and other minority groups, as we will see in chapter 10 on the criminal justice system. Discrimination in housing destroys communities, social networks, familial wealth, upward mobility, and the American Dream, and contributes to the sky-high rates of homelessness seen among many marginalized groups in the United States.

Would You Live There?

Absent a housing unit of their own, people experiencing homelessness still need shelter. In evaluating the various types of housing options available to our unhoused neighbors, and in considering why many individuals experiencing homelessness prefer to live on the streets, the operative question to reflect on here is: *Would you live there?*

Let's begin with homeless shelters, the best-known option for housing our unhoused neighbors. To stay at a shelter, you must abide by many restrictions: shelters tend to regulate when you can eat, sleep, and bathe. You must leave very early in the morning and stay away for most of the day, but be back before curfew; otherwise you risk being denied entrance. Do you have a husband or wife or boyfriend or girlfriend? In all likelihood, you will not be able to stay together at the same shelter. Shelters routinely split up families based on age and gender, so you may not be able to keep your children with you as well. Do you have a beloved dog or cat? They are probably not welcome at the shelter. Do you have many belongings? Most shelters limit how much stuff you can store on-site. Do you value your privacy and safety? What about a sense of community? You will probably be surrounded by a rotating assortment of other shelter residents with no regard to mental illness, substance use, disability, employment, sleep habits, history of violence, and the like. And if you follow all these rules, you are rewarded by being able to stay at the shelter anywhere from a month to six months before you will need to leave.

Shelters tend to be paternalistic, engendering a loss of freedom and agency among vulnerable people who have few other options. As a result, many people experiencing homelessness prefer the relative independence of the streets . . . when they can. Cities across the country force people experiencing homelessness into shelters, often accompanied with threats of legal consequences if the person refuses and tries to survive outside a shelter.[28] For example, officials in Orange County (California) and Las Vegas have forced people experiencing homelessness into shelters through fines and possible jail time.[29] While living on the streets is clearly not a safe or acceptable option, compulsory enrollment in a large congregate shelter could be considered yet another form of punishment for the "crime" of experiencing homelessness.[30]

Besides shelters, another temporary housing option for those experiencing homelessness is tent encampments. Occasionally, "tent cities" are sanctioned by local governments, although this remains rare and is often met with fierce neighborhood opposition. In Portland, Oregon, for example, the Right to Dream Too is a small grouping of tents located on a partial city block close to the central downtown business district. Living within its carefully constructed boundaries and monitoring system, residents have access to kitchen facilities, an office-type space with computers, electricity, and a relatively robust sense of community. In Denver, Colorado, Safe Outdoor Spaces, approved by the mayor and city council, are tent encampments that include bathroom facilities, access to food, and security.

Much more common are tent encampments that have not been officially approved. These makeshift situations usually lack access to bathroom facilities, garbage disposal, utilities of any kind, or anything that resembles a kitchen. These unsanctioned encampments are generally heavily surveilled by law enforcement. Although these encampments are far from ideal, for their residents, they are often preferable to crowded, unsafe, isolating shelters.

Tent encampments often draw the ire of local housed residents, schools, and downtown business establishments. The absence of sanitary facilities means that trash, human waste, and other detritus often surround such encampments. Concerns around threats to public safety, health standards, and commercial activity posed by encampments usually lead to efforts to dismantle or "sweep" encampments through police enforcement of local anti-camping ordinances. Frequently with few other viable options for shelter, the displaced residents of a razed encampment will simply move a few blocks to another location, only to be confronted again by law enforcement a few days later, thus giving rise to a "whack-a-mole" situation.

Safe parking sites, where people experiencing homelessness can sleep in their vehicles without fear of harassment, are growing in number as another form of "transitional" housing. Some forward-thinking communities are also building tiny homes as a type of interim housing, which generally provide an excellent relative level of stability, safety, and health standards for residents and the surrounding neighborhoods. Accessory dwelling units (ADUs), euphemistically called "granny flats," such as apartments over garages or small guest cottages, are also being promoted to increase the supply of affordable housing. The creation of these alternative forms of housing is growing across the country, but much more expansion will be needed to meet current demand. These alternative types of transitional housing provide a modicum of stability for those who are unable to gain access to their own affordable housing units.

The High Cost of *Not* Housing

One of the perennial challenges around whether to build housing for people experiencing homelessness and other extremely low-income residents is the cost of developing such housing. Opponents tend to point to the billions of dollars that would be needed. Local, state, and national budgets cover a vast array of pressing needs, and officials are often caught off guard by even the most conservative estimates of the price tag of providing sufficient housing for all who need it. To be sure, building new housing is quite expensive, given the increasing cost of materials, labor, licensing fees, permits, zoning, and local fees to tap into water, electrical, and sewer systems.

Yet study after study has found that the costs associated with providing housing and services are substantially less than the costs that are incurred by *not* housing people. In 2017, for example, the United States Interagency Council on Homelessness (USICH) concluded that each person experiencing chronic homelessness costs taxpayers $30,000 to $50,000 per year. Some scholars believe that figure is even higher, perhaps closer to $80,000 per year or more.[31] These exorbitant costs include health care and hospitalizations, law enforcement and incarceration, sanitation and emergency services, and shelters and other homeless services. In groundbreaking research, Dennis Culhane, one of the nation's leading researchers on homelessness, found that the cost of providing housing and services to people experiencing homelessness is estimated to be almost 50% lower than the cost associated with health care and incarceration alone if nothing is done.[32] A 2020 study in Canada indicates that "on average, it costs $87,000 per year to support a person using hospitals, jails, courts, and emergency services, because they don't have a home. But once that person has a home, the cost of their housing and [support services] decrease to approximately $30,500 per year, representing a 65% reduction."[33]

Beyond just the considerable financial costs, failing to provide housing and other basic services to unhoused people exponentially increases the human suffering of those living on the streets. Just as Elizabeth was forced to undergo chemotherapy treatment for cancer while living in a congregate shelter where she felt unsafe, the quality of life for people experiencing homelessness suffers immensely by not providing decent housing and basic services. This includes physical, mental, and behavioral health deterioration and premature death. In fact, most studies put the life expectancy of people experiencing homelessness as 20 to 30 years shorter than their stably housed counterparts, a jaw-dropping difference.[34] According to a 2019 report, the average life expectancy for individuals experiencing homelessness in Los Angeles County was 48 years for women and 51 years for men, compared to a life expectancy of 83 for women in California and 79 for men in California.[35] To put this gap into perspective, in the year 1900, the average life expectancy for white women in the United States was 48.7 years, nearly identical to the average life expectancy for women experiencing homelessness in Los Angeles County in 2019 (for Black women in 1900, it was 33.5 years).[36]

Given these tremendous financial and human cost savings, why have we not invested more in housing "the homeless"? In purely economic terms, the return on such an investment would be huge: one analyst suggested in 2021 that it would cost about $20 billion to provide housing for all people experiencing homelessness,[37] a bargain compared to the tens of billions of dollars spent nationwide each year on homelessness to maintain our very broken status quo.

Finances alone are not the only significant barrier to ending homelessness: stifling state and local bureaucracy—and the lack of political will and community buy-in to change it—thwarts our ability to develop enough housing. Lengthy and expensive permitting processes, overly restrictive zoning ordinances and land use policies, never-ending red tape, and exorbitant tap fees fuel America's affordable housing crisis.[38] Local residents protest any proposed housing development for "the

homeless" in their neighborhoods, however modest. And elected officials pander to the NIMBYism of their most vocal stably housed voting
constituents to stay in office.

Housing for everyone in the United States would represent one of
the most important steps we could take toward improved health care,
racial justice, and stronger communities. Unfortunately, the current
mindset is that housing is something to be earned, despite the hurdles in
accessibility and affordability for millions of people. As a result, homelessness continues to be one of the most costly (and ongoing) human
rights crises of our time.

And what about housing for Elizabeth? As it turned out, Elizabeth's
story has a happy ending. Her chemotherapy was successful, and she
is now cancer-free. In 2020 Elizabeth signed up for the Miracle Friends
phone buddy program, through which she was connected to Joan. Joan
became Elizabeth's "dearest friend," bonding over a shared love of the
ocean, outdoor walks, practicing their Spanish, teaching, and family.
Joan decided to nominate Elizabeth for Miracle Money, the basic
income pilot by Miracle Messages. As she reflected on her experience
getting connected with Joan and being notified of her basic income,
Elizabeth quipped, "Wow, miracles don't fall from the sky, they come
from the phone."

Through Miracle Money, Elizabeth received $500 a month for six
months. Despite this relatively small amount and short timespan, Elizabeth was able to use her monthly basic income to obtain eligibility
at a senior housing provider that required a minimum monthly contribution. Elizabeth moved into her "forever home" in early 2021, a
spacious studio apartment with its own bathroom, small living room
space for lounging, and "galley kitchen," which boasts a "full-sized
fridge, oven, and dishwasher, and just enough counter space to make
a Thanksgiving dinner on," reports Elizabeth. Joan helped her furnish
the apartment, move her belongings, and unpack. The apartment was
converted from an old hotel under Project Homekey, a program in California that emerged during the COVID-19 pandemic, which provided
local government agencies with funds to purchase and rehabilitate
housing units and convert them into permanent, long-term housing for

vulnerable people experiencing or at risk of homelessness.[39] Elizabeth's apartment happens to be in a complex in Redwood City, just a few miles from the apartment where she previously lived for fourteen years and where she once served as a public school teacher.

We will return to the topic of solutions for our affordable housing crisis in the final two chapters of this book. For now, our attention turns to another critical aspect of Elizabeth's story: the intersection of homelessness and health care.

KEY TAKEAWAYS

Homelessness is defined by a lack of stable housing and is highly correlated to high housing costs. As such, affordable housing is the key ingredient to end homelessness.

Affordable housing is becoming increasingly inaccessible, with long public housing waitlists, disinvestment from the federal government, an inadequate supply of affordable units in the private rental market, landlord bias toward Housing Choice Vouchers, inaccessibility of federal benefit programs, unjust evictions that inhibit renters from renting in the future, and the consequences of a history of racism and discrimination in our housing policies.

Individuals who earn minimum wage or have low incomes cannot afford to rent in the vast majority of communities in the United States; many low-income renters are severely rent-burdened, spending more than half their income on rent.

Common temporary housing options for people experiencing homelessness include homeless shelters and unsanctioned tent cities. Neither of these options is ideal. Homeless shelters impose many paternalistic restrictions on their clients, split up families, and are often characterized by crowded and unsanitary living conditions, while unsanctioned tent cities offer few if any resources or utilities, are heavily surveilled, and result in the further criminalization and displacement of people experiencing homelessness.

More effective approaches to transitional or temporary housing for people experiencing homelessness include "safe parking" initiatives, tiny home villages, and accessory dwelling units.

The high costs associated with providing housing and basic wraparound services to people experiencing homelessness are substantially less than the exorbitant costs we pay to maintain our unhoused neighbors on the streets each year, vis-à-vis the health care system, the criminal justice system, and other emergency services, as part of a deeply broken and costly status quo.

7

Work, Wages, and Wealth

AFTER FINISHING HIS AFTERNOON SHIFT at McDonald's, Gabe, a soft-spoken, heavyset teenager with a boyish smile, stepped into the restroom to bathe himself using the sink as best he could. After freshening up, he walked out to the edge of the parking lot where Lainie, his mom and best friend, was sitting in their old pickup truck. Gabe smiled meekly and gave his mom a quick hug. For Gabe and Lainie, the truck was more than a vehicle: it was their home, the place where they slept, ate, occasionally argued, and lived in San Jose, California, the second most expensive rental market in the country.[1] It was where Gabe did his schoolwork, stretched for high school wrestling meets, texted his friends, contemplated his future, and returned each day after his shift at McDonald's. This was the paradox of Gabe's young life: a teenager who spent most days after school serving Big Macs and McFlurries, only to rarely have enough to eat himself.

In the United States, the wealthiest country in the history of the world, a loving mother and son like Lainie and Gabe who both work hard and have jobs may still not make enough money to afford stable housing together.

"Get a Job!"

Every week, there seems to be a news report from somewhere in the country of angry local residents protesting plans to develop housing, shelters, or other support services for people experiencing homelessness, a topic we looked at in the NIMBYism section of chapter 3. A common sentiment in these protests is that people experiencing homelessness should just "get a job"—the presumption being that people experiencing homelessness do not work, for if they did, they probably wouldn't be homeless. As one example, here's the local news report from a July 2014 protest in New York:

> The homeless shelter at the Pan Am Hotel came under fire Monday night when hundreds of residents rallied outside a meeting between shelter operators and the city, and residents inside blasted officials, even booing a woman who urged compassion for families using the services. The meeting at the Elks Lodge on Queens Boulevard and Goldsmith Street was called by Community Board 4 after the former hotel, which up until weeks ago was advertised as a hostel, was quietly turned into a homeless shelter for families without notice to the community. Outside the meeting, which was open only to those who had pre-registered, *several hundred protesters chanted and held signs voicing opposition to the shelter—and exchanged words with more than 20 shelter residents who came to offer their side, with children yelling "shame on you," "get a job," and "pay your rent."* One child held up a sign saying "2, 4, 6, 8, who do we NOT appreciate, hobos hobos hobos."[2] [emphasis added]

Lainie and Gabe have been on the receiving end of such hostility on numerous occasions. As Lainie described it, "All the time, people would tell me: 'Get a job.' I just cried, I just cried. A couple of times, I would actually sit there and say: 'You know what? I do have a job. We're just down on our luck right now. Not all homeless people are homeless because of choice.' They would just walk away."

People experiencing homelessness are often assumed to be responsible for their own suffering. The protesters' chants of "get a job," "pay your rent," and "shame on you" speak to the stereotype that people experiencing homelessness are lazy, irresponsible, and blameworthy.

In reality, up to half of people experiencing homelessness in the United States have jobs. A 2021 study from the University of Chicago found that 40.4% of unsheltered people had formal labor market earnings from either part-time or full-time work in the year they were observed homeless, as did about 53% of people living in homeless shelters, a finding that "contrasts with stereotypes of people experiencing homelessness as too lazy to work or incapable of doing so," as described in the report's findings.[3] Based on their review of a large number of studies, Tobin and Murphy suggest that around 45% of individuals experiencing homelessness receive income from having at least one job,[4] and many of the rest, about 40%, cannot work as a result of disability.[5] There is a good reason why homeless shelters witness their lowest occupancy rates during the first week of each month: that is when the many residents who are working receive their paychecks and can afford to stay elsewhere for a few nights.

What the aforementioned protesters may not realize is that individuals experiencing homelessness *do* face monumental barriers to employment, which result in much higher rates of unemployment than the general US population. And of those who do manage to persevere and find employment, the vast majority work at the very bottom rungs of the labor market and are unable to make ends meet.[6]

According to a recent memo from the Homelessness Policy Research Institute at the University of Southern California, "Unemployment is a prominent factor in the persistence of homelessness across the country. In Los Angeles County, 46% of unsheltered adults cited unemployment or a financial reason as a primary reason why they are homeless."[7] Once a person becomes homeless, they face gigantic barriers to employment—it is truly remarkable that so many resilient people experiencing homelessness are able to find jobs and work. These barriers include the experience of homelessness itself,[8] physical or mental health issues, administrative burden, challenges related to reentry from incarceration or hospitalization, daunting skill and experience requirements without access to training and education, and pervasive negative stereotypes and discrimination from employers (*Can they work? Do they want to work? Are they reliable? Will they be able to integrate well into the workplace? How will they dress? Will they be clean?*).[9]

And for the vast majority of individuals experiencing homelessness who are employed, simply having a job does not guarantee sufficient resources to afford housing. Paltry wages and nonexistent savings are no match for the high (and rising) cost of housing in the US. Over the past 50 years, the federal minimum wage has fallen significantly behind the *living wage*, defined as the minimum income necessary for a worker to meet their basic needs in a particular community. In every state, the minimum wage is less than 50% of the living wage a single income household of four would need to meet their basic needs, which includes the cost of housing, food, utilities, transportation, health insurance, childcare, and emergency expenses.[10]

Adjusted for inflation, the federal minimum wage of $1.60 per hour in November 1968 is worth about $13.60 per hour in February 2023 dollars.[11] Yet in 2023 the federal minimum wage is $7.25 per hour, or roughly 47% less than the value of the minimum wage from 55 years ago.[12] The federal minimum wage has not increased since 2009. According to the Economic Policy Institute, "The latest consumer price index data reveal that the value of the federal minimum wage is now at its lowest point since February 1956."[13] The Congressional Budget Office estimates that increasing the minimum wage to $15 would lift over 6 million people out of poverty over the next 10 years, including many of the roughly 45% of people experiencing homelessness who work.[14]

Many people experiencing homelessness work jobs that pay even below the minimum wage, a result of their immigration status, holding a tip-based job, being paid under the table, or working in the informal economy. And they are not alone: "In 2018, 1.7 million U.S. workers received wages at (or even below) the federal minimum wage."[15] Kathryn Edin and H. Luke Shaefer documented the implications of below minimum wage work in shocking economic terms: "In early 2011, 1.5 million households with roughly 3 million people were surviving on cash incomes of no more than $2 per person per day in any given month. That's about one out of every twenty-five families with children in America."[16] A recent study by the National Alliance to End Homelessness highlights the implications of these paltry wages: the bottom 20% of non-homeless wage earners spent

87% of their total income on housing, leaving them about $1,300 remaining each year, or about $100 a month for everything else—food, clothing, health care, child care, transportation, paying off debt such as student loans or medical debt.[17]

Gabe was working full-time while also attending college to become a medical assistant. Between school tuition and daily expenses, for Gabe and Lainie, who collectively made below the living wage, this translated to sometimes having nothing to eat: "There was times where we'd sit at McDonald's and eat ketchup packets, until somebody felt sorry for us. It was horrible."

In stark contrast, between 1979 and 2019, compensation for the top 0.1% of income earners increased by 345% in the US. Meanwhile, wages for the bottom 90% of income earners increased only by 26%.[18] In 1965 the ratio of the average CEO salary to a typical worker salary was 20:1. By 1989 that ratio had grown to 58:1. In 2018 that ratio had exploded to 278:1.[19] In terms of actual salaries (i.e., not adjusted for inflation), the bottom 90% of workers saw their salaries increase from $31,265 to $40,085 between 1979 and 2020. For the top 1% of wage earners in that same period, salaries increased from $656,823 to about $3.2 million.[20] According to social capital scholar and political scientist Robert Putnam, "If today's income were distributed in the same way that 1970 income was distributed, it is estimated, the bottom 99 percent would get roughly $1 trillion more annually, and the top 1 percent would get roughly $1 trillion less."[21]

Instead, for most of the people experiencing homelessness who do work, like Gabe and Lainie, the jobs they hold do not pay anywhere near a living wage, and often not even the minimum wage. And so, in and of itself, work is not a solution to homelessness or poverty in the US, at least not at current wage levels.

Impenetrable Benefits

The federal public benefit system is intended to provide financial assistance to those in need. Temporary Assistance to Needy Families (TANF),

Supplemental Nutrition Assistance Program (SNAP), Special Supplemental Nutrition Program for Women, Infants, and Children (WIC), and Medicaid, among others, are there to help impoverished people, including those experiencing homelessness or housing insecurity.

Ideally, any difference between the basic cost of living in an area and what individuals experiencing homelessness and other extremely low-income people currently make in that community could be made up by public benefit programs. Unfortunately, that is not happening right now. Only about 25% of people experiencing homelessness who qualify for housing subsidies under current rules are actually receiving these subsidies.[22] And this is just the tip of the under-enrollment iceberg.

Data about TANF is particularly telling. TANF is the successor to the original federal welfare program and remains one of the largest public benefit programs in the US. However, according to the Center for Budget and Policy Priorities, there has been a steady decline in the proportion of poor families who are receiving this support, a trend that has accelerated over the past few decades. In 1979, 82% of poor families were receiving the precursor to TANF, which dates back to 1935 and was established by the Social Security Act. In 1996, 68% of poor families were receiving this benefit. But in August 1996, President Bill Clinton signed the "Welfare to Work" bill, a major welfare reform that added significant new work requirements for receiving TANF. By 2020, only 21% of poor families nationwide were receiving TANF assistance, and in 16 states, the figures were as low as 10%.[23] Furthermore, as the result of this legislation, the state family assistance grant under TANF fell from $16,567 in 1996 to the equivalent of $9,893 in 1996 dollars in the year 2020, a 40.3% decline, and the monthly number of families receiving TANF fell from a high of 5.1 million in March 1994 to 1.0 million in November 2020.[24]

In 2017 the Colorado Center on Law and Policy created the Gap Map (gapmap.org), which identifies the number of persons enrolled in a particular public benefit program as a percentage of the overall number of persons eligible in each of the 64 counties in the state. The five major benefit programs mapped are Medicaid (for health care), SNAP (for food security), TANF (for financial security), WIC (for additional food security), and CCCAP—the Colorado Child Care Assistance Program (for early learning). In the urban area of Denver, the estimated caseload compared to total eligibility—the gap in receiving benefits—was 90% for Medicaid, 65% for SNAP, 64% for TANF, 54% for WIC, and 12% for CCCAP between 2014 and 2016. In more rural areas like Garfield County, the percentages were even worse: 88% for Medicaid, 52% for SNAP, 19% for TANF, 55% for WIC, and 5% for CCCAP. In other words, apart from Medicaid, not many more than 1 in 2 Coloradans, and as few as 1 in 20, is receiving the vital benefits for which they qualify.

One reason for the low enrollments is that many people experiencing homelessness or housing insecurity face major barriers in applying for and being accepted into benefit programs that can often feel convoluted to access. These include the lack of a permanent mailing address, which makes it difficult to receive official announcements and enrollment documents; the lack of reliable transportation; the lack of government-issued identification cards, including birth certificates, driver's licenses, and social security cards; and the administrative burden—the lack of help in determining their eligibility, filling out complex forms, making appointments, and coordinating the process. These barriers prevent people experiencing homelessness from accessing crucial benefit programs, and often, employment.

Another common challenge with benefit programs today is what is called the "cliff effect," which occurs when an individual or household loses eligibility for a public benefit program once their income surpasses the threshold set by the Federal Poverty Guidelines, which are used by the government to determine financial eligibility for certain federal programs. In some cases, every additional dollar earned through wages[25] may be offset by an equivalent or even greater loss or reduction in benefit value. In effect, this disincentivizes low-income workers from trying to work more and earn more money, so as to avoid "falling off the cliff" and potentially losing their access entirely to health care, nutrition assistance, or other essential benefits. Benefit cliffs penalize people experiencing homelessness from trying to earn their way out of their precarious situation.

It is easy to glaze over all these statistics and barriers, however dire they may seem. In simple terms, benefit cuts, under-enrollments, and cliff effects inhibit people in extreme poverty from receiving the government assistance they need, making them worse off today than they would have been 30 years ago in their ability to receive and access life-saving benefit programs. For people experiencing homelessness like Gabe and Lainie, this means that they can work but not earn enough to make ends meet, and *still* not receive the relatively small amount of additional support from the government that they are eligible for and need to cover their basic needs. When asked what it was like living in their pickup truck in the same McDonald's parking lot where Gabe worked, Lainie replied: "It was hell."

Death and Taxes

Along with barriers to employment, shockingly low wages, and hard-to-access (and -keep) public benefits, people experiencing homelessness face major barriers to getting back on their feet by federal spending priorities that disproportionately favor the wealthy. The previous section focused on problems with public benefit programs that are designed to help extremely low-income people get by. In reality, the total amount that the federal government actually spends on these public benefit programs is a drop in the bucket compared to the benefits offered to wealthy individuals and families. To use a few loaded terms for a moment to emphasize a point, *the homeless* receive far fewer *handouts* than *the housed* in the United States.

In 2015 the federal government spent $270 billion on all housing subsidies, which includes public housing and housing vouchers like Housing Choice Vouchers for low-income individuals. Seventeen percent, or $46 billion of this $270 billion, went to low-income renters, while the other 83%, $224 billion, went to wealthy homeowners, primarily through the tax code with deductions like the mortgage interest deduction.[26] In an article entitled "How Homeownership Became the Engine of Inequality," sociologist and *Evicted* author

Matthew Desmond points out that the total subsidy for the mortgage interest deduction exceeded "the entire budgets for the Departments of Education, Justice, and Energy combined" in 2015, and that the homeowner's net worth was 36 times greater than the average renter's that year.[27]

Other benefits in the tax code for the wealthy include deductions for yacht taxes, rental properties, business meals, and gambling losses, and exclusions for retirement plans and for large portions of estates. According to the Congressional Budget Office, in 2019 "about half of the total benefits from income tax expenditures accrued to households in the highest quintile of tax preparers [or about 50 million people[28]] [. . .] whereas nine percent of such benefits accrued to households in the lowest quintile."[29]

* * *

In no small part as a result of who the government prioritizes, over the past four decades, inequality in the US has skyrocketed. In 1983, the top 1% of households by net worth owned 33.8% of all the wealth in the country, while the bottom 80% of households owned 18.7%. In 2019, the top 1% owned 38.2%, while the bottom 80% owned 11.1%. Thus, in 36 years, the bottom 80% of households went from owning 55% to owning 29% of what the top 1% own in the US.[30]

To be sure, homelessness is at the intersection of broken systems like housing, criminal justice, and mental health. But it also intersects with low wages, paltry public benefits, and an unfavorable tax code. Although this latter connection may be less obvious at first, at some level, if people experiencing homelessness simply had more money or benefits, they would not be currently unhoused, or perhaps would never have been in the first place.

In summary, our neighbors experiencing homelessness *do* work, but their jobs often only pay a minimum wage, not a living wage. With only a minimum wage salary, many cannot secure housing, let alone purchase their own homes, which keeps them from a major source of wealth generation. Public benefits provide relatively little assistance, and many people experiencing homelessness do not receive the benefits for which they are eligible. America's tax code provides little assistance, as it favors the wealthy far more than it does the poor.

For Gabe and Lainie, this means that the front seat of their old, shared Ford pickup, parked just outside the 24-hour Lawrence Expressway McDonald's, the very same McDonald's Gabe worked at, was the only home they could afford. Every morning, the two of them would wake to the familiar brown stucco, slightly faded golden arches, and single-occupancy bathroom that would serve as their sole shower, laundry room, water fountain, and respite, simply because in America, homelessness often does not end by just "getting a job."

KEY TAKEAWAYS

Many people believe getting a job is an easy fix-all solution to homelessness, but in reality, about half of all individuals experiencing homelessness are already working but do not make enough to afford housing, while the rest face significant barriers to employment such as the experience of homelessness itself, physical or mental health issues, reentry challenges from incarceration or hospitalization, lack of access to training and education, and discrimination from employers.

Several economic factors have a major impact on people experiencing homelessness and housing insecurity, including wage structures and the failure to provide a living wage, benefit programs and the degree to which they provide adequate support, and the inequity within how and for whom wealth accumulates in our country.

America's minimum wage—which is 50% less than what the living wage would need to be in every state in the US—is unlivable, and in part responsible for the homelessness crisis.

The federal public benefit system, intended to help those in poverty, is significantly underfunded and shamefully inaccessible to people experiencing homelessness due to bureaucratic barriers such as a lack of a permanent mailing address, reliable transportation, and documentation, along with difficulty with determining eligibility, completing complex application processes, and the ease in which life-saving benefits can be lost.

The US tax system disproportionately supports the wealthy, promotes income inequality, and exacerbates the housing crisis, thereby increasing the likelihood of homelessness for many low-income individuals and families.

8

Health Care

BORN IN ALLENTOWN, PENNSYLVANIA, and raised on Governors Island, New York, Jennifer was "a military brat" who spent her childhood moving along the eastern seaboard. She grew up with a strong sense of community: "If you needed a babysitter, if you needed a dog walker, if you needed a house sitter, if you needed your grass cut, I'd be there."

During her first pregnancy, Jennifer discovered that she suffered from hyperemesis, a very acute morning sickness that required supplementary hydration and nutrients. "The sickness was every single day, all day, and I was still working a full-time job. A lot of times during my lunch break, I would have to catch a cab to GW Hospital. I was going there so often that I didn't even have to check into the emergency room. I could just walk right upstairs to the maternity ward and get an IV because drinking was too hard on my stomach. That would be my lunch. At work, at my desk, in a cubicle, I would have a trash can for trash and a trash can for my vomit."

It was during this pregnancy that Jennifer lost over 70 pounds. She started to miss days of work and was forced to use up all her paid sick leave and vacation days in an effort to improve her medical condition. After a nearly five-year tenure at the State Department, Jennifer was summarily laid off for being "unreliable," though she would characterize it quite differently: "Although they would never say it, what they meant was that I was a medical liability."

Shortly before her last day of work, Jennifer gave birth to a daughter. Yet her discomfort did not go away. She started experiencing irregular bowel movements and severe headaches. Hospital visits became more frequent, and Jennifer doubted that the culprit was just lingering effects of hyperemesis and postpartum recovery. In her heart, Jennifer knew she had a serious medical problem that was not yet diagnosed. The hospital staff began to prescribe her narcotics, unsure of what else to do.

"A young third-year student, a blond-haired, blue-eyed resident said to me, pointing to his head, 'I think you need to see a different kind of doctor.' But I knew the pain was real, and I knew in my heart that something was seriously wrong. [. . .] I was frustrated but I thought about what he said and started to believe him, only for a second. But that second was long enough for my frustration and sadness to manifest into anger and rage." Jennifer described her fragile health from that time: "I was jaundiced, my kidneys were shot, and I hadn't had a bowel movement in four months. I was beyond tired and desperate." Finally, feeling exasperated after yet another weekly visit to the emergency room without any further clarity on what else might be ailing her, Jennifer refused to leave unless she could see a specialist. "You want me to leave, call the police or call my doctor! Your choice, but I'm not just walking out."

Jennifer saw a specialist, and additional tests were performed. The specialist returned a few hours later to Jennifer's room and announced that he had found "something that piqued his interest" and said he would like to take a closer look. A lump was found on her pancreas. It was malignant. After several years of doctors misdiagnosing and dismissing her physical discomfort, and many months of their prescribing her with narcotics and dismissing her concerns, Jennifer heard the dreaded *c* word: she had stage three pancreatic cancer.

As the cancer had not yet metastasized to blood vessels, lymph nodes, or other organs, Jennifer elected to have emergency surgery to remove the primary tumor. Thankfully, the surgery was successful, but Jennifer soon faced another challenge: she was temporarily unable to work given her fragile health and recovery post-surgery. She quickly depleted her very modest savings and still could not keep up with rent at her co-op. Less than six months after her surgery, Jennifer was evicted. At first she couchsurfed with a handful of friends and family members, but that "didn't work out well." So, as a new mom, Jennifer and her young daughter moved into a homeless shelter in Washington, DC.

Homelessness: The Worst Kind of Medicine

A serious illness or medical emergency can quickly turn the previously inconceivable prospect of homelessness into a stark reality for far too many Americans, as was the case for Jennifer, Elizabeth from chapter 6, and Ray from chapter 2.

As but one example, housing insecurity and even homelessness are such common outcomes of a cancer diagnosis that there is even a term for it: "cancer-related financial toxicity." According to a 2017 study, "between 20% and 30% of women diagnosed with breast cancer will lose their jobs, with poor women four times more likely to become jobless after a breast cancer diagnosis than their wealthier peers."[1] The loss of employment can lead to the loss of stable housing, which in turn results in the loss of a place to rest post-surgery, a place to store medications, to cook nutritious meals, to sleep soundly, and to feel safe, as well as a whole host of other negative outcomes that have awful implications for one's health. Even the time and cost of transportation to and from hospitals and doctors' offices can create a major barrier for those without homes. In a vicious cycle, medical emergencies and declining health lead to homelessness and housing insecurity, which in turn leads to even further deteriorated health.

Once a person is experiencing homelessness, physical sickness becomes a facet of daily life. Epidemiological data suggest that adults who are unhoused experience 60% to 70% higher rates of cardiovascular events compared with the general population, while conditions such as diabetes and high blood pressure develop in a timeframe on par with people who are 20 years older.[2] Individuals experiencing homelessness also have higher rates of depression, suicide, and anxiety, a 50% increased risk of dementia, a 32% increased risk of stroke, impaired executive functioning, accelerated cognitive decline, and pro-inflammatory gene expression.[3] Housing status is considered by medical practitioners to be a more accurate metric for establishing disease risk than diet, exercise, medical history, or even biological age.[4] Housing is health care, and its absence is a death sentence.

Relational poverty is another silent killer of people experiencing homelessness, often overshadowed by physical ailments and infectious disease. It's why those with fragile relationships and little money have an indiscriminate 50% increased risk of death across all disease states and injuries, and why the Centers for Disease Control encourages the formation of social connections to slow the decline of health.[5] Loneliness can be deadly, too.

As a result of these myriad health threats, people experiencing homelessness have a five times higher likelihood of premature mortality in comparison to securely housed Americans,[6] and an average life expectancy of around 50 years of age, or roughly 30 years less than people who are securely housed.[7] Interestingly, the average life expectancy in the United States was around 50 years in 1909 and nearly 80 years in 2009, also a 30-year difference, which some urban planners have attributed to the widespread implementation of minimum housing standards and proper sanitation.[8] As sociologist Paul Muniz points out in a 2021 paper, "It is therefore not surprising that [. . .] unsheltered persons in Boston faced an age-adjusted risk for death nearly 10 times greater than the general population, implying an average life expectancy of 53 years."[9]

According to the California Policy Lab brief "Health Conditions among Unsheltered Adults in the U.S.," 84% of the 209,000 unsheltered individuals in the US experience at least one physical health condition, compared to 19% of 199,000 sheltered individuals.[10] Without a safe place to stay, those without shelter are forced to seek refuge wherever they can: on park benches, in cars, underneath bridges, on sidewalks, in abandoned buildings. Unsheltered homelessness leaves individuals at a greatly elevated risk for injury, hypothermia, frostbite, falls, assault, all sorts of diseases and maladies, and self-harm. And the longer a person experiences unsheltered homelessness, the more likely they are to suffer from malnutrition, parasitic infections, and dental and degenerative joint diseases.

Homeless shelters would appear to be an obvious solution for the severe health risks of unsheltered homelessness—by definition, a person staying at a shelter is no longer unsheltered. However, shelters offer little respite.

Many shelters are dilapidated, unhygienic, and chaotic: faulty fire alarms, bedbugs and other unsanitary conditions, incessant noise, poor air quality, and erratic heating and cooling systems make wellness and recovery difficult. For those requiring regular medical treatment, the loss, misplacement, or contamination of medication, needles, and syringes can be fatal. Shelters are often understaffed and operating on limited resources. In the context of COVID-19, individuals experiencing homelessness who were living on the streets suffered substantially less from the ravages of the pandemic than those who were staying in shelters,[11] at least in part because of the crowded, unclean conditions of many shelters.

> Franklin, a young man who stayed in a shelter in Washington, DC, for over a month, offers us an insider's harrowing account on what shelter life can be like: "Sometimes there were fifty or sixty guys in line at any one time [to get into the shelter] [. . .] and there was jostling in line and people got in fights [. . .] A couple of times, a guy would come in with his buddy, and he couldn't get a bed, so he would sleep on the top of the bed, and his buddy would sleep on the bottom. Sometimes, you might see three guys in one small bed [. . .] You could touch the next bed easily . . . they were like little bunk beds, like little cots [. . .] If you rolled over, you might be in the next guy's bed [. . .] After you go to your bed, you dust it off, spray it [. . .] because there's lice, crabs, bed bugs everywhere [. . .] There was blood on the sheets . . . blood stains that came from an infection [. . .] They wouldn't change the sheets or the blankets. [That shelter] was

a place that I never took a bath or showered, because the bathroom was so filthy [. . .] about half the guys in the rooms and hallways were high on something [. . .] guys used to get physically ill in the night, usually seizures [. . .] The paramedics and ambulances would come roughly two or three times a night."[12]

Health care and homelessness are intertwined: one cannot be resolved without the other.

"Frequent Flyers" of the Emergency Room

Angelo experienced chronic homelessness in Solano County, California, while suffering from an alcohol addiction. The police frequently found him passed out drunk in public and would bring him to the hospital emergency department (ED). There, he was allowed to safely detoxify and was treated for his other health conditions. He would be discharged to the streets, rather than to an alcohol detoxification or rehabilitation program. Soon enough, the police would once again find Angelo passed out in public, in need of another visit to the emergency room.

For years, this happened on a regular basis. Because Angelo was experiencing unsheltered homelessness, his alcoholism, diabetes, and heart disease only worsened, which in turn necessitated more visits to the ED. Over a three-year period alone, Angelo's medical care cost taxpayers over $1 million. He became known as the "million dollar homeless patient."[13]

Throughout the US, hospital EDs see patients like Angelo on a nightly basis. Hospital staff know them on a first-name basis and collectively call these individuals "frequent flyers," or "high utilizers" to be a bit more considerate. In fact, more than 50% of all ED visits from people experiencing homelessness come from less than 10% of individuals.[14] Tony, an unhoused frequent utilizer of the ED in Sacramento, put it bluntly: "I'm kind of ashamed to say this, but sometimes it was just cold, and I [got] drunk. I just want[ed] to be warm and safe."[15]

According to a 2021 report entitled "Identifying Homeless Population Needs in the Emergency Department Using Community-Based
Participatory Research," people experiencing homelessness and housing insecurity represent an extremely disproportionate and growing
share of ED visits nationwide.

> ED utilization by homeless patients is three times the US norm
> [average] and has increased 80% over the last 10 years. Home-
> less patients are more likely to be "frequent users" (≥ 4 visits/
> year) or "super users" (≥ 20 visits/year) of the ED, and thus uti-
> lize more resources. Homeless patients have twice the number
> of ED evaluations and are four times more likely to re-present
> to the ED within 3 days of a prior evaluation compared to their
> housed counterparts. [. . .] At one urban ED, 14% of total
> patients were living on the streets or shelters and 25% were
> concerned about becoming homeless within 2 months. Only 4%
> of frequent ED users are discharged with a plan that specifically
> addresses their housing.[16]

As a result of limited social workers, limited shelter beds, and limited options for more stable care, the ED has become a shelter of last
resort, where people experiencing homelessness can reliably access a
bed, food, protection from the cold and inclement weather, and the
company of other people, only to leave in the morning. They know that
if they go into the ED, they won't be denied care, and there is a lot of
care that is needed: as noted previously, the health of our unsheltered
neighbors is generally wretched and worsening, thus offering further
context for their disproportionate utilization of the ED within our current system.

Using the emergency room as a waiting room or rest stop is incredibly expensive and obviously not ideal. However, it is important to
note that individuals experiencing homelessness are not maliciously
racking up medical costs for taxpayers to cover, or gleefully returning
to the ED for the third time this month for the fun of it. On a day-to-
day basis, people experiencing homelessness must expend significant
time and energy trying to figure out where they are going to sleep, get

food and water, go to the bathroom, make a few dollars, ensure their belongings do not get lost or stolen, get warm, avoid potential physical threats, and survive. The mental and physical exertion of homelessness leads many to postpone much-needed medical attention, contributing to the increased use of urgent care and emergency room facilities as conditions worsen and become chronic.

And for many ED high utilizers who are experiencing homelessness, even if they have free health insurance through Medicaid (the federal insurance program for low-income individuals), coordinating their own care needs is often unrealistic: making appointments, keeping appointments, following up with case workers, getting plugged into the care system, retaining benefit cards and identification documents, and dealing with other administrative loads. Unfortunately, in our current system of health care, there are few options that do a better job of meeting our unhoused neighbors where they are at than the ED.

When people experiencing homelessness like Angelo and Tony are provided supportive housing, their emergency visit rates decline significantly. As one example, starting in 2012 Los Angeles County began identifying frequent utilizers of the ED, moving them into supportive housing and providing additional physical and mental health services there. Among the 3,500 individuals experiencing homelessness who were moved off the streets into housing, ED visits declined by a whopping 70%, saving the county $6.5 million, or $1.20 for every dollar spent on the program.[17] Once placed into supportive housing, these formerly unhoused individuals experienced great health improvements: they reported fewer hospitalizations, fewer unmet physical and mental health needs, and being significantly happier.[18]

Housing would be the best medicine for the vast majority of our neighbors experiencing homelessness. But sadly, as a nation, we have left that medicine cabinet locked and nearly empty. And the literal medicine of our health care system is extremely expensive and difficult to access.

Barriers to a Better Way

Housing is health care, to be sure. But also health care is health care. Yet the United States fails to provide an affordable and accessible system of health care for those who need it most. A multitude of hidden barriers make receiving federal benefits and quality health care outside of the Emergency Department a herculean task for people experiencing homelessness. For example, many individuals do not know how to apply for federal benefits or find the process too difficult on their own. Supplemental Security Income (SSI) applications are notoriously complicated, and people experiencing homelessness are more likely to be denied due to procedural, not medical, reasons. Extremely low-income individuals may also face issues in qualifying, depending on the state. In our patchwork of a national health care system, in many states a person cannot get Medicaid based on income alone, thus disqualifying many non-disabled individuals experiencing homelessness who need health care.

As the country with the most expensive health care system in the world and the only industrialized nation without universal health coverage, the United States and its medical system make out-of-pocket costs for medical visits unfeasible. In fact, "about 40 percent of Americans report skipping a recommended medical test or treatment and 44 percent say they didn't go to a doctor when they were sick or injured in the last year because of cost."[19] In addition, "twenty percent of adults had major, unexpected medical expenses in the prior 12 months, with the median amount between $1,000 and $1,999."[20] For Elizabeth, these statistics translated to the loss of savings, inadequate access to cancer treatment, and ultimately homelessness.

Medical debts, incurred and shouldered by families, not only prevent individuals from receiving further medical treatment but detract from other necessary expenses including rent payments, grocery tabs, and utility bills. The median hospital stay in the US for the year 2020 averaged $11,700.[21] One illness, one hospital stay, depending on the severity, duration, and path of treatment, could take the average

American family without insurance and living well below the poverty line an entire lifetime to pay off. And personal GoFundMe campaigns are not a viable strategy to pay such bills (much less a tolerable option in the wealthiest country on earth): out of the 437,596 GoFundMe campaigns to pay for medical costs between 2016 and 2020, less than 12% were successful.[22]

Much of the data examined and referenced in this chapter refers to homelessness as a single entity, referencing a monochromatic perspective of the health effects of experiencing homelessness in America. In reality, there are numerous factors that either directly or indirectly affect the health care journey of each person experiencing homelessness: from age to disability to state and city of residence to length of time experiencing homelessness to race and ethnicity. To provide a small sense of this diversity of experience and condition, we return to the stories of Jennifer and Elizabeth.

Jennifer, a Black woman, intrinsically knew that her stomach pain (which was later revealed to be pancreatic cancer) was serious. Yet her concerns were dismissively brushed aside by her physician: "I knew there was something wrong. I was losing so much weight so fast. That's what really scared me. Within six to seven days, I was right back in the same emergency room. The doctor said, 'We're not going to give you more prescriptions. We're not going to give you any more medications. You need to stop coming. I think you're seeing the wrong kind of doctor.'" She gestures to her head. "He was so convinced he was right, and he convinced me. He really did. I believed him. I did. I went home feeling defeated. I was depressed, but I could not sleep. I could not sleep."

Elizabeth, also a Black woman, also felt a deep distrust in the health care system, stemming from her own subpar experience: "I learned the reality of disparity in the health care system. My health care was delivered through a county system. The county system I was in, they only depended on a fecal blood test. Every four years: nothing, nothing, nothing. I was 10 years overdue for my colonoscopy. It was like a bad movie: 'I'm sorry, Elizabeth, you have cancer.'"

Jennifer's and Elizabeth's encounters with the medical system are not unique.[23] Over the past two decades, thousands of studies have demonstrated that Black people and members of other minority groups receive lower quality medical care than whites, independent of disease status, setting, insurance, and other clinically relevant factors. This differential treatment resulting from racism, discrimination, and deeply ingrained bias contributes to the mistrust of doctors and other medical institutions by many marginalized groups. It is hard to trust a system that has consistently harmed, ignored, and deprived you . . . and that does not look like you: nearly 40% of the entire US population is non-white, yet less than 11% of all board-certified physicians in America are Black or Hispanic collectively.[24] Once again, we are reminded that homelessness deeply intersects with many ailing systems in our country, a situation that is greatly exacerbated for marginalized groups.

KEY TAKEAWAYS

The relationship between health care and homelessness is a vicious cycle: A diagnosis of a serious illness leads to homelessness for many people in the US, and having to endure a serious illness while experiencing homelessness greatly exacerbates symptoms and makes recovery an ever more difficult task.

Homelessness—which exposes individuals to chronic loneliness; unsafe and harsh conditions; little to no access to showers, hygiene, or first-aid products; and overcrowded and unsanitary shelters—is a major risk factor for chronic and infectious disease. In fact, housing status is a more accurate metric for establishing disease risk than diet, exercise, medical history, or even biological age.

With poor health, competing priorities, mental exhaustion from the daily demands of homelessness, and few alternatives, many people experiencing homelessness disproportionately utilize emergency departments, leading to exorbitant costs paid by taxpayers with little improvement of the health conditions of such high utilizers. Housing is health care, and would greatly reduce these costs and health inequities.

Even when benefits and health care are available, bureaucratic barriers, lack of transportation, missing identification documents, having no address or mailbox, and the sheer cost of out-of-pocket health care make it practically inaccessible for many people experiencing homelessness in the US.

Inequities in our health care system and discriminatory health practices that have disproportionately impacted Black individuals and members of other minority groups have led to a wide distrust in doctors and medical institutions, making quality health care even more inaccessible for a large portion of the population.

9

Mental and Behavioral Health

A FEW YEARS AGO, a stubbled, slender man named Joseph approached Kevin and his team toward the end of a meal service event at Saints Peter and Paul Church in San Francisco. Joseph said that he was interested in taking Kevin up on his offer to help people experiencing homelessness attempt to reconnect with their loved ones through Miracle Messages. In the course of their conversation, Joseph described living on the streets with untreated severe mental health challenges, including schizophrenia. With his downcast eyes and tinge of sadness in his voice, Joseph reminded Kevin of his beloved late uncle Mark.

Although Kevin had met hundreds of people experiencing homelessness since he started Miracle Messages in December 2014, he could not recall too many others who were quite so forthcoming so quickly about their mental health, particularly what it was like living with schizophrenia on the streets.

And so, toward the end of their conversation together, Kevin decided to ask Joseph a question that he had been wanting to ask someone ever since he started this work: "What do you wish people understood about you that they currently don't? In other words, if you could share a message with people who are currently housed and not living with schizophrenia, who may not understand what life is like for you as a person experiencing homelessness and living on the streets with a severe mental health challenge, what would you want to say to them?"

Joseph paused for a moment, and slowly raised his gaze. Softly, he replied, "I just wish people knew that I was so much more of a threat to myself than I would ever be to them."

Untreated Mental Illness

The vast majority of individuals with serious mental illnesses like schizophrenia are not violent toward others. On the contrary, they are more likely to be victims of violence.[1] But Joseph is not alone in feeling the harsh stigma of severe mental illness, which affects millions of people in the United States, both housed and unhoused alike. But because of their lack of stable housing, people living with both severe mental health challenges and housing instability face colossal challenges in obtaining the treatment they need to improve their symptoms and well-being, which in turn makes it extremely difficult to permanently exit homelessness. The combination of homelessness and mental illness is a vicious, costly, dehumanizing cycle.

For most of us who are stably housed and not living paycheck-to-paycheck, if we suffer from mental illness and are experiencing an episode, we have the opportunity to treat it relatively easily: we can draw the blinds, stay in bed, take a few pills, lock the door, close our eyes and breathe, turn on the heater or get cozy under a blanket, properly hydrate, eat a nutritious meal, call a friend, have a family member or partner check in on us, feel hygienic and refreshed with our own toilet, shower, sink, soap, and toothbrush, put on clean clothes, turn on our bedside lamp, read a few pages from a favorite book, listen to a meditation on our smartphone, get a good night's sleep, and in the morning drive our car to see our therapist or open our laptop for a virtual group counseling session or schedule an appointment with our trusted doctor. Stable housing allows mental illness to be stabilized, too.

For our unhoused neighbors, mental illness mostly goes untreated.

People experiencing homelessness have relatively high rates of mental illness, as well as substance use disorders, which co-occur at a high prevalence with mental illness as they share some underlying causes. Based on data from a 2011 report from the federal Substance Abuse and Mental Health Services Administration, education professors Kerri Tobin and Joseph Murphy indicate that the mental illness rate among the 582,462 people experiencing homelessness each night in the US is around 30%,[2] and about half of those individuals also have a substance use disorder. Even so, Tobin and Murphy point out that these percentages are "considerably less than commonly assumed or portrayed."[3] It is also worth noting that about half (46%) of the entire US population will meet the criteria for a diagnosable mental health condition at some point during their lives.[4] For alcohol use disorder, the lifetime prevalence is nearly 30%.[5] For drug use disorder, it's 10%. It is critical to remember that these issues affect unhoused and housed people alike.

Homelessness itself comes with frequent experiences of trauma, violence, and victimization, all of which create and exacerbate mental and behavioral health issues, which are made even worse by the grossly inadequate and inaccessible options for treatment. Individuals suffering from both a mental illness and a substance use disorder are at an even greater risk for suicide, suicide ideation, and chronic homelessness, while having a "dual diagnosis"—a person who has both a substance use disorder and a mental illness concurrently—increases the severity of their psychiatric symptoms, health problems, and likelihood of incarceration.[6]

Mental health and substance use treatment, including prescription drugs, long-term psychiatric care, and inpatient treatment programs, is notoriously expensive. People experiencing homelessness are less likely to have insurance and more likely to face transportation barriers.[7] When living on the streets, basic survival needs like food, water, and shelter come before mental and behavioral health needs. Barriers to treatment exacerbate psychiatric and behavioral health symptoms and make exiting homelessness even more challenging.

Overcrowded congregate shelters and the streets fail to provide the safety and privacy needed to address mental or behavioral health issues, adding yet another barrier to treatment. Elizabeth described her constant concern for herself and her belongings in congregate shelters:

> "There was always dread, deep dread: 'would this still be there, would that still be there?' Just fear, all the time. You never know what's going to happen, what you're going to walk into. People need security and their own space. It's more than about getting shelter. You need space to recover. You need to be alone with your own thoughts, where you can process. You cannot do that in a congregate environment."

What individuals like Elizabeth and Joseph need are stable places with basic human necessities such as a shower, toilet, and bed, along with a sense of privacy and safety. Studies have consistently shown that those placed in supportive housing reduce their use of substances over time, and even reduce their mental health symptoms as well.[8] It is also more costly to taxpayers to not house individuals with mental illness. People experiencing homelessness with chronic mental illness have 32% higher health care costs compared to those in supportive housing, in part because of how difficult it is for people experiencing homelessness to recover from their mental or behavioral health symptoms.[9]

As a nation, we have fundamentally failed to address the systemic need for decent and affordable mental health and substance use treatment. Instead, we are more likely to attribute poor mental health and addiction among people experiencing homelessness to personal failures, rather than untreated health issues that many housed people also face. In the absence of quality systems of care or basic compassion from their local communities, people experiencing homelessness with mental health and/or substance use issues tend to self-isolate and self-loathe, are less likely to seek help, and experience worse health outcomes.

Deinstitutionalization

In the 1960s and onward, *deinstitutionalization* describes the federal effort to close down deteriorating state mental health hospitals, with the goal of moving patients to federally funded local community mental health clinics. Though state hospitals were a deeply flawed, often carceral method for treating people—many of us have seen *One Flew over the Cuckoo's Nest*—deinstitutionalization was dysfunctionally implemented, without adequate funding for community-based alternatives. Robert Felix, the man behind the federal mental health program, claimed that community mental health clinics would "eventually be available throughout the length and breadth of the land."[10] In reality, only half the proposed clinics were created, they were never fully funded, and few facilities served people with severe needs.[11]

Instead, over the past four decades, mental health and substance use services have been increasingly privatized and unavailable to those with little to no economic resources. Between 1955 and 2010, the number of public psychiatric hospital beds dropped from 340 beds to 14 beds per 100,000 people,[12] while the number of private beds has skyrocketed.[13] This has resulted in overwhelming psychiatric boarding in hospital emergency rooms, where patients experiencing mental health crises await beds for up to a week or more.[14]

A similar trend is seen in substance use treatment centers. For example, in New Jersey the number of beds available for substance use treatment for the poor and uninsured decreased by 40% between 2010 and 2016, with only 619 state-funded beds available statewide.[15] Several public treatment centers have been bought by larger for-profit private institutions. The most intensive treatments with the most promising results are reserved for the rich and well-insured, such as the Betty Ford Clinic, which costs $32,000 per month and looks like a luxury home. "It comes down to a funding issue," said Michael Cartwright, CEO of Addiction Centers of America. "Addiction is one of the few diseases that's underfunded at every level and those funding streams have not changed in 15 years. It's not even so much a New Jersey problem as it is a United States problem."[16]

From Hospital Beds to Behind Bars

People with severe mental illness went from receiving treatment in deplorable state hospitals to living in deplorable conditions on the streets and moving in and out of emergency departments and incarceration, almost always with little to no ongoing psychiatric care.

Studies found that over 25% of patients who were released from state-run mental health institutions through deinstitutionalization exited into homelessness.[17] This means that overwhelmed hospital emergency departments (EDs) have been flooded with individuals experiencing homelessness with mental illness who are in crisis; they often have to wait days to be admitted to a psychiatric facility. In addition, according to a 2012 Wake Forest University Health Sciences study, psychiatric patients who are waiting in EDs remain there 3.2 times longer than non-psychiatric patients.[18] Once patients are discharged, proper care would require regular outpatient visits with a psychotherapist or psychiatrist, and other types of follow-ups lasting several years or even a lifetime. Like people with chronic physical health conditions described in the previous chapter, effective coordination, stabilization, and wellness are incompatible with the experience of homelessness.

As a result, people cycle through a revolving door of homeless shelters, EDs, jails and prisons, and other services. "This constant changing of venues is one factor that makes the psychiatric treatment system so ineffective and expensive," writes E. Fuller Torrey, a psychiatrist and founder of the Treatment Advocacy Center.[19] As one example, in 2007 Los Angeles spent between $35,000 and $150,000 for every mentally ill individual who cycled between homeless shelters, jails, emergency rooms, and psychiatric hospitals.[20] Those figures are even larger today.

Though many deinstitutionalized patients became homeless, many more ended up in jails and prisons. In the 1970s, the number of incarcerated individuals with severe mental illness was around 5%. In the 1980s, this figure rose to 10%, and in the 1990s, to 15%. Between 2007 and 2012, the estimate rose to 20%–40%.[21] In some sense, patients with severe mental illness have not been deinstitutionalized, but "transinstitutionalized," moved from one institution to another (from state-run mental health facilities to incarceration).[22]

In fact, there is not a single county in the US where a public psychiatric institution holds more people with mental illness than the county jail.[23] For example, upon the closure of the Northwest Georgia Regional Hospital, the number of prisoners with mental health problems increased an estimated 60%. And when the Georgia Mental Health Institute closed, the number of inmates in the county jail needing treatment for a mental illness increased by 73.4%.[24]

Individuals with serious mental illness are 10 times more likely to be in a jail or prison than a hospital bed.[25] Physician and epidemiologist Tala Al-Rousan and her colleagues conducted a prevalence study in a state prison system that they claim is the "nation's largest mental health institution." They highlight that with the highest incarceration rate in the world, the United States has created a public health crisis in which "correctional facilities have become a front line for mental health care."[26]

Looking at the prevalence of mental illness for Iowa inmates, Dr. Al-Rousan and her colleagues found that almost half of inmates were diagnosed with a mental illness (48%). Of those diagnosed with a mental illness, 29% had a serious mental illness, such as depression, PTSD, or personality disorders. These rates are much higher than in the general population, where 20% have a mental illness and 5.6% have a serious mental illness. After being placed into the criminal justice system, inmates faced increased structural and interpersonal discrimination, high early mortality rates, comorbid psychiatric diagnoses, and greater intensity of psychiatric symptoms. The effects of incarceration create additional barriers to accessing housing and employment while simultaneously worsening the physical and mental health of the incarcerated individuals with mental illness. The result: incarcerated individuals with mental illness face greater risk of homelessness—and continue to receive subpar mental health treatment, cycling through a revolving door of prison, inadequate treatment programs, emergency care, and homelessness.

"Armed Social Workers"

One notable consequence of transinstitutionalization is the growing involvement of the police in the nation's mental health crisis. When someone calls 911 for a mental health emergency in the US, the police are likely to show up. Regardless of the de-escalation training a particular police force may or may not have received, the very presence of the police can escalate a situation.[27] Police officers are often inadequately trained to deal with mental health crises. To borrow a phrase from one law enforcement official, the police have become "armed social workers" with little to no training in social work.[28]

The number of people taken to hospital emergency departments by the police for psychiatric evaluation has boomed, and the police have become the "world's largest psychiatric outreach team."[29] Though some police departments offer training for mental health crisis intervention, tragedies involving individuals with mental illness are alarmingly high. Studies in Seattle and New York report that a third of people killed by the police were mentally ill. Nationally, somewhere between 25% and 50% of fatal police shootings involve someone with an untreated severe mental illness.[30] Individuals with serious mental illness are 16 times more likely to be killed by law enforcement than those without such an illness.[31] Community violence perpetrated by individuals with untreated mental illness has also increased in the decades since deinstitutionalization, including a number of high-profile homicides and other violent crimes.[32]

In this way, transinstitutionalization and its aftermath have led to the criminalization of mental illness. The closing of state mental hospitals and the failure to provide adequate alternative treatment facilities has meant that former state hospital patients have been released without follow-up, many of whom have subsequently been arrested and imprisoned or all too often shot to death by untrained police officers. Some of these patients have nowhere to live but on the streets or in shelters, and are unable to access the ongoing treatment they need to stabilize.

Fortunately some progress is being made. Crisis intervention teams and mandatory mental health training among police departments have become increasingly popular. Police departments have begun hiring mental health professionals to assist with increasing mental illness calls in the community. And law enforcement agencies have begun providing social services to mentally ill individuals. One such program in California's Ventura County Sheriff's Department provides mentally ill inmates medicine and free rides to appointments at treatment facilities following their release from jail. Hillsborough County in Florida offers a similar program, which reported a significant drop in recidivism. Mental health courts have also been created and have proven to decrease arrests and incarcerations of mentally ill individuals.[33]

These are all positive developments, and as coauthors, we recognize the vital, hard, and often thankless work that law enforcement does to maintain public safety and connect struggling individuals with social services. In Kevin's experience, police departments have been some of Miracle Messages' most enthusiastic partners: through officers' daily interactions with people experiencing homelessness, they intrinsically understand the need for cost-effective services like family reunifications, phone buddy programs, and direct cash transfer programs, and are desperate for new, promising tools in their toolkits to better help people and stop the revolving door between homelessness, incarceration, and emergency departments. Clearly, our society has not set law enforcement up to succeed by expecting them to be the sole providers of mental health intervention and treatment for people experiencing homelessness in this country.

Substance Use and Addiction

"My addiction didn't start until my 40s. I buy this house. I'm married to my wife. I have a family. Everything's kinda-sorta going okay, but not really. I had marital problems on and off throughout my marriage. We've had financial struggles on and off. It's expensive having two kids. It's expensive to have a mortgage. In early 2015, I had surgery on my foot, and I was prescribed a 30-day supply of oxycodone for the pain when I left the hospital. And I didn't use those pills as directed. Addiction was the primary driver into my homelessness. [. . .] I actually became homeless because one night, I snuck out of the house and stole money from my wife's purse. I took the car, and I went to the Tenderloin neighborhood of San Francisco, and I didn't go home for 11 days. I went on an 11-day bender of fentanyl and heroin and crack cocaine. She filed a missing person's report on me. The police came and got me, and I went home. My wife waited for me with a bag, saying: 'I got you a bed in a drug rehab. You either go to rehab, or you get out.' And, at that moment, I was in full withdrawal from heroin. And I chose heroin. I chose my addiction—it was that powerful. I walked out of the house, and for the next six months, I was living in the doorway on Golden Gate Avenue."

Tom grew up in San Francisco in the 1980s. His parents were kind, loving, and attentive; not rich, but not poor, either. In reflecting on his own struggles with drug addiction, Tom believes his family history of alcohol addiction and unresolved traumas influenced the choices he and his three siblings made, as two of them also struggled with addiction and are currently in recovery.

"I got off the streets because of intervention. It's not like I walked into a rehab and said, 'Hey, I want to get clean.' I got caught up in the criminal justice system and had to go to jail for three months. I was scared. I was so scared. We have to start being honest about what's happening on the street. Honesty is where we have to start. We have to put down our ideologies and recognize that, in addition to there being systemic racism issues and housing problems, we have a huge, tremendous problem in this country. There are [millions of] people who are addicted to drugs in the United States right now, and it is unequivocally complicating the issue of homelessness. And recovery from addiction is the way out. It's really the way out because that recovery includes housing, too. It's one thing to meet people where they're at, but it's another to not leave them there. Not leaving them there means, not only do we want to save their lives, but we want to change their life for the better. It's about changing lives."

Tom is not alone in his story. Substance use among unsheltered individuals living on the streets is rampant. For some individuals, addiction is a primary cause of homelessness, as was the case for Tom. For others, drug and alcohol use are primarily effects of homelessness: the unfathomable daily trauma, physical pain, and psycho-social suffering of living on the streets are too much to bear and lead many to self-medicate through substances. Kerri Tobin and Joseph Murphy write that "substance use, considered 'both a consequence of and a leading factor in the continuance of homelessness among individuals,' is even more prevalent than mental illness, with 50% of the total homeless population,[34] and 79% of veterans experiencing homelessness, believed to have substance use disorders."[35] In another study conducted in the streets and shelters of Boston, approximately half of the unhoused respondents reported having used or abused illegal drugs.[36]

Our nation's severely inadequate treatment options for substance use are especially evident in today's opioid epidemic, which has disproportionately ravaged the lives of people experiencing unsheltered homelessness. According to the CDC, nearly 69,000 people in the US died due to an opioid-related overdose in 2020, which equates to approximately 188 deaths per day. Nearly three-quarters of fatal drug overdoses involved opioids in 2020, an increase of 31% from the previous year.[37] And persons experiencing homelessness were nine times more likely to die from an opioid overdose compared to stably housed individuals.[38]

Very few people experiencing homelessness receive the treatment they need to recover from substance use.[39] Similar to the move in mental health care toward deinstitutionalization in the 1960s and 1970s, in the early 1970s Congress passed the Hughes Act and the Uniform Alcoholism and Intoxication Treatment Act, which together called for the creation of a vast nationwide network of detox and treatment centers, shifting the responsibility for treating alcohol addiction from the prisons ("drunk tanks") to the health system. However, as was the case of the national network of community mental health centers that never fully materialized, adequate detox centers and treatment beds for substance use across the country were never created.[40]

Instead, punishment became the status quo. President Richard Nixon declared a "War on Drugs," which led to the rapid criminalization of drug use, which especially targeted Black men and communities of color. People struggling with drug addiction were not referred to appropriate treatment centers but were incarcerated. Today one in five incarcerated people—approximately 400,000 individuals in state and federal prisons, jails, and youth facilities—are locked up for a drug offense.[41] And as many as 65% of the prison population has an active substance use disorder.[42] Given the prison-to-homelessness pipeline we will explore in the next chapter, many of these inmates with active substance use disorders will be discharged to the streets, where their substance use will get worse, go untreated, and result in further incarceration, hospitalization, and/or premature death.

These statistics are especially cruel when considering that recent research has offered overwhelming evidence that substance and alcohol use disorders have genetic origins, and that addiction literally overtakes the brain, changing both its structure and function. Twin studies found that between 40% and 60% of susceptibility to addiction can be explained by genetic heritability.[43] Addiction does not result from a lack of willpower but from the physiological and functional changes to the brain as a result of a substance that hijacks the brain's pleasure center, making the addicted individuals seek more and more. And some neurological systems are more prone to be unduly affected by substances than others, as Tom presumed was his case.

When addiction is viewed as a personal failing, and mental illness goes untreated but remains highly stigmatized, people experiencing homelessness who suffer from mental illness and/or substance use disorder face nearly insurmountable barriers to housing and employment. According to a study of unhoused individuals with mental illness, a majority of participants (61.5%) reported being discriminated against for being homeless or in poverty, 50.6% reported being discriminated against for their skin color, and 43.7% reported being discriminated against for mental illness or substance use disorder. The authors of this study concluded that their results "underscore poverty and homelessness as major sources of perceived discrimination, and expose underlying complexities in the navigation of multiple identities in responding to stigma and discrimination."[44] Holding multiple stigmatized identities makes discrimination and its negative social, psychological, and physical effects even more salient, keeping its victims excluded, underemployed, unhoused, and often feeling hopeless.

The social disconnection and deep stigma accompanying mental illness and addiction may be the most harmful of all. Johann Hari, the author of *Chasing the Scream*, argues that the opposite of addiction is not recovery, but connection.[45] In order to heal, stabilize, and get the support they need, people experiencing homelessness with mental illness and/or substance use disorders need to be embraced in our society, not excluded and further marginalized. Without supportive relationships, people will further rely on drugs, alcohol, and other self-harming behaviors to try to numb their pain, thus leading to even worse health outcomes. Relational poverty, stigma, shame, and exclusion greatly exacerbate addiction and mental illness for people experiencing homelessness, and make both nearly impossible to manage, treat, and live with.

KEY TAKEAWAYS

Individuals with mental illness face significant housing and employment discrimination, making them more likely to experience homelessness.

People experiencing homelessness with mental illness, which encompasses substance use disorders, face a slew of barriers in obtaining treatment, including high costs, lack of access to insurance, prescriptions, and transportation, the competing priorities of meeting basic needs, and the increased privatization of treatment—all of which, in turn, worsen psychiatric symptoms and make it much more difficult to permanently exit homelessness.

Without adequate care, individuals with severe mental health disorders cycle through a revolving door of homeless shelters, emergency departments, jails and prisons, and other services—a cycle that is incredibly wasteful and costly.

Deinstitutionalization contributed to increased rates of homelessness and has led to the de facto process of transinstitutionalization, where a large percentage of individuals with mental illness and substance use disorders are simply being housed in jails and prisons.

With a shortage of trained outreach and mental health professionals, police have been increasingly involved in the nation's mental health crisis, yet officers are not adequately trained or equipped to deal with individuals with mental illness. Tragically, a large proportion of people killed by the police are mentally ill.

Substance use disorders are a type of mental disorder and have genetic origins, but have been historically punished and criminalized rather than adequately treated.

10

Criminal Justice

TIMOTHY, A MIDDLE-AGED BLACK MAN with a portly build, graying beard, and kind eyes, said he wanted to record his Miracle Messages video to his daughter Makayla, whom he never stopped thinking about during his many years behind bars. Looking straight into the camera, Timothy's eyes smile as he speaks about his daughter, lighting up as he recalls memories of the little three-year-old he has not seen in over 18 years. Timothy leans forward and begins addressing his daughter:

> "I love you. I miss you. I've never stopped loving you. You have family here in Northern California that want to see you. They've been waiting to see you. They love you, and, please, call me, or I'll call you, as soon as you can. I love you. I've always loved you. I picked your name. It took me seven months. Your mother gave me two baby name books, and I wouldn't take 'em. Your grandmother spoiled you. Your great-grandmother spoiled you. Everybody at the church we went to when you were a baby were your relatives. There's people here waiting for you. [. . .] I love you. Your momma, I still care for her as a human being. Please call me. There's nothing but goodness here for you. Your cousin, if you come, she has a place for you at her house. She planned and hosted your baby shower when you were in

your mother's stomach. She was there at your birth, as well as your grandmother. You were born at the same hospital as me, San Francisco General. You have a lot of family here, and they love you. They remember you, and they want to see you again. Please call me. Come home when you want to. I love you."

For many years, Timothy had cycled in and out of jails and prisons. He'd lost custody of Makayla and had been out of contact with both her and her mother for most of his time behind bars. After being released from state prison, Timothy was unable to find employment or housing anywhere. His record followed him, reminding potential employers and housing providers of his past when all he wanted was to find his daughter and move on. He served his time, but his time never stopped serving him.

Some nights, Timothy had enough money for a hotel room. But often not. He spent over five years living on and off the streets. Yet anyone who knew Timothy knew that regardless of the hurdles before him, he maintained hope by always holding on tightly to the memory of Makayla, "the best thing that ever happened" to him. She was his guiding light to keep living, to not give up. His daughter was his "why."

The Revolving Door

In the United States, there is a revolving door between homelessness and the criminal justice system: individuals like Timothy cycle between incarceration and shelters—jails and prisons to shelters and the streets and back again. The numbers are harrowing: between 15% and 20% of state and federal prisoners experienced homelessness immediately prior to their incarceration. Forty percent said they had been homeless at some point during the past several years. This represents an overrepresentation of people experiencing homelessness moving into incarceration of at least 10 times the standardized estimate for the general US adult population.[1]

Looking at the numbers from the other direction, among unsheltered adults in the Los Angeles Continuum of Care, nearly two-thirds report involvement with the criminal justice system. For people released from prison, 15% face homelessness at some point within their first year of release, with two-thirds of these individuals reoffending within the year on average.[2]

The cost of this revolving door is exceptionally high. As one example, the City of Denver spent an average of $7.3 million a year to provide basic services to 250 people cycling between chronic homelessness and jail, or nearly $30,000 per person per year, between 2015 and 2019.[3] This vicious cycle can go on indefinitely, leading to astronomical costs and strain on our criminal justice and homeless services systems.[4]

From Homelessness to Incarceration

One of the most ubiquitous developments in the history of homelessness over the last 20 years has been the efforts at local levels across the country to punish people experiencing homelessness for life-sustaining activities, making it essentially illegal to be experiencing homelessness in more than half of cities nationwide.[5]

As we highlighted in chapter 3 on the topic of exclusion, hundreds of local jurisdictions nationwide have adopted anti-homeless ordinances such as camping bans, sit-and-lie ordinances, anti-panhandling laws, and prohibitions on sleeping on the streets, living in vehicles, using public restrooms, moving household goods at night, and even public feedings in the name of public safety and sanitation. In 2022, 78-year-old Norma Thornton was arrested for feeding people experiencing homelessness in Bullhead City, Arizona, under their recent ordinance barring the distribution of prepared food in public parks. Thornton's attorney characterized the city's efforts as "criminalizing kindness."[6] In 2014, 90-year-old Arnold Abbott, a World War II veteran and homeless activist, was arrested in Fort Lauderdale, Florida, for feeding people experiencing homelessness at a public beach through his nonprofit organization, Love Thy Neighbor. "One of the police officers said, 'Drop that plate right now,' as if I were carrying a weapon," said Abbott.[7]

In the absence of sufficient housing, shelter, restrooms, and other necessary resources, the overwhelming impact of these anti-homeless laws has been to criminalize individuals experiencing homelessness for trying to fulfill their basic needs for living: sleeping, eating, urinating, defecating, sitting, and more. People who are forced to live on the streets violate laws simply by trying to stay alive.

In its most recent survey regarding the criminalization of homelessness, the National Homelessness Law Center reported on its analysis of 187 urban and rural cities around the country. Of the surveyed cities, 72% have laws restricting camping in public, and 51% have a law restricting sleeping in public. Sitting and lying down in public are outlawed in 55% of the cities, and 83% restrict begging in public. Even sleeping in one's own car is restricted in half of the cities surveyed, and 83% prohibit public urination and defecation. As the report indicates in its executive summary, "Many people experiencing homelessness have no choice but to live outside, yet cities routinely punish and harass unhoused people for their presence in public places. Nationwide, people without housing are ticketed, arrested, and jailed under laws that treat their life-sustaining conduct—such as sleeping or sitting down—as civil or criminal offenses. In addition, cities routinely displace people experiencing homelessness from public spaces without providing any permanent housing alternatives."[8]

Anti-homeless laws are inhumane, dangerous, punitive, and discriminatory. Criminalizing homelessness effectively moves people to distant and confined spaces, strips them of their full rights, and bars them from activities that are essential to life. The result is stockpiled fines, hefty criminal records, and lost or confiscated personal property that creates additional barriers to stable housing and employment.

Anti-homeless laws are likely unconstitutional as well. Since 2015, "no panhandling ordinance challenged in court has withstood constitutional scrutiny under the 1st Amendment."[9] In 2021 the Ninth Circuit Court of Appeals affirmed the property rights of individuals experiencing homelessness, ruling that a 2016 Los Angeles ordinance that permitted city agents to remove bulky items like mattresses, dog crates, storage bins, and carts likely violated the "unreasonable searches and seizures" protections of the Fourth Amendment.[10]

And in one of the most significant challenges to anti-homeless ordinances, the Ninth Circuit ruled in *Martin v. City of Boise* that in the absence of available and adequate shelter alternatives, "it is cruel and unusual punishment under the 8th Amendment to punish someone for life-sustaining activities like sleeping, resting, or sheltering oneself."[11] The decision, hailed as a breakthrough for those sleeping on the streets, prevented police from enforcing camping bans if no other shelter or housing was available.[12] To be sure, in most communities, there are simply not enough shelter beds, tiny homes, safe parking spaces, and transitional housing beds available to meet current demand. The 2020 Point-in-Time survey estimated a nationwide deficit of 184,000 beds, which means that at least 30% of people experiencing homelessness lack access to any kind of shelter.

At some level, criminalizing homelessness abdicates society's responsibility to solve a problem of its own creation.

Through criminalization, homelessness becomes no longer a community's problem but a problem for law enforcement and the criminal justice system. The moral quandary of how to ensure all people have their basic needs met is ignored and replaced with arbitrary ordinances, hostile architecture, and outlawing life-sustaining activities. And when a person experiencing homelessness inevitably violates a local anti-homeless ordinance and is apprehended, they are squirreled away to a prison or jail cell, out of sight and out of mind . . . at least temporarily. Sara Rankin from Seattle University School of Law calls this process *transcarceration*, or moving from one kind of incarceration to another— the same basic concept as transinstitutionalization, which we explored in the previous chapter.[13]

From Incarceration to Homelessness

In a groundbreaking article entitled "Return to Nowhere: The Revolving Door between Incarceration and Homelessness," part of the "One Size Fails All" report series from the Texas Criminal Justice Coalition, one of the coauthors recounts a particularly illuminating story of one woman's experience being released from state jail:

> She was scared to get out. She had just done six months on a felony prostitution charge. Her pimp had taken her to a different

city to "hit licks" (commit theft) and she was arrested. He didn't bond her out or put any money on her commissary account. On her day of release from state jail, the Texas Department of Criminal Justice dropped her off at the bus station with a ticket back to the county where she was arrested, not her hometown. When she got off the bus, she had no money, no clothes, no food, no place to go. She went to the shelter, and it was first-come-first-serve and had no beds. She immediately went to "turn a trick" just to meet her basic needs. She said that she couldn't stand to sleep with strangers for money without getting high and found all the wrong people rather quickly: "they all hang around the bus station, it's all right there." She was "free" for only three days before being arrested again for prostitution and possession of a controlled substance less than a gram. She returned to state jail, only to be released again to the same situation.[14]

Like Timothy's story from the beginning of this chapter, this woman's account shows that the revolving door between homelessness and incarceration flows both ways in the United States. Nationwide, an estimated 20% of those released from prison become homeless.[15] But the percentage can be significantly higher than that:[16] In New York City for example, in 2017 more than half of the people released from prison headed straight to the city's shelters upon release.[17] It is hard enough for returning citizens who have a stable home and supportive family to return to post-incarceration. But for many individuals like this woman in Texas, there is relational poverty, no housing, and no real hope of getting out from under the criminal justice system.

To understand how and why so many millions of people have moved from jail and prison cells to living on the streets and in shelters, it is helpful to look at the data around incarceration rates in the United States. The numbers are staggering.

The United States incarcerates more of its people than any other developed nation in the world, by far. By the end of 2019, there were almost 6.4 million adults in the criminal justice system in the US,[18] almost 70% of whom were on probation (3.5 million) or parole (880,000).[19] With over 2 million people in prisons and jails in the US, if the prison population were a city, it would be the fifth-largest city in the United States, just below Houston but bigger than Philadelphia or Phoenix. The 2 million people in the US who are currently incarcerated represent a 500% increase over the last 40 years.[20] While the other 4.38 million adults in the criminal justice system like Timothy may be officially outside the walls of prisons and jails while they are on probation or parole, they are far from free, much less able to get back on their feet.

In the United States, having a criminal record casts a very wide, lingering shadow. A criminal record can make it impossible to secure housing, access life-saving benefits, gain stable employment, and more. As one indication of how destabilizing incarceration is, individuals who have been incarcerated once are 7 times more likely to experience homelessness, while those incarcerated more than once are 13 times more likely.[21] Finding housing or employment is especially challenging for people convicted of a sex offense, who in many states are banned from public housing and from obtaining subsidized housing vouchers for life, despite good data on the relative absence of reoffending, about 5% within three years.[22]

As Michelle Alexander points out in her landmark book *The New Jim Crow: Mass Incarceration in the Age of Colorblindness*, "Most people branded felons, in fact, are not sentenced to prison [. . .] [they are] barred from public housing by law, discriminated against by private landlords, ineligible for food stamps, forced to 'check the box' indicating a felony conviction on employment applications for nearly every job, and denied licenses for a wide range of professions."[23] These barriers, specific to incarceration, are compounded by the many barriers to housing and employment poor people face in this country in general: credit checks, income requirements, high security deposits, and the like.

The negative impact of these barriers is severe. For Timothy, his inability to secure stable employment and housing—and, in turn, generate bridging social capital with coworkers and neighbors—left him in a very precarious situation, which directly resulted in homelessness. With no place to call home, no savings, and no connections, many individuals (over 50,000 each year) upon release from prison or jail head straight to the nearest homeless shelter.[24] And small wonder: as we mentioned in chapter 6, public funding for corrections increased by $19 billion (or 171%) during the Clinton administration, while funding for public housing decreased by $17 billion (61%), thus "effectively making the construction of prisons the nation's main housing program for the urban poor," to once again quote Michelle Alexander in *The New Jim Crow*.[25] Meanwhile, the average cost to taxpayers to house a person in jail is $83,000 per year.[26]

These barriers, faced by many, are further compounded by systemic racism in the criminal justice system and other sectors of society. For instance, in the United States, Black people in particular are significantly overrepresented among both the prison and homeless populations by revealingly similar ratios. In California, Black people account for only about 6% of the overall population, but 30% of the prison population . . . and nearly 30% of the homeless population.[27] As Michelle Alexander pointedly asks, how does a system that is purportedly colorblind achieve such disparate racial results?

Part of the reason for this is that "predominantly Black neighborhoods are simultaneously over-policed when it comes to surveillance and social control, and under-policed when it comes to emergency services," says Daanika Gordon, an assistant professor of sociology at Tufts University.[28] This contributes to the disproportionate impact of police violence and subsequent involvement in the criminal justice system in Black, Hispanic, and Native American communities. As a result, upon release from prison or jail, people of color in the US are much more likely to live in a perpetual state of second-class inferiority under a lifetime of "legalized discrimination," deprived of essential benefits like SNAP (food stamps), barred from serving in the military or on a jury, denied employment and housing opportunities, and, in far too many cases, left to experience homelessness.[29]

The trauma of all of this is not just financial, professional, and civic, but also relational: incarceration removes a person from their loved ones, often causing profound feelings of shame. Any family members, friends, or work colleagues who choose to remain by the formerly incarcerated person's side will inevitably feel the strain of their unmet needs, caused by the legalized discrimination that makes reintegrating into society incredibly difficult. Formerly incarcerated individuals must rely on loved ones—whom they would ideally focus on reestablishing relationships with first—to meet their basic needs. As a result, conflicts like arguing, fighting, divorce, separation, and estrangement become more likely, making it even more difficult for the formerly incarcerated person to get back on their feet and stay out of prison or jail and avoid homelessness. In short, imprisoning a person also imprisons their families and social support systems long after serving their sentence and being released.

So it is especially difficult to imagine the tremendous emotional and psychological pain of what it must be like for a person experiencing homelessness in this broken system: to be incarcerated for possessing a small amount of marijuana or cocaine, spend a few weeks in jail, get saddled with more fines and court costs, and get denied for early release for failure to make bail and pay the hefty fees. Then, after finally being released with a few bucks in their pocket, and perhaps doubling up for a few weeks with an increasingly stressed-out friend before getting kicked out after fighting about rent or chores, spending many hours attempting to get into a shelter but being turned away because it is full, and ending up in a small tent in an encampment on a busy street, only to be monitored and harassed by the police for disobeying the anti-camping ordinance, and eventually ending up back in jail . . . the revolving door revolving yet again.

KEY TAKEAWAYS

In the US, there is a high-cost "revolving door" between homelessness and the criminal justice system: individuals cycle between jails or prisons, shelters, and the streets.

Individuals experiencing homelessness are criminalized for behaviors which they have no choice but to engage in—such as sleeping outside or in cars, panhandling, and setting up tent encampments—contributing to the revolving door.

Criminalizing homelessness abdicates society's responsibility to solve a problem of its own creation. Harmful "quality-of-life" offenses attempt to move homelessness further to the margins— out of sight, out of mind—and reinforce the fallacy that punishing "the homeless" is a justified consequence of their "bad behavior."

Just as homelessness leads to incarceration, incarceration leads to homelessness; this is due to the racist and discriminatory multisystem consequences of being involved in the criminal justice system, which include being barred from public housing, being denied federal benefits including using housing vouchers, having to "check the box" on employment applications, and being discriminated against by private landlords, all of which disproportionately harms Black, Hispanic, Native American, and other minority groups.

11

Youth Development

TODAY, RAND IS A FATHER and a social worker, a man with blue-rimmed glasses and a deep love for community, who didn't think he would one day be "on the other side of the table," helping boys and girls who remind him so much of his younger self.

Rand grew up in a household characterized by neglect. In his words:

"My life started after my two parents abandoned their first children, separately. My mom had a child, and she left her in Maryland, in a hospital, and my biological father was about to get married, and the woman was already pregnant, and he abandoned both of them. They met during that time period. [. . .] They were not well: self absorption, vanity, sex addiction, chronic lying to themselves and to each other. My parents struggled with their honesty, their virtue, chastity, having lots of different affairs and taking me to different relationship spots with their boyfriends and girlfriends. It was confirmation that I was not wanted."

Once, Rand said, he broke his arm, but couldn't find his parents anywhere. "I was alone way too much as a little kid." At 11 years old, Rand "spent a lot of time alone, sleeping in bushes, behind gas stations, parks, other people's places." At 12 or 13 years old, Rand tried to kill himself for the first time. He couldn't take the abandonment any longer. He was temporarily placed in a psychiatric facility: "I think my family was happy that I was gone. They told Human Services: 'Don't bring him back. We don't want him.'" At 15 years old, Rand entered the foster care system. Rand lived in what he described as "quasi-confinement" in a cramped group home on the outskirts of Denver, "a disgusting, terrible, violent, sad place," where he, alongside 12 other boys, would spend their days and nights alone in a basement. "It was miserable," he said.

Long before he slept in bushes, was locked up at a psychiatric facility, or placed in a dysfunctional group home, Rand lacked a safe place to live. Although he sometimes had a physical roof over his head, four walls do not make a house a home. So the quote shared in this book's preface that launched Kevin into creating Miracle Messages—"I never realized I was homeless when I lost my housing, only when I lost my family and friends"—does not apply to Rand: he *never* had supportive family and friends to begin with. For Rand, his family was part of the problem, not part of the solution. In this very real sense, Rand was born without a home.

The Face of Homelessness

What percentage of people experiencing homelessness do you imagine are under 25 years old? As a society, we tend to greatly underestimate the number of children and youth who are experiencing homelessness. The story of Rand is heartbreaking, harrowing, and unique in its particulars, but his experience of homelessness is tragically shared by millions of youth across the United States each year.

Youth are one of the largest segments of people experiencing homelessness in the US. According to HUD's 2022 Annual Homelessness Assessment Report to Congress, there were 98,244 children under the age of 18 experiencing homelessness, based on that year's Point-in-Time survey data, and an additional 40,177 aged 18 to 24.[1] Those under the age of 18 constitute 16.9% of the total unhoused population on any given night. If you add in those between 18 and 24, they're 23.8% of the total population. In other words, under the very narrow HUD definition and Point-in-Time count, roughly one in six of all those experiencing homelessness are under 18, most of whom are in families, and about one in every four people experiencing homelessness is under 25 years old.

If we use the broader US Department of Education definition of homelessness that includes people who are doubled or tripled up with others, and includes those who experience homelessness at any point over the course of the year and not just on any given night, then the children and youth homelessness numbers are much larger. For the 2020–2021 school year, the National Center on Homeless Education found that 1,096,669 public school children experienced homelessness,[2] and another 1 million children under the age of six years old experienced homelessness,[3] out of the approximately 6 million people who experience homelessness each year in the United States. This is 34.9% of the total population, or more than one in every three people experiencing homelessness under the Department of Education's definition and our estimates. And by some reports using even broader definitions, the numbers may be even larger than that.[4]

Being undercounted is just one of the many ways children and youth are left out of the narrative of combating homelessness in the US. But regardless of common misperceptions of how many young people—both in families and unaccompanied—actually experience homelessness, some of the primary risk factors for homelessness at any age begin very early in life.

Childhood trauma is a major predictor of youth and adult homelessness. Among people who experience homelessness, the proportion with high adverse childhood experiences (ACE) scores—which is a tally of different types of childhood abuse, neglect, toxic stress, and other types of trauma—is significantly greater than the general population. Examples of adverse childhood experiences include experiencing or witnessing violence, having a parent or guardian incarcerated, or instability due to parental separation. The more of these experiences a child has, the higher the ACE score—Rand's ACE score would be very high.

And the higher the ACE score, the higher the likelihood that a child will experience mental health problems, developmental delays and learning disabilities, disruptive behavioral issues, and general health problems, and, as an adult, not complete high school, not have a college degree, be unemployed, experience poverty, experience homelessness, and have a harder time exiting homelessness.[5]

In one study, over half of unsheltered youths interviewed indicated that some form of trauma played a part in leading them to homelessness.[6] When trauma and instability collide, youth experiencing homelessness have a harder time developing healthy coping mechanisms. This can lead to deteriorating mental health, and turning to alcohol and drugs to numb the pain. In one study in 2014, out of 601 unhoused youth aged 16 to 25, 60% met the clinical criteria for a substance use disorder, with 50% addicted to alcohol and 60% addicted to drugs.[7]

The psychological burden of homelessness takes an especially heavy toll on youth who also face discrimination for their racial and sexual identity. For unhoused youth of color, the mental health harm is amplified. Racial stigma, just like perceived homelessness stigma, is associated with increased depressive symptoms, regardless of gender, age, or other forms of discrimination.[8] In some cases, even youth who do not feel stigmatized for their housing status may still have poor psychological and physical health if they feel stigmatized for their race. This means that youth of color, who are overrepresented in the unhoused population to begin with, are likely to suffer more emotionally and psychologically if they experience homelessness.

This dual stigmatization creates psychological barriers in children of color that often keep them from accessing social and health services. After facing various forms of stigma throughout their lives, many unhoused young people of color fear how they will be perceived or treated by social workers. The cycle is dangerous: the more stigmatized a youth is, the more at risk they are for various mental and behavioral health problems, and the greater level of distrust they are likely to develop in "the system" and other people, which leads to developing unhealthy coping mechanisms and further disconnecting, which results in greater stigmatization.[9]

LGBTQ+ youth are at a disproportionate risk of becoming homeless, often due to their family's rejection of their sexuality. While LGBTQ+ youth make up an estimated 9.6% of the nationwide population, they make up approximately 40% of the homeless youth population.[10] Multiple studies have linked family rejection of LGBTQ+ youth with a higher risk of various behavioral problems. One study found that compared to those who reported no levels of family rejection, rejected youths were 8.4 times more likely to have attempted suicide, 5.9 times more likely to report high levels of depression, 3.4 times more likely to use illegal drugs, and 3.4 times more likely to report having engaged in unprotected sexual intercourse.[11] On top of this, LGBTQ+ youth face a greater level of stigma based on their housing status than their peers, studies have found. As with racial stigma, these various sources of trauma and stigma exacerbate, overlap, and lead to a higher probability of mental illness, substance use, and other high-risk behaviors.[12]

Even when they attempt to receive support, LGBTQ+ youth are often discriminated against, stigmatized by, or become targets of social violence. While there aren't sufficient shelter beds for adults experiencing homelessness, the situation is even worse for LGBTQ+ youth. For instance, transgender and gender-nonconforming youth are barred from some single-gender shelters, which puts them at elevated risk for transphobic violence and discrimination.[13] And as we described in chapter 3 on exclusion and chapter 10 on criminal justice, for youth living in public spaces, the daily activities of washing, eating, and sleeping can be illegal. As a result, unsheltered young adults and children are pushed toward more dangerous living environments, which makes them even more vulnerable to violence, sexual assault, and human trafficking.[14]

Foster Care and Schools

Tragically, "the back door of the foster care system is the front door of the homeless system," as the National Center for Housing and Child Welfare states.[15] A staggering 36% of young adults who age out of the foster care system report experiencing homelessness by the time they are 26 years old. For Black youth in foster care, this risk of homelessness is even higher, about 60%.[16] Certainly, no one deserves to experience homelessness, and we hope this book has already provided you with all sorts of helpful insights, stories, and deepened understanding of this issue. But the next time you hear someone talk about homelessness as "a choice" or in even more derogatory terms, consider asking if they believe that the more than one in three young people who age out of foster care into homelessness are somehow making a choice or are otherwise "failed" individuals.

Beyond homelessness, a slew of other challenges affect foster youth at far greater rates than their non-foster youth peers. Foster youth—youth who are in state-authorized temporary living situations away from their parents or legal guardians[17]—are at a much higher risk of developing disabilities that significantly impair their learning and psychological wellness than non-foster youth. Among 17-year-old foster youth, a heartbreaking 6 in 10 have had at least one lifetime psychiatric disorder, like major depression, anxiety, PTSD, or ADHD, while 3 in 10 have more than one such disorder.[18] In terms of educational attainment, 50% of the general population hold a postsecondary degree; for youth who age out of foster care, it's only 8%.[19]

Foster care and education are intimately intertwined systems—even if their agencies are historically siloed. School can provide an invaluable base of stability for foster and homeless youth, and education systems can be an excellent buffer against other failed systems.[20] And conversely, the more schools a youth cycles through, the more likely they are to experience homelessness. "Perhaps the single most important thing that each of us can do to improve the educational outcomes for foster children is to ensure that their school placement remains stable," as stated in "Improving Educational Services for Foster Children: An Advocate's Guide."[21]

Unfortunately, unstable school placements often accompany unstable living situations. For instance, special education services are critical to learning and development, but they are often delayed at each new school because of bureaucratic delays in transferring records between schools and districts. As a result, every new school may need to reevaluate a foster youth's condition, forcing the student to wait weeks or months before receiving the services they need.[22] And even if there are minimal bureaucratic hurdles, the student must still try to adjust to new teachers and pedagogies, new classmates, new friends, a new campus to navigate, and more. These changes can be socially isolating and very harmful to learning. As Rand describes it, "You just feel like so many things are not in your control. You need to wait until they can find a place that will 'accept you.' You need to be 'accepted by the system.'"

While reasons for each move vary, "more than a third of foster children and youth experience more than two placements each year, meaning their living arrangements change at least twice a year,"[23] while an average foster youth moves 6.5 times while in care.[24] Each school move results in a four- to six-month loss of academic achievement for foster care youth.[25]

Multiple studies have shown that the academic involvement of foster parents is central to a foster child's academic success, particularly since many youth in foster care will become unhoused after leaving the foster care system.[26] While there are many foster parents who do maintain active roles in their foster child's academic life, sadly a majority of foster youth report that their parent or guardian has never attended a parent-teacher conference.[27] This absence of parental or guardian support is devastating, especially if it is not partially offset by the stabilizing presence and social support of a trusted coach, teacher, mentor, relative, or family friend.[28] Years ago, Kevin heard an experienced leader in the foster youth space say something that has stuck with him ever since. To paraphrase: *The number one factor in predicting whether a child in foster care will succeed in the system and afterward in life is whether they have someone who goes to bed at night and wakes up in the morning thinking about their well-being, who isn't a paid government caseworker.* Relational poverty is poverty, whether for unhoused adults or at-risk youth.

Punishing At-Risk Youth

Cycles of homelessness often begin in youth. Studies of unhoused populations in various cities find that up to 50% of homeless adults first experienced homelessness as teenagers; for people experiencing chronic homelessness, this correlation is even stronger.

Unfortunately, schools tend to punish rather than embrace at-risk youth, pushing them further away from the very stability and support they desperately need, and increasing the likelihood that they will experience homelessness and/or will have a harder time exiting homelessness.

A child who exhibits behavioral issues in school could face suspension, expulsion, and even time in the juvenile justice system. These measures interrupt a student's academic progress and social integration, and they reflect a trend where schools without sufficient resources resort to a "one strike and you're out" response to deal with students they deem *problematic*. Research over the past few decades has shown that schools are increasingly suspending and expelling students for seemingly trivial conduct, such as "disrespect," "disobedience," and "disruption."[29]

The problem with such overuse of disciplinary actions is that it creates a dangerous precedent that leads to later involvement in the criminal justice system. A groundbreaking Texas study found that 23% of students who are disciplined in middle or high school eventually come in contact with a juvenile probation officer; out of those who were not disciplined, only 2% did.[30] One reason why this happens is that disciplined students feel alienated from their school and their peers. Once a student drops out, they are often left with no educational alternatives, making it more difficult for them to secure decent-paying jobs in the future, and more likely to become involved in the criminal justice system, which as we looked at in the previous chapter, often opens a revolving door involving homelessness. A 2016 report indicates that "high school dropouts are three and one-half times more likely than high school graduates to be arrested, and more than eight times as likely to be incarcerated. Across the country, 68 percent of state prison inmates have not received a high school diploma."[31] Roughly 50% of the general population hold a postsecondary degree (educational instruction beyond high school),[32] while only about half of those experiencing homelessness have a high school degree.[33]

Black youth, especially Black males, are some of the most disciplined students. Although Black students constitute 16% of the students in public schools, they make up 32% to 42% of the students who are suspended or expelled. White students, by comparison, constitute 51% of the student population and 31% to 40% of suspended or expelled students. The picture is even more grim when it comes to out-of-school suspensions (as opposed to in-school suspensions or detentions). Black students are suspended and temporarily barred from school at a rate three times greater than white students.[34] While Black children are criminalized for their behavior, white children with the same behavior are often given second chances or are provided with psychological or behavioral health resources. Black students are much more likely to be punished in schools than white students.[35] As a ratio of the overall student population, Black students are overrepresented in school disciplinary actions by a factor of three, a ratio similar to what Black people face in the criminal justice system and homelessness.

The lack of stability in school makes some children more likely to fall into the criminal justice system or homelessness (or both). When a child leaves the education system without a high school diploma, it becomes much harder for them to earn a postsecondary degree through college or university, an apprenticeship, or a trade school, as well as a living-wage job and stable housing. The situation is particularly bleak for former foster youth, who are much less likely to have family support to fall back on or at least a stable home where they can return and get back on their feet. Once a youth ages out of foster care, they are usually left without any safety net as they step into adulthood; it is little wonder that over one-third of them will experience homelessness. And according to interviews with unsheltered youths from 11 different cities, 44% said they had been incarcerated in jail, prison, or a juvenile detention center, and nearly 62% had been arrested at some point in their lives.[36]

Like Rand, many (but not all) young people who experience homelessness grow up in disruptive, unstable, and unsafe homes. They often have siblings to look after and very little physical or psychological space to focus on homework. Children who grow up in foster care are likely to switch schools multiple times, leading to loneliness and a constant fear of not fitting in. Being placed into new schools midyear disrupts the flow of curriculum, leaving many kids with gaps of information that impact their long-term ability to learn and succeed in schools. It's no wonder that kids growing up in unstable home environments, especially those in foster care or who experience youth homelessness, have an increased risk of homelessness in adulthood.

As the head of a homeless service agency in Colorado recently put it, "The number one contributing factor to chronic adult homelessness is youth homelessness."[37] In other words, if we can reduce the number of youth who experience homelessness, we will reduce the number of adults who experience homelessness.

KEY TAKEAWAYS

As a society, we greatly underestimate the number of people experiencing homelessness who are children and youth; in fact, under the HUD definition, about 25% of the homeless population is under 25 years old.

Childhood abuse, neglect, and other types of trauma greatly increase the risk of homelessness for youth and adults.

Unhoused LGBTQ+ youth and youth of color—who are at disproportionate risks of experiencing homelessness—have poorer psychological and physical health and are less likely to access important services due to the cycle of trauma, discrimination, distrust, and stigmatization they experience.

The foster care system is a point-blank gateway to homelessness, wherein roughly one-third of aged-out former foster kids will experience homelessness by the age of 26.

The foster care and education systems are intimately intertwined—the more schools a youth cycles through due to foster care displacement or disciplinary measures, the more likely they are to suffer academically, and later, to experience homelessness.

School disciplinary measures interrupt a student's academic progress and social integration, pushing at-risk youth into the juvenile or criminal justice system, and ultimately, a much greater risk of homelessness. Black students in particular are overrepresented in school disciplinary actions by a ratio similar to what Black people face in the criminal justice system and homelessness.

PART III

SOLUTIONS

12

Fixing Broken Systems

HOMELESSNESS IS A MICROCOSM OF what ails America. The issue is complex, multifaceted, highly nuanced, and interwoven with many other broken social systems, as the previous chapters have shown. There is no silver bullet for ending homelessness, any more than there is a quick fix or one-size-fits-all solution for poverty, mass incarceration, racism, income inequality, the mental health crisis, drug addiction, health care disparities, or childhood traumas.

As such, the challenge of ending homelessness can feel impossible at times, *too big to succeed*. Instead, we can be left banging our heads at the maddening disconnect between the reassurances we hear from officials in their latest five-year plans to solve homelessness and the jarring reality that we see every day: our neighbors living and dying on the streets; tens of millions of dollars spent (or much more[1]) with no end in sight, let alone tangible progress being made; and human suffering on a vast, nearly unimaginable, heartbreaking scale.

Not that we need any external validation of our collective frustration on this issue, but just in case: Leilani Farha, a Canadian lawyer and the former United Nations special rapporteur on adequate housing from 2014 to 2020, described the state of homelessness in San Francisco and Oakland in the same breath as the worst slums in the world.[2] "There's a cruelty here that I don't think I've seen," Farha said, referring to the anti-homeless laws that criminalize sitting on the side-walk or distributing food to unhoused residents. "Every single person, whether it was in passing or in a long conversation, said they just want to be treated like a human being," said Fahra. "What does that say? That is bleak."[3]

To be sure, homelessness can feel exhausting and overwhelming. We as coauthors feel this way at times, too. But in our experience, we have found one surefire way to not feel helpless, but to actually feel a sense of hope, to recognize that every system is made up of human beings, that the world is not static and things can change for the better, to believe that each of us can truly make a difference: by getting close to our neighbors who are actually experiencing homelessness.

Homelessness cannot be solved from a distance. Jeffrey, Ray, Ronnie, Linda, Elizabeth, Gabe and Lainie, Jennifer, Joseph, Tom, Timothy, Rand, and others featured in this book each have their own story. The closer we get to our unhoused neighbors living on the margins, the more likely we will be to "hear things that we won't otherwise hear" and "see things we won't otherwise see," which is "critical to our knowledge and our capacity to problem solve," as Bryan Stevenson, author of *Just Mercy*, counseled in a talk on the importance of "getting proximate."[4]

So as we look at how we might fix the many broken systems that intersect with homelessness, we return to the individual stories of our unhoused neighbors for guidance.

Housing for All

Less than six months after emergency surgery to remove a malignant tumor on her pancreas, Jennifer, whom we met in chapter 8, ended up at a homeless shelter in Washington, DC, with her young daughter. They stayed there for about two and a half years, a "horrifying" and "eye-opening" period of her life. "There were just too many issues there," Jennifer reflected. "There were rodents, bedbugs, cockroaches,

and other bugs all over the place, and the staff didn't seem to care."
Shocked by the poor conditions and apparent apathy from staff members, Jennifer's mantra became "Why can't we do this?" Jennifer began
organizing other residents to protest the conditions and fight for their
rights. The status quo didn't make sense to Jennifer: "I kept wondering,
the figures say that it costs $60,000 to $65,000 to house a family at
the shelter for a year, and yet I know that I could be in housing, and it
would cost my daughter and me about $12,000 a year to live where we
were evicted from. Where's my $12K?"

Finally, in 2016, Jennifer received a Housing Choice Voucher that
enabled her daughter and her to move into a small apartment in the
Capitol Hill neighborhood in DC. Jennifer has been stably housed ever
since, which has allowed her to pursue exciting new career opportunities: speaking publicly about her experiences within the medical system
and at a shelter, working as an after-school instructor and consultant,
and doing community organizing on behalf of working families. Nine
years after her surgery and cancer remission, she still feels a great deal
of physical discomfort, "but the only thing I will take for it is Tylenol
and Motrin. I don't want to become addicted to other kinds of stuff."
She hopes to someday relinquish her subsidized apartment and find her
own market-rate housing—as soon as she is able to afford it.

Jennifer's story reminds us that a lack of a home encompasses much
more than a mere lack of shelter. Home is a place to recuperate after an
emergency surgery, a place to heal from years of chronic pain, a place
to get a good night's rest before tomorrow's job interview, a place to
work hard for and feel dignified in, a safe, sanitary place for a single
mom to raise her beloved child.

Ending homelessness begins with making sure everyone has a home,
a place to be.

More affordable housing

Given the nationwide deficit of over 7 million affordable housing units
to meet current demand, it is imperative that we create more affordable
housing for people with low incomes.

We would like to explore three major reasons why we have such a dearth of affordable housing. First, the cost of construction is sky-rocketing, due to the cost of building materials, the cost of labor, and the expense of various zoning restrictions and local fees. It is nearly impossible at present to build low-income housing without support from all levels of government in the form of tax credits, reduced fees, and expedited project reviews. That support must be expanded, along with embracing sophisticated construction methods and alternative types of housing units like ADUs and tiny homes, so affordable housing can be built more quickly and less expensively. Second, only about 25% of eligible low-income families and individuals receive any type of housing subsidy.[5] This is outrageous, and must change. And third, we must do more to help low-income renters facing eviction stay in their apartments, as preventing homelessness is one of the most cost-effective tools we have in resolving our housing crisis.

The cost of construction

One approach to reducing construction costs is to utilize less expensive construction materials. In Austin, Texas, for example, the Community First! Village by the nonprofit Mobile Loaves & Fishes is the country's largest master-planned development designed specifically for men and women coming out of chronic homelessness, and it has become a national model. In the most expensive city in the state, each of its 3D-printed homes only costs about $4,000.[6] Almost 200 people have been provided homes, at a cost of approximately $720,000. To put that into perspective, the average cost to build a unit in a large permanent housing complex is about $300,000, a figure that is substantially higher in high-cost regions like San Francisco and Los Angeles.[7] If only 1,000 of these 3D-printed homes were built each year, 1,000 households could be housed for about $4 million, as opposed to $300 million using traditional building materials. If this were replicated in each city in the US with a population of at least 100,000 residents, over 300,000 new, very low-income houses would be created each year, at a potential cost savings of billions of dollars. This would be enough to significantly reduce the number of people experiencing homelessness within a few years—assuming local communities embraced them (more on how that might happen in the final chapter of this book, Healing Our Humanity).

Other efforts underway to reduce the cost of building affordable housing include retrofitting shipping containers into homes. Smaller, more basic container homes can range between $10,000 and $35,000 to build. Large homes built with multiple containers and amenities can range in price from $100,000 to $175,000 to build, still a significant savings compared to the cost of building typical wooden homes. In fact, many shipping container homes cost half as much per square foot (or less) than traditional buildings. Other advantages of shipping container homes include the chance to reuse materials (there is a large surplus of empty containers[8]), their durability, and the fact that their prefabrication size is widely standardized.

Tiny homes are yet another way to reduce construction costs. Tiny home villages are sprouting up across the country, and at an average cost of $21,160 per home, they are cheaper to construct than traditional apartment units.[9] Oakland's Tuff Shed camp, made up of 20 Tuff Sheds, housed 40 people at a time, and 76% of the residents moved into permanent housing over the course of a year.[10]

Beyond building materials, the other way to reduce construction costs is by streamlining the siloed, expensive, and unnecessarily bureaucratic purchasing and licensing process. Community land trusts can buy up land near public transportation hubs, such as light rail stations, and lease the land to prospective builders for pennies on the dollar over a long period of time, thereby substantially reducing the total cost of a large apartment building.[11] Local zoning code restrictions, parking space requirements, and the local fees for tapping into utilities can be reworked to ease the financial and time burden of new construction.[12] In its national survey of such efforts, the Urban Institute highlights three examples of regions making these much-needed changes: Minneapolis, Minnesota, for its efforts to eliminate single-family zoning; Fairfax, Virginia, for easing height and density restrictions near transit stations; and Seattle, Washington, for allowing smaller, denser family dwellings.[13] Finally, allowing accessory dwelling units (ADUs), or "in-law suites," to be built in the backyards and above garages of single-family homes is a relatively cheap way to increase the housing supply, which can provide safe, stable housing to formerly unhoused neighbors and families and those on the brink of homelessness.[14]

One might ask, so why aren't these types of tangible, cost-effective solutions being developed all over the country? Part of the reason is that some of the technology is new and still being tested. For instance, the first 3D-printed housing unit for someone experiencing homelessness was created in 2019,[15] and there is some evidence that the materials used in 3D printing may not be strong enough to sustain high-rise buildings.[16] In addition, 3D printing requires fewer construction workers, which could put many workers out of work without proper planning and skills training. A fundamental shift in the building materials used in construction across the country will take time, as well as retraining the workforce.

And finally, at some level, innovative approaches to building new types of housing for people experiencing homelessness are not widely embraced because people experiencing homelessness are not widely embraced. In other words, it is often politically easier to enact new anti-homeless ordinances and crackdowns than fight for more constructive approaches (literally) that may require some sacrifice from housed voters, such as building affordable housing units on their streets.

Housing subsidies and supply

In recent years, there has been a national rallying cry to create more Housing Choice Vouchers, the modern equivalent of what was once known as Section 8 vouchers. A strong proponent of this strategy is Matthew Desmond in his best-selling book *Evicted*. Jennifer, as one example, was able to secure long-term housing through a housing voucher.

But even today there are simply not enough affordable housing units available for everyone who currently has a voucher. Adding more housing vouchers will raise the demand side of the equation but will not affect the supply side, where we are facing a massive nationwide deficit. Although there is a clear need for more housing subsidies for people experiencing homelessness, and although housing vouchers are a primary vehicle for such assistance, simply providing a person experiencing homelessness with a housing voucher does not guarantee a housing unit, much less increase the supply of housing units, and it does nothing for the people who do not win the lotteries to get them. We need to both increase the number of vouchers *and* add many more units of low-income housing.

Two of the most common sources of low-income housing are public housing and housing built through low-income tax credits. In 2023 there are 1.82 million residents in public housing units nationwide,[17] many of whom reside in housing that is deteriorating or already dilapidated. The federal government spent $31.6 billion on public housing in 2020,[18] but funding for major repairs declined by about 35%, and "about 10,000 public housing apartments are lost each year due to deterioration."[19] With a nationwide shortage of over 7 million affordable housing units today, we cannot afford to lose units from our current supply of public housing due to repairs and updates not happening.[20] We must appropriate additional funds to maintain current units and resuscitate public housing. Public housing should not be neglected.

Because the shift from public housing to housing vouchers did not, in and of itself, produce new housing, the federal government responded by offering low-income tax credits to developers, to subsidize the cost of construction in exchange for tax breaks. Since its creation in 1986, the Low-Income Housing Tax Credit program has developed or preserved 37,727 properties and an estimated 2.3 million housing units.[21] These tax credits have been a boon to developers as they try to piece together funding for the construction of units.

The Low-Income Housing Tax Credit program is not perfect: a major flaw is that the credits are only good for a specific time period, usually either 20 or 30 years. At the end of that time, the credits disappear, and the building owners can convert the units into higher-end market-rate housing to realize a higher revenue return, thus making them unaffordable for those in poverty and homelessness. Still, if there is no extension of the tax credits, thousands of units will no longer be available every year to house the very poor and those experiencing homelessness. Human Rights Watch estimates that some 400,000 apartments that renters are able to afford today as a result of tax credit programs are at risk of losing their affordability by 2030, or approximately 20% of the total number of such units. We must extend these critical tax credits.

The supply of permanent supportive housing—or housing in which various wraparound services are offered to residents, such as health and behavioral health assistance and help with access to public benefits—must be expanded substantially as well. Housing First, the strategy that places priority on getting people experiencing homelessness into housing as the essential first step before addressing other needs, is the country's major programmatic emphasis for such housing. However, there are important cautions to consider. One is the potential for grouping and concentrating people experiencing homelessness in the same location, in effect "ghettoizing" places where "they" live. Building large congregate facilities that provide housing exclusively for people experiencing homelessness runs the risk of concentrating people without giving them access to networks of support and community that can be invaluable.

Most facilities should have mixed-income tenants, so that every resident has the chance to form friendships with and see models of living at various income levels. There is an important social capital argument here. If a person who was formerly experiencing homelessness lives next to a wealthier neighbor, the person who was formerly unhoused has a better chance of finding employment because wealthier friends tend to have access to stronger professional social networks, among myriad other benefits.[22] And the wealthier neighbor has the opportunity to put a real face, name, and story to a widely misunderstood issue in our society, thus helping to destigmatize homelessness. Relationships like these between people of different socioeconomic statuses foster *weak ties* with social capital benefits to both parties—this is the same rationale colleges and universities use in selecting a diverse pool of students for each class year.

Scattered site housing—or affordable housing that is built throughout an urban area, including in nonminority neighborhoods, rather than being concentrated in a single area—is one way to ensure mixed income housing.[23] As a 1996 HUD report titled "Scattered-Site Housing" cites, "Tenants in scattered site housing feel welcome in their new homes and prefer their new neighborhoods, where they expect their children to benefit from safer surroundings and better access to quality schools."[24] But developing individual units in various locations across an urban environment brings its own set of challenges. Delivering wraparound services to many people scattered all over a city can create transportation and logistical issues, even if mobile service vans can help alleviate some of these concerns. Also, as mentioned in the HUD report (and likely, a recent edition of your local newspaper!), scattered site housing frequently encounters strong initial community opposition, in part due to fears that such housing and the tenants who live there will bring lowered property values and higher crime rates.

Even if developers and service providers obtain community buy-in and dispel fears, however, the process can be agonizingly slow. Which brings us to a second caution of over-relying on permanent supportive housing. Unfortunately, experience suggests that, even with tax credit financing and the support of a land trust, it takes years for the construction of new low-income housing. Meanwhile, there are literally hundreds of thousands of people in need of temporary housing who are living and dying on the streets and in encampments totally unsuitable for human habitation. And while we have a vast array of congregate shelters, shelters are not for everyone and probably not ideal for anyone, as we indicated in chapter 6. Instead, we believe that we need many types of temporary and transitional housing, a need that goes far beyond typical homeless shelters.

Over the last few years, we have seen real advances in generating transitional housing. One innovative example is Goodness Village (www.gvlivermore.org) in Livermore, California, Kevin's hometown, an intentional housing community that was developed on acreage provided by a local church. Goodness Village includes 28 single-occupancy permanent tiny homes measuring 160 square feet (8 feet wide by 20 feet long, and 13.5 feet high). Each home includes a restroom, shower, kitchenette, HVAC (heating, ventilation, and air-conditioning), and a porch. In addition, 24-hour wraparound services and vocational skill building programs are offered. In Los Angeles, the Safe Parking LA project (www.safeparkingla.org) now has 10 safe parking lots with the total capacity to accommodate 209 cars per night, allowing persons experiencing homelessness to safely park and rest in their vehicle in a parking lot. Safe Parking LA is the largest such program in the city, but the need is still greater: in 2020, over 25% of LA County's homeless population of 66,436 people lived in their vehicles,[25] and across the US, "vehicle residency is one of the fastest-growing forms of homelessness," according to Sara Rankin, an associate professor of law and director of the Homeless Rights Advocacy Project at Seattle University School of Law. [26] And in multiple cities in California, DignityMoves (www.dignitymoves.org) builds interim housing communities using state-of-the-art prefabricated modular construction and partners with local services agencies to operate the sites and improve outcomes for their clients. The result is what they call "dignified interim supportive housing" that can be built fast and economically.

Identifying and developing new affordable housing units quickly, offering wraparound services from a variety of providers, rigorously tracking individualized client data through a by-name directory, and getting different agencies and organizations to collaborate effectively are not easy, but are critical. To address these issues, Community Solutions, a widely acclaimed nonprofit, is working with over 100 cities and counties nationwide as part of their Built for Zero movement to solve some of the most persistent challenges that stand in the way of ending homelessness: "prevent inflow into homelessness from happening in the first place; build and sustain homeless response systems that can continuously end, rather than manage, homelessness for populations across a geography; and quickly deliver affordable housing that can close the housing gap" (https://community.solutions). In a similar vein, Urban Vision Alliance (www.urbanvisionalliance.org) is working in San Francisco to create an effective homelessness management system by breaking down silos, lowering costs, and increasing transparency with large-scale collaboration. Organizations like these reflect the urgent need for broad public-private coalitions and frictionless coordination between cities, counties, and homeless service providers to make homelessness rare, brief, and non-recurring.

Finally, in their efforts to end homelessness, communities should resist the temptation to embrace one type of housing (e.g., permanent supportive housing) at the expense of everything else (e.g., transitional housing like tiny homes and motel rooms). We see this most notably in the widespread focus solely on the first pillar of Housing First ("permanent housing with no housing readiness requirements") while overlooking the other four core pillars in the strategy ("consumer choice and self-determination," "recovery orientation" through harm reduction or abstinence, "individualized and client-driven supports," and of particular note for this book, "social and community integration").[27] *Housing First* should not be interpreted as *Housing Only*.

We believe this narrow oversimplification of Housing First reflects a relatable desire among exasperated local residents, elected officials, and funders alike to find an elusive silver bullet for ending homelessness that, quite frankly, does not exist. Instead of searching for the perfect tool for tackling homelessness everywhere, we suggest looking at the role NIMBYism and anti-homeless sentiment often plays in driving this pressure to solve "the homeless problem" in as minimally intrusive way as possible, while hypocritically fighting against the development of low-income supportive housing in their local area.

In community after community, even well-meaning residents have banded together to fight the proposed placement of a housing project, a tiny home village, a sanctioned tent encampment, or a safe parking lot in their neighborhood. As Matthew Desmond writes in his latest book, *Poverty, by America,* "Democrats are more likely than Republicans to champion public housing in the abstract, but among homeowners, they are no more likely to welcome new housing developments in their own backyards." In fact, in one study that Desmond cites, liberal homeowners were less supportive of a hypothetical 120-unit apartment complex in their neighborhood than were conservative renters.[28] As Desmond surmises, "Perhaps we are not so polarized after all. Maybe above a certain income level, we are all segregationists."[29]

While we recognize that residents should have a say in what types of projects are built on their block, relatively narrow self-interests should not constantly trump the greater good. As coauthors, we are stead-fast in our commitment to the provision of permanent and transitional housing for those who need it, in neighborhoods and communities of all socioeconomic levels. The emergence of the YIMBY movement, Yes in My Back Yard, is positive,[30] and seems to grasp a basic truism around homelessness: once "they" are housed, they are no longer homeless.

Keeping people in their homes

Prevention is a critical, incredibly cost-effective, and obvious approach to addressing homelessness. As just one example of why preventing home-lessness to begin with is so critical: between the 2019 and 2022 Point-in-Time (PIT) counts, the Department of Homelessness and Supportive Housing (HSH) in San Francisco reported helping "more people than ever before in a three-year window exit homelessness through housing, prevention, or reunification with support systems. Over 8,000 house-holds exited homelessness from January 2019 to January 2022 [. . .] However, HSH's placements to housing have not been able to keep pace with inflow of people who become newly homeless or return to home-lessness throughout the year. HSH estimates that while 7,754 homeless individuals were observed on the night of the [2022] PIT Count, as many as 20,000 individuals may experience homelessness in San Francisco over the course of a full year. Analysis of these figures suggests that for every household San Francisco is able to permanently house through its Homelessness Response System, approximately four households become homeless."[31] Across the country, the large number of people who are moving into housing is offset by the much larger number of people who are falling into homelessness each year.

We must do more to prevent homelessness to begin with. In May 2009 President Obama signed the Homeless Emergency Assistance and

Rapid Transition to Housing (HEARTH) Act into law, which specifically targeted money for homeless prevention. But it is not easy to predict which high-risk households will end up losing their home. As researchers Marybeth Shinn and Jill Khadduri indicate, "in the 35 years since the nation started funding homelessness prevention, few programs have been rigorously evaluated."[32]

Although there are now some efforts to develop algorithms to improve our ability to ascertain exactly who will end up without housing,[33] the need for homelessness prevention is as great as ever, including in early childhood. Facing over a decade of neglect, Rand, whom we met in chapter 11, grew up in an environment rife with trauma and physical and emotional abuse. What he needed most was a sense of stability that could have been achieved through improved oversight of foster care, stronger wellness monitoring and support networks at school and at home, and bridge programs to help vulnerable youth as they age out of foster care. Homelessness prevention should come in many forms and should extend from birth through old age.

One example of a novel, win-win approach to helping nontraditional applicants get into stable housing is landlord recruiters, or individuals who are tasked with contacting landlords to persuade them to rent units to prospective tenants whose rental history has not been exemplary or who are coming off the streets with bad credit, who are involved in the criminal justice system, or who face other barriers to housing. One such landlord recruiter, Cathy Blair, spoke to the dual advocacy she engages in as part of her job: "I am actually working on the side of the landlord, both to make sure their units are rented and rented to people who will become good tenants. Once I have a prospective tenant, I use their positive qualities to persuade the landlord to rent to them. I advocate for the family during lease up to help landlords understand what is going on with the background check and minimize the feeling of risk. Once the lease is in place I am an advocate for the landlord to assist with on-time rental payments and mediation efforts when compliance issues arise."[34] Blair is under contract with the City of Aurora, Colorado, and has found apartments for more than 420 individuals and families over the past six years. We hope to see the use of landlord recruiters expand more broadly.

Once people are in their apartments, the next step is stability, or making sure that they are able to remain there. One of the biggest threats to such stability is the prospect of eviction. An eviction is not an unfortunate one-time event but a devastating cycle. An eviction notice stays on your rental record, leading to future rental discrimination by potential landlords. Since most job applications require an address, a lack of housing and its emotional and physical consequences make it incredibly challenging to get a stable, well-paying job. Without a decent job or other reliable source of income, there is limited hope for paying rent in the private market. With years-long lists for public or subsidized housing due to chronic underfunding, there is simply nowhere for an evicted individual with no social support to live. As previously mentioned, most formerly unhoused tenants appear in eviction proceedings without legal representation, and consequently lose over 90% of the time. However, if the tenant is able to secure adequate legal representation, they successfully defeat the eviction almost 90% of the time. Recall the story of Elizabeth from chapter 6, who had to defend herself in eviction court shortly after receiving her cancer diagnosis, only to lose her case and be evicted. Eviction defense funds must be established to help ensure that every tenant who is being threatened with eviction has at least minimal support. And everyone should have access to legal representation, regardless of their housing or socioeconomic status. As one pioneering example in San Francisco, Open Door Legal (www.opendoorlegal.org), cofounded by Adrian Tirtanadi and Virginia Taylor, is working to dramatically reduce poverty by pioneering the country's first system of universal access to legal representation.

Changing the tax code to increase housing equity

Under the current tax code, the wealthiest Americans can take advantage of the largest deductions. One of the most regressive examples in the tax code is also the most-used itemized deduction: the mortgage interest tax deduction. "Abolishing the mortgage-interest tax deduction, which subsidizes the home-buying of the already wealthy and well-capitalized, would allow the federal government to double the size of its housing-assistance programs for the poor," as an article in the *Economist* concluded.[35] Despite widespread condemnation by economists,[36] the mortgage interest deduction perseveres, in large part due to the massive lobbying efforts of groups like the National Association of Realtors, which outspends the pharmaceutical industry and the National Rifle Association in terms of lobbying dollars.[37]

Another method for increasing equity through the tax code is the creation of tax credits for low-income renters. This is different from Housing Choice Vouchers, which provide housing subsidies rather than tax credits. A version of the Earned Income Tax Credit for low-income renters could provide substantial assistance to the people who have the greatest housing precarity today, preventing evictions and entry into homelessness for many.

Also, the Child Tax Credit is currently tied to a family's earnings and income tax liability, which denies the lowest income households from the full credit and withholds invaluable help from some of the children who need it the most, "hurting their long-term health, educational, and economic outcomes while doing virtually nothing to boost parental employment."[38] We agree with the Center on Budget and Policy Priorities that "policymakers should prioritize expanding the Child Tax Credit for children who receive a partial credit or none at all because their families' incomes are too low." Furthermore, the pandemic-era expansion of this tax credit under the Biden American Recovery Plan, which raised the Child Tax Credit from $2,000 to $3,000 per child for children over the age of 6 and from $2,000 to $3,600 for children under the age of 6, and raised the age limit from 16 to 17, should have been extended indefinitely (it expired at the end of 2021).[39] For those who worried that the money provided through this tax credit would have been used unwisely, the Center on Budget and Policy Priorities found that 91% of families with low-income (less than $35,000) used their monthly Child Tax Credit payments to cover the cost of basic necessities, including housing, food, utilities, and clothing.[40]

Right to shelter and right to housing

There are legislative actions that can be taken as well. In New York City, everyone has a right to shelter, meaning that any individual experiencing homelessness who seeks shelter on any given night must be provided for through the city-run homeless shelter system.[41] In Massachusetts, families have a similar right to shelter; individuals do not. Although such enforceable guarantees are imperfect tools in the fight to end homelessness, they can save countless lives and provide a modicum of support and resources for people who might otherwise have none. Robert Hayes, the lawyer who successfully fought for the right-to-shelter order in New York City in 1979 through the New York State Supreme Court decision issued in *Callahan v. Carey*, recently laid out the conundrum and significant costs of providing the right to shelter, while reaffirming his belief in it: "The perennial debate is—does the right to shelter actually help subvert what people really need? Does it kick the housing can down the road? Does it hide a problem? Yeah, it does. But what's the cost of not doing that?"[42]

Another possible legislative step is establishing the right to housing. The United Nations, in article 25 of the 1948 Universal Declaration of Human Rights, states, "Everyone has the right to a standard of living adequate for the health and well-being of himself and of his family, including food, clothing, housing and medical care and necessary social services."[43] In the United States, President Franklin Delano Roosevelt used part of his 1944 State of the Union address to propose a Second Bill of Rights, or Bill of Economic Rights, in which he specifically called for "the right of every family to a decent home."[44]

Today, Rhode Island, Illinois, Connecticut, and Puerto Rico have Homeless Bills of Rights that include a provision about the right to housing, as do France, Scotland, and South Africa. The California legislature tried to develop something similar in 2021, but it died in committee.[45] During the COVID-19 pandemic, the Open Society Foundations created model legislation with sample legal provisions that could be used to protect the right to housing, with sections on evictions, rental and mortgage payments, housing and housing services, and homelessness.[46] Although this model legislation was intended for use during the pandemic, it could catalyze other legislative efforts to enshrine the right to housing for all.

Martin v. Boise, the landmark decision of the Ninth Circuit Court of Appeals in 2019, forbade the enforcement of police sweeps in communities where there were insufficient shelter opportunities for persons living on the streets and in unsanctioned encampments. This decision had a profound effect on those states and cities in the West and Northwest within the purview of the court. As the National Homelessness Law Center described its impact after the US Supreme Court upheld the ruling by denying a petition by the City of Boise to review the case, "people experiencing unsheltered homelessness—at least in the 9th Circuit—can sleep more safely without facing criminal punishment for simply trying to survive on the streets."[47] But there is no national legal decision upholding the *Martin* standard, nor are there decisions of the same ilk in other court districts. We hope to see this change.

Although we would argue against the enactment of local ordinances that criminalize homelessness, where they are allowed to stand, police enforcement must change. Law enforcement teams should be equipped with the training, support, staffing, and partners to adequately approach and handle situations involving people with long histories of trauma, neglect, severe mental illness, and/or homelessness. For example, in Eugene, Oregon, a program called CAHOOTS (Crisis Assistance Helping Out on the Streets), a crisis mobile-assistance team working in collaboration with the police, was developed in 1989, and it has been the model for similar efforts in Denver, Oakland, Olympia (Washington), Portland (Maine), and others.[48]

Housing Choice Vouchers, which allow low-income individuals to live in standard apartment complexes by spending only 30% of their income on rent, have great theoretical potential. But in practice, according to a 2018 study prepared for HUD by the Urban Institute, between two-thirds and three-quarters of landlords in several major US cities reject voucher applicants.[49] In an effort to make it easier for people experiencing homelessness to rent housing units, some states have enacted local ordinances to "ban the box" (also called Fair Chance or

Clean Slate ordinances), making it illegal to ask whether a prospective tenant has a housing voucher. Yet only a handful of states have some type of legislation that protects potential renters in this way, and no federal law bars landlords from discriminating based on whether an applicant is using a housing voucher.[50] Each state should pass "ban the box" source-of-income laws, treating voucher and non-voucher applicants equally, and preventing discrimination based on rental payment source.

Thinking outside the box

It is also imperative for the private sector to get more involved in investing in low-income housing. One compelling example is the Denver Social Impact Bond project.[51] In the initial pilot, investors provided upfront risk capital to housing developers to build new affordable housing and to nonprofits to provide appropriate wraparound services for chronically homeless residents. The government guaranteed to repay the initial investment with interest if the housing project reduced jail bed days and increased the length of time in housing, thus saving taxpayer funds by lowering health care and incarceration expenditures. The private investment was a kind of low-interest, high-risk loan, with specific targets created for repayment. This pilot was so successful that the city provided additional funds to expand social impact bonds to reach more tenants.[52]

One factor that enabled the Denver Social Impact Bond project to come together was that the nonprofits, investors, and other organizations were established and trusted enough for the city government to be willing to work with them, without fearing they would go out of business or not honor their commitments. Even so, this multistakeholder, performance-based contract took considerable time to establish. We believe Social Impact Bonds are a model of the type of public-private partnership that should be considered by other communities in the future.

We also need to prioritize community development. A home is not just a house; four walls and a roof may be enough for a physical structure, but they do not make a home. Homelessness is a housing crisis, but it is not just a housing crisis: community reintegration is essential as well, which is all too often an afterthought of new housing projects. Beyond affordable housing, safe and supportive neighborhoods are needed for all people to thrive. One such example is the Community First! Village, mentioned earlier in this chapter, which provides affordable housing and abundant community for its formerly unhoused residents. There are a bus stop, laundry facilities, car maintenance, walking trails, an organic farm, a family health resource center, and a woodworking shop. The Community First! Village is a vibrant hub where people *want* to visit and live, not an "out of sight, out of mind" forgotten place—you can even book a tiny home, yurt, or Airstream for a minimum of two nights as a guest for $75 on up (https://communityinn.mlf.org). Another example is Angelica Village in Lakewood, Colorado (www.angelicavillage.org), an intentional community that houses several refugees, immigrants, and individuals and families who have experienced homelessness in residential facilities in close proximity to each other and "fellow community partners who bring their social capital and support." Their inspiring mantra is "give what you can, receive what you need."

Finally, to ensure that everyone truly has access to safe, stable, and affordable housing, we must look for ways to remove the legacy and lingering effects of racism in the housing sector. While adequately understanding and addressing racism and other forms of discrimination in the housing sector (and criminal justice system, and foster care system, and many other service systems) are beyond the scope of this book and have been expertly researched elsewhere,[53] a few promising interventions bear mentioning.

We believe in the importance of inclusionary zoning at the local level. Requiring that new housing construction include a percentage of low-income housing would advantage many groups who have experienced discrimination.

Another approach to righting the wrongs of centuries of discrimination is affirmative action. Allowing people of color to be given special consideration has been a major social policy debate in this country for decades, especially in college admissions. As suggested by Professor Ira Katznelson, affirmative action should be one consideration among many in making decisions about which individuals and families experiencing homelessness should be given priority in awarding housing vouchers.[54] Another similar strategy would be to provide preferential treatment to voucher holders who find available housing in more non-poor neighborhoods, especially if those neighborhoods have real residential diversity.[55]

One of the policy suggestions that arouses considerable controversy is reparations, or what *The Color of Law* author Richard Rothstein calls remedies.[56] We believe that some highly targeted partial compensation to low-income African Americans and Native Americans would greatly reduce their disproportionate representation among the population experiencing homelessness. One such strategy would be to reduce monthly rent charges for African American and Native American renters who are trying to utilize housing vouchers, such as reducing the 30% income contribution requirement to 15% or 20%, with the government picking up the rest.

Housing is essential for ending homelessness. In addition to providing a safe and secure environment for people, housing is health care, as we can see in Elizabeth's story. Housing is also racial justice, a great equalizer that enables people of all backgrounds to reach their potential. Housing is key to economic prosperity and professional advancement. And housing is key to moving from relational poverty to relational wealth, encouraging community formation, and ensuring the safety, stability, and success of families and individuals. To end homelessness, we must do a better job of providing safe, secure, and affordable housing throughout the US. No one deserves to be without a decent home.

Making Work Work

Gabe and Lainie, whom we met in chapter 7, were never able to work their way out of homelessness, despite moving to more affordable locales: from a McDonald's parking lot in San Jose, California, to a stint in San Diego, to a rural patch of Oregon, where they currently reside. For most of the past decade, this hard-working mother and son have lived in their vehicle. Both have developed serious health issues as a result: severe foot pain, repeat visits to the emergency room, and 20-something-year-old Gabe now needing a hip replacement. As Lainie recalled, "We spent most of the time in the car. Gabriel and I would cuddle up in the front seat to stay warm. In the summertime, we were sitting there, sweating like dogs. Sometimes, we'd sit there and just scream." In addition to suffering through physical health issues, Lainie and Gabe occasionally had to flee from domestic violence. Lainie, desperate for another source of income and missing romantic companionship, would find a boyfriend, who sometimes would stay with them in their vehicle. These relationships often turned violent, forcing Lainie and Gabe to flee to a new city.

Gabe and Lainie were able to build a handful of modestly helpful relationships along the way, including with an acquaintance in Oregon they met at a 7-Eleven who invited them to move in with her in exchange for cleaning the house and helping with groceries. For much of 2022, Gabe and Lainie doubled up with their new acquaintance, contributing by taking her to and from work, shuttling her kids to school and playdates and back, paying for groceries for her family, and cleaning the house on a daily basis. They were just beginning to mend from their decade-long ordeal of living in their vehicle. Unfortunately, tensions rose in the cramped living quarters shortly after they adopted a puppy, and the acquaintance said they "were being bullies to her kids for making them clean their mess after we just cleaned," according to Gabe. Two weeks before Thanksgiving, Gabe and Lainie and little Athena were kicked out of the house. For the rest of the year and through the holidays, they were back to living in their car.

Gabe is a student and also works full-time, with the hope of one day becoming a chef. Lainie continues to work full-time too, and they dream of one day opening a food truck together. The month before they got kicked out of their acquaintance's house, they had a kickoff fundraiser for the food truck at a local park, in which they made burgers, sliders, ribs, chicken, salad, and mac salad to raise funds and feed some of the unhoused community. But it did not go well. Gabe texted Kevin the day after the event: "well it was a bust like always I guess once a failure always one." A few days later, after regaining some perspective, Gabe and Lainie resolved to do once again what they always have done: simply work harder.

Fortunately, a few weeks after getting kicked out of their shared apartment, Gabe and Lainie received a promising call from the local St. Vincent de Paul informing them that they qualified for a below-market unit. After submitting their rental application (including a letter of recommendation from Kevin, which Gabe requested since he needed two from people "who aren't related"), they spent the next few months waiting and going back and forth with St. Vincent de Paul; according to Gabe, "We were approved and signed the paperwork as possible tenants, and we kept having to go back in to file our corrections and then wait a week and do the same thing for about a month and a half until we finally got it right, and then we got the call saying we were approved and could sign our lease but we had to wait another week because they didn't have the staff to come out because they are based [an hour away in Oregon]."

Finally, on February 12, 2023, Gabe, Lainie, and Athena the pup moved out of their vehicle and into a three-bedroom, two-bathroom unit for $663 a month plus $40 a month in utilities, with the rest subsidized by St. Vincent de Paul. After months of delays, Gabe said, "We told them please just let us in and if not let us know. We told them that they were killing us not letting us in. I think that's what got them to accept us." Now stably housed, Gabe gushed about the local social support they have received: "[We] got our place fully furnished for free through the help of our church and community." In his most recent update to Kevin, Gabe said that they are "doing good, my mom has a job interview tomorrow."

Gabe and Lainie's story reminds us that, for many people experiencing homelessness, hard work alone does not pay off, at least in terms of getting and staying stably housed. Despite working extra shifts, starting side hustles, and working multiple jobs for over a decade, Gabe and Lainie were not able to work their way out of homelessness—additional support in the form of social capital and a local housing program were critical for them to get housed. Insufficient wages, amid a backdrop of high costs of living, kept Gabe and Lainie in a state of perpetual hard work, neglected health, and with little choice but to remain living and sleeping in their vehicle.

Roughly 45% of adults experiencing homelessness are receiving income from employment.[57] In order to empower people like Gabe and Lainie to have any real chance of getting off the streets through work alone, our country must increase the minimum wage and benefits available for extremely low-income people. We must also reduce the numerous barriers that people experiencing homelessness face to higher-paying work opportunities, or even being able to work at all.

In every single county in the United States, the minimum wage is inadequate for renting even an average one-bedroom housing unit. Gabe and Lainie's story exemplifies this. Although some states and local communities have increased the minimum wage for their workers, many have not, and $7.25 an hour is a paltry sum in the face of ever-increasing costs. To help end homelessness and lift millions of individuals and families out of extreme housing instability, it is imperative that the federal government increase the minimum wage to at least $15 an hour, or approximately what the federal minimum wage of $1.60 per hour in November 1968 would be in 2023 dollars.

In addition to low wages, there are several other significant barriers to employment and public benefit programs that individuals experiencing homelessness face. One is the lack of adequate identification. Keeping track of important documents such as ID cards and drivers' licenses can be difficult for someone whose only safe storage is a large plastic bag that they carry around in an overflowing shopping cart. Another major barrier is the lack of a fixed mailing address. Some agencies provide services to overcome these types of barriers, but not all do. For example, the St. Francis Center in Denver helps their unhoused guests secure IDs, use its address as their mailing address, and safely store their bags of personal belongings on-site. These types of reasonable accommodations from homeless service providers are invaluable; similar arrangements should be offered discreetly and where feasible by employers as well, such as safe storage places on company grounds and problem solving with new hires who lack a permanent mailing address.

Another barrier that unhoused workers face is navigating their working hours. Individuals who are living in shelters tend to be under very strict curfew hours, which are sometimes at odds with their employment hours. Employers and shelter managers must develop greater flexibility to help unhoused workers overcome this barrier. For example, shelter managers should allow employed residents to arrive after doors are officially closed, to specifically reserve quiet places for these latecomers to sleep, and to allow these residents to sleep in later in the mornings, aligned with their work schedules. Similarly, employers should adopt flexible work schedules to enable employees who may be living in shelters to transition between nighttime shifts to daytime shifts as needed. Again, discretion is critical here: unhoused employees should not feel pressured to "out" themselves in order to access these provisions, risking stigma and shame. As one Reddit user in the r/homeless group described it, "Many shelters kick you out for missing their curfew which is often as early as 7pm. Good luck managing that if you have a job. 'I can't work late because my homeless shelter will kick me out.' Aaaand now your coworkers know you're homeless."[58] Where possible, flexible working hours should be offered to all employees who can reasonably do their jobs outside a set schedule, without the need for explanation.

Low-barrier work opportunities for people experiencing and exiting homelessness are also popping up in cities around the country. For example, the Denver Day Works (https://bayaudenterprises.org/day -works/) in Colorado is a jobs program that hires unemployed, unhoused workers to do landscaping and clean up trash in public spaces. Each worker is paid the minimum wage on the day of work, given breakfast and lunch, and offered help with finding other jobs and accessing benefits. Another example is Downtown Streets Team (www. streetsteam.org), whose mission is "ending homelessness through the dignity of work and the power of community," which contracts with cities and counties in Northern California to offer community beautification and cleanup projects led by their members experiencing homelessness and at-risk of homelessness. One especially laudable facet of

Downtown Streets Team is their Weekly Success meetings, which celebrate their members' wins from the past week and provide resources and access to case management, system navigation, basic needs assistance, and employment placement services from trained case managers and employment specialists. And in Detroit, Empowerment Plan (www .empowermentplan.org) is a holistic workforce development organization that provides full-time employment and services for individuals recovering from homelessness; it produces innovative sleeping bag coats, which are distributed to unsheltered folks individually around the world. As they proudly proclaim, "We don't hire people to make coats, we make coats to hire people." Denver Day Works, Downtown Streets Team, and Empowerment Plan are a few innovative examples of the type of low-barrier workforce development programs that serve a critical need for people experiencing homelessness. We hope to see programs like these replicated nationwide.

Benefit systems

A fundamental problem for people experiencing homelessness is the lack of financial resources. Even if a person experiencing homelessness is able to work full-time, the pay is almost universally insufficient to afford decent housing and break the cycle of homelessness. Supplemental assistance programs are essential, but today most government-backed benefit programs are inadequately funded, poorly structured, and often inaccessible.

Most of the federal benefit systems, including Temporary Assistance for Needy Families (TANF), Supplemental Nutrition Assistance Program (SNAP), Women Infants and Children (WIC), and Medicaid are all based on eligibility determined by the Federal Poverty Level, or the "poverty line." However, since its inception, the level has been set based on the cost of a month's worth of groceries, given a minimum nutritional diet,[59] with the expectation that these groceries will constitute one-third of the family's expenses for the month. Although the Federal Poverty Level has increased over time because of the rising cost of groceries, there is no recalibration based on the rising cost of other essentials, such as housing, medical care, childcare, and the like. Recent data demonstrate how inaccurate the Federal Poverty Level is as a true reflection of monthly expenses. Based on a US Bureau of Labor Statistics 2022 report, considering all types of consumers, food constituted 12.4% of all the year's expenses in 2021; both housing (33.8%) and transportation (16.4%) far exceeded food expenses, and personal insurance and pensions (11.8%) came close to equaling the money spent on food.[60]

In other words, the actual dollars spent on food in 2021 were just about one-third of what the Federal Poverty Level uses as its base calculator. Changing the formulation of the Federal Poverty Level to reflect actual expenses, akin to how most states use a self-sufficiency index today,[61] would increase program eligibility and bring much-needed benefits to an even larger number of extremely low-income people in need.

The Federal Poverty Level needs a major reworking. We must also allocate much more funding for each of the major benefit programs, and just as importantly, fix the profound flaws in multiple benefit programs that prevent millions of eligible individuals and families from being able to receive help. As we indicated in chapter 7 as one example, having only one out of nearly every five TANF-eligible recipients actually receive cash assistance from this essential anti-poverty program is totally unacceptable; the Clinton-era "welfare to work" reform provisions have failed, and TANF as a program should be completely overhauled. It is imperative that federal benefit programs actually reach and benefit all those who are in need of the relatively modest but potentially lifesaving support these programs can offer. And low-income families and individuals should not have to worry about drastic cuts to their benefits or even losing eligibility due to marginal increases in their finances, whether through wages or from participating in a basic income program.[62] Waivers should be easily accessible and liberally granted by local, state, and federal agencies to avoid harmful "cliff effects" as benefit income thresholds are reworked.

Basic income

We turn now to one of the most promising poverty alleviation tools available: offering a basic income to people who need it most. A common concern around basic income programs for individuals experiencing homelessness is the misguided belief that, without proper safeguards or oversight, unconditional cash will be overwhelmingly used to purchase drugs, alcohol, or other illicit substances. This could not be further from the truth. In the New Leaf Project, which we cited earlier in this book, 50 people experiencing homelessness were provided a one-time lump sum of $7,500. The results speak for themselves: 52% spent money on food and rent, 15% on medications and bills, and 16% on clothing and transportation, while spending on alcohol, cigarettes, and drugs decreased by 39%.[63] Seventy percent of participants were able to become food secure.

Similarly positive results happened in the inaugural Miracle Money pilot, which combined a $500 a month basic income for six months alongside regular calls and texts from a volunteer phone buddy. For Ray, the monthly payment of $500 meant the difference between the fear of living on the streets with congestive heart failure and a return to stable health in the shared housing unit he was able to afford with a housemate. Ray was also able to return to the workforce full-time and reconnect with his teenage daughter. Today, Ray finds joy in his new career as a hospital director and recently celebrated his two-year anniversary of housing. "It's been a blessing. My health has improved, surrounded by wonderful people that I love," reports Ray.

For Elizabeth, the $500 monthly payment meant the difference between the ongoing terror of living in a shelter as a single woman and the psychological safety of having her own home in which to rest and store her belongings. With her basic income, Elizabeth was able to qualify for senior housing and make her minimum monthly contribution, reenter the workforce as a community educator through a county vocational program, more fully recover from her cancer treatment, and volunteer as a lived experience advocate for the US Census Bureau. Today Elizabeth lives in a refashioned hotel room, with her own kitchenette, a bed, a table for eating, and a place to cook her meals. Her health has significantly improved, noting that her "appointments are now starting to taper off," relieving her administrative burden and giving her the opportunity to "work on getting back to working." Now settled, Elizabeth has the mental space to think about her goals for the future. Five hundred dollars a month for just six months opened doors for Elizabeth that were, for a painful period of time, unimaginable.

With secure housing, Ray, Elizabeth, and the other formerly unhoused Miracle Money recipients have been able to focus on themselves, their careers, their dreams, and their plans. Their stories exemplify the transformation and long-lasting success that basic income programs can have on the lives of people experiencing homelessness, with a relatively minuscule amount of money spent. Basic income programs should be embraced nationwide for the majority of people experiencing homelessness. The next phase of the New Leaf Project is underway. The Denver Basic Income Project recently launched, which will distribute a whopping $12,000 over the course of a year to 820 individuals and families experiencing homelessness, and is backed by a $2 million contribution from the Denver City Council.[64] And many inspiring pilots are in the pipeline or already making waves around the country. Even Miracle Messages' modest basic income and phone buddy program is expanding. Miracle Money: California will distribute more than $1 million directly to 100 individuals experiencing homelessness in Los Angeles County, San Francisco, and Oakland, as one of the largest 100% privately funded basic income pilots for people experiencing homelessness in the US.[65] In addition to receiving $750 a month for 12 months, unhoused recipients will receive regular one-to-one phone calls and text exchanges with caring volunteers around the world through the Miracle Friends phone buddy program, as part of a randomized control trial in partnership with the University of Southern California. We are excited for the impact these pilots will make and hope they will influence future policymaking.

Health Care, Not Incarceration

Medical emergencies can lead to job loss, eviction, and homelessness, as we witnessed through the stories of Elizabeth and Jennifer. And homelessness itself leads to dire health outcomes. Ray reflected on how precarious his health situation was while experiencing homelessness with chronic obstructive pulmonary disease (COPD): "Without continuing the medical support and continuing my medication, at some point or another, my sickness was going to come back to me, and especially with the sort of lifestyle where you're just out on the streets, it takes a toll on your body, and it certainly did for me."

To end homelessness, high-quality, affordable, and widely accessible health care for people experiencing homelessness is essential. Over the last 40 years, one of the most significant advances in providing health care for people experiencing homelessness has been the advent of numerous Health Care for the Homeless programs around the country. These programs meet people where they are at, offering those "too sick for the streets" but "not sick enough for the hospital" a secure place to rest, recuperate, and recover. The nation's first such medical respite program was founded by Dr. James O'Connell in Boston in 1985. Since then, Health Care for the Homeless programs have become the successful backbone of the country's effort to address the diverse health needs of our unhoused neighbors. With the rise in the number of unsheltered people and the aging and ailing of the population of people experiencing homelessness in the US, the demand for Health Care for the Homeless–type programs is greater than ever. These lifesaving programs should be significantly expanded through continued federal and state funding.

We also advocate for funding accessible low-income primary care clinics, which include many coordinated services under one roof (dental, general care, gynecology, pediatrics) that promote comprehensive care for people living in shelters and without reliable transportation.

One of the more successful approaches to supporting the health care needs of people experiencing homelessness has been the utilization of outreach teams that combine medical care with social services and can respond to crisis situations as an alternative or complement to law enforcement. As one example, the Street Crisis Response Team in San Francisco sends a paramedic, behavioral health clinician, and formerly unhoused peer specialist to address behavioral health emergencies, with an aim of reducing emergency room visits and criminalization in favor of referring people to long-term treatment centers.[66] Similar programs pair law enforcement officials with social workers or mental health professionals to respond to cases of extreme mental health decompensation on the streets. Consider Ronnie and Jeffrey—two men who struggled with addiction who both eventually died on the streets as a result of their substance abuse. Outreach programs won't instantly "solve" mental and behavioral health crises or "cure" addiction, but they will ensure that people like Ronnie and Jeffrey are compassionately treated as fellow human beings, and are reached and cared for without any barriers to service.

Mental health

It is also imperative that we find a happy medium between the unforgiving state mental institutions of the past and today's unacceptable status quo where people with untreated severe mental illnesses are left to live and die in broken-down tents and tarps on city streets, endangering themselves and others.[67] Partnering law enforcement with social workers and mental health workers seems like a reasonable step in the right direction, as does developing independent community-based outreach programs. But outreach must also be coupled with more hospital beds, recovery and treatment program spots, and compassionate albeit controversial interventions like involuntary temporary psychiatric holds and even involuntary treatment for individuals experiencing severe mental health crises who pose a serious threat to themselves or others, and who are unable to care for themselves to a degree that risks serious self-harm.[68]

Recently several high profile Democratic elected officials in New York City, Portland (Oregon), California, and elsewhere have cited the need to use mental health laws to facilitate involuntary treatment for people experiencing homelessness in these limited circumstances.[69] Involuntary treatment options could include "therapy, social workers, housing referrals, medication or other interventions, either in hospitals or on an outpatient basis," writes Katherine Drabiak, a health law and medical ethics professor at the University of South Florida. "Though involuntary treatment violates autonomy, it can also help people regain it through stabilization and recovery."[70] Furthermore, since involuntary treatment can be easily misused, it is critical that health care professionals determine that the individual is in desperate need of hospitalization before they are committed. Katherine Koh, a psychiatrist at Boston Health Care for the Homeless and Massachusetts General Hospital, said that "for some patients, you need to intervene in order to protect them and maximize the chance that they're going to survive and to minimize harm," but that "the key is not just getting people off the streets but keeping them off the streets and in care"—meaning that any involuntary treatment must be coupled with greatly expanding the availability of psychiatric hospital beds, increased funding for outreach teams and mobile crisis care, and a coordinated plan that goes beyond the initial commitment, including housing.[71] We agree with these nuanced sentiments.

Behavioral health

For individuals experiencing homelessness with substance use disorders, treatment programs have proven to be effective by emphasizing the importance of concurrently meeting various needs like "assistance with accessing food, clothing, shelter/housing, identification papers, financial assistance and entitlements, legal aid, medical and dental care, psychiatric care, counseling, job training, and employment services."[72] Creating more affordable and accessible public facilities to care for those with substance use disorders (and serious mental health issues) must be a priority. Expensive, $10,000-a-month on up private treatment facilities serve a certain segment of the (housed) population, but recovery should not be a money-making enterprise, available only to the well-off and well-insured. Tom, whom we met in chapter 9, memorably shared his thoughts regarding the need for more substance use intervention programs: "We need to meet people where they're at, but we can't leave them there."

For both Tom and Ronnie, getting clean happened in prison, a sad commentary on the dearth of substance-use treatment options available in the US. Tom now celebrates over five years of sobriety and is a vocal advocate for recovery, homelessness, addiction, and drug policy. For years after his release from prison, Ronnie was able to maintain his sobriety, running and training often, and working out of a small studio space on Haight Street where he made his incredible art and interacted with many friends and admirers. Tragically, in 2014, his son was murdered, and within a few years, Ronnie fell on tough times. He lost touch with friends, withdrew, and relapsed on his substance use. The last year of his life was spent in a makeshift tent encampment on the corner of 16th Street and Capp in the Mission District, still making amazing art, and getting ready for the first major exhibit of his artwork, at the MOMA PS1 gallery in New York City. He died on the streets one month before the scheduled opening.

Tom and Ronnie's stories, divergent in their outcomes, demonstrate the complicated role of prison as the de facto substance use treatment program in the US. Recovery cannot happen alone, especially when life feels like a series of one step forward, two steps back. Getting clean is one thing; long-term healing from deep trauma and substance dependency is another. Yet zero tolerance is the only option for many people behind bars struggling with substance use. We strongly encourage the development of therapy and detox care for people while they are incarcerated, as it is important to help people struggling with addiction get clean and address underlying traumas and other psychological issues that may have contributed to their addiction in the first place, and which do not magically disappear otherwise. The path to sustained healing and recovery requires it.

At the same time, we must also figure out ways to break the cycle of incarceration and zero tolerance to homelessness and drug abuse. As Tom stated: "I go to jail, I get out of jail, they release me back into homelessness. I'm in withdrawal from heroin at that point, and so I do the only thing I know how to do at that point—I go back to the same block where all the drug dealers were." One of the newer approaches to this problem is the use of diversion interventions, including mental health courts that help increase the quality of life of those involved, lead to decreased recidivism, and lower taxpayer costs.[73] Another perspective is suggested by Iain De Jong in *The Book on Ending Homelessness*: "If we are serious about ending homelessness [. . .] we would be well-served to teach people how to be housed and use substances—like the 17 million or so other citizens on a nightly basis that do so."[74] In other words, substance abuse and mental illness are not confined to those experiencing homelessness, but afflict millions of stably housed people in the US. Given the vicious cycle between homelessness, increased drug abuse, untreated mental illness, and incarceration, we must ensure that everyone has access to a baseline of safe and stable housing, regardless of any other challenges they may be facing—or rather, as an essential prerequisite for seriously facing them.

Whole Person Care, a five-year pilot program implemented in Placer County, California, identifies vulnerable individuals based on records of emergency room visits, use of social and behavioral services, substance use programs, and probational courts. Data is used to coordinate physical health and social services for patients—from medical care to housing resources—all under one system. Former patients who have completed the program are hired to improve Whole Person Care, integrating lived experience into the narrative of care. This is a promising new approach to coordinated and accessible health care for people experiencing homelessness.[75]

As a society, we must meet the substance use and mental health crises with treatment, not punishment. It is simply unconscionable that 65% of the prison population has an active substance use disorder.[76] For inspiration, we look toward how our society has handled drunk driving over the past 40 years, an activity with a much higher likelihood of injury than the personal use of drugs, as Michelle Alexander highlights in *The New Jim Crow*. Programs like Mothers Against Drunk Driving, memorable national advertising campaigns ("friends don't let friends drive drunk," "buzzed driving is drunk driving," "drive sober or get pulled over"), popular social support programs like Alcoholics Anonymous and Al-Anon, and a wide variety of recovery programs across the country have led to great progress on this issue. "Since 1982, drunk driving fatalities on our nation's roadways have decreased 45%, while total traffic fatalities have declined 12%. Among persons under 21, drunk driving fatalities have decreased 83%," according to the Foundation for Advancing Alcohol Responsibility, a distillers-funded nonprofit fighting to eliminate drunk driving and underage drinking.[77] We believe a similar approach of building awareness, fostering conversation, expanding treatment options, and destigmatizing people who struggle with substance use and/or mental illness through peer support—rather than relegating them to jail cells and the streets— could save countless lives.

Reforming the Criminal Justice System

Stop criminalizing homelessness

As we shared in chapter 10, there is a "revolving door" in the US between homelessness and the criminal justice system, whereby individuals cycle between jails and shelters and prisons and the streets. People experiencing homelessness are criminalized for behaviors they have no choice but to exhibit—such as sleeping outside or in their vehicle or in a tent encampment.

We must stop criminalizing homelessness in our communities by eliminating the dangerous anti-homeless ordinances that limit the ability of our unhoused neighbors to engage in life essential activities like sleeping, sitting, eating, and asking for charity. Enforcement of these dehumanizing prohibitions for reasons of "public health and safety" only serve to push unsheltered individuals to the next street corner (or city limits) in the whack-a-mole approach to policing. Anti-homeless ordinances do nothing to address homelessness or its underlying causes. We advocate for utilizing the funds that are currently being used for police enforcement of these likely unconstitutional local statutes for improved services and increased housing instead.[78] We encourage local jurisdictions to do away with anti-homeless architecture—that park bench does not need a divider—and provide public toilet facilities, trash receptacles, and the like. We would argue for the adoption of a nationwide expansion of the ruling in the *Martin v. Boise* case: if a local community has insufficient shelter space to temporarily house all those experiencing homelessness, then enforcement of local "quality of life" laws should be curtailed. In general, we believe that the many ordinances and statutes that criminalize our fellow human beings for life essential activities that we have not otherwise properly provided for as a society should be eliminated.

Close the revolving door

Just as homelessness leads to incarceration, incarceration leads to homelessness; this is due to the multisystem consequences of being involved in the criminal justice system, which include being barred from public housing, being denied federal benefits, having to "check the box" on employment applications, and being discriminated against by private landlords. As we saw in chapter 10, there is a strong connection between homelessness and the criminal justice system that runs in both directions. Closing the revolving door will be difficult, but we do see ways to improve the system.

First, it is important to reduce the penalties for minor offenses and provide diversion courts in which offenders have alternative options for serving out sentences. Second, we must develop strategies for improving the relationship between unsheltered individuals experiencing homelessness and law enforcement.[79] Training and adequate staffing of police officers, offering community forums for information sharing, and establishing lived experience advisory boards are three possible tactics.

Another aspect of the criminal justice system that needs fixing is the high cost of being incarcerated. When a person experiencing homelessness is incarcerated, they face a wide variety of court costs and fines that make it difficult to stay out of jail. In his 2021 book, *Profit and Punishment: How America Criminalizes the Poor in the Name of Justice*, Pulitzer Prize–winning journalist Tony Messenger spent years in county and municipal courthouses documenting how poor Americans are convicted of minor crimes and then saddled with exorbitant fines and fees, not unlike the debtor's prisons of a few hundred years ago. If they are unable to pay bail, they are often sent to jail, where in many states they face pay-to-stay fees (such as a daily charge for lodging), in a cycle that creates a mountain of debt that can take years to pay off. Exploding a small fine into a $50,000 debt for a woman who shoplifted an $8 tube of lipstick is unconscionable.[80] Fines and legal fees must be reduced, one's ability to pay should be considered by the courts, and basic human decency should not be forgotten.

Unfortunately, planning for a person's successful release from incarceration to housing is a step that has not been handled well. Discharge planning is haphazard or minimal throughout the country, leaving many returning citizens with virtually no options but the streets. It is unacceptable that as many as 15% of formerly incarcerated individuals face homelessness within their first year of release from prison or jail. Special attention must be paid to creating housing opportunities for this vulnerable population, and providing guidance and support for inmates as they prepare to reenter society, such as job training and completing benefit applications like Social Security, Disability, and Medicaid. Simply put, we believe all people in our society should have access to the basic human rights of work, education, food, health care, and housing, regardless of what they may have been convicted of through our broken and discriminatory criminal justice system.

Timothy, whom we met in chapter 10, lived through the realities of the revolving door. Incarcerated at a young age, Timothy served his time, and when his sentence was through, he was ready to restart his life. Yet despite his intentions, the weight of his felony record trailed him wherever he went, affecting his employment, health, and relationships with family. Timothy experienced homelessness for the last year of his life, after being in prison for over a decade. There was no discharge plan, no support for his transition "beyond the cell." Through Miracle

Messages, Timothy reconnected with his daughter, and while they were able to share many phone calls in what he described as "the best year of [his] life," Timothy never got the chance to see his daughter once again in person before passing away. While it is difficult to say for certain how Timothy would have ended up had he been given the proper discharge planning and follow-on support he deserved, what we do know is that the revolving door can and should be closed.

Ensuring a Successful Start

To end homelessness, we need to prevent it. The reality is that, for most people, the groundwork for adult homelessness begins during childhood, so we must develop better ways to ensure successful starts. As Rand shared from his experience: "I was just waiting. There's not a lot of information shared. There's a lot of confusion, a lot of gray. In the system, there were kids that hadn't been there long. There were kids that had been there in foster care way too long. There were a lot of kids that had been oppressed and abused, and again, too, disproportionately minorities. The turnover is just atrocious. And it's like, dang, America, you're doing this to kids. It's bad to do to anybody, but to kids?"

Foster youth are among the most at-risk people in our society. Although foster youth may have housing while in foster care, their situations are often precarious and relatively unstable, which is especially harmful during the formative development years of childhood. One simple suggestion is to increase the age limit for aging out of foster care from 18 to 21 or later, as many states have already done,[81] in part to enable more time for creating a viable plan for life after foster care. Rand, whom we met in chapter 11, is now a social worker, working directly to support children experiencing homelessness who remind him so much of his younger self. Reflecting on his past, Rand notes: "It took many, many weeks [to find a placement], and some people denied me because of my past; some were full. It still happens today. There's so many kids and not enough homes." According to one review of the literature on foster care, over 20,000 youth age out of the foster system each year without reaching a permanent placement in a family, and 51% of youth who age out of foster care will do so without a plan for permanency.[82] Looking back on his own story, Rand recommends extending the age limit for foster care to 26.

The Foster Care Independence Act of 1999 created the John H. Chafee Foster Care Program for Successful Transition to Adulthood, which provides funding to states and tribes to assist youth in foster care and young adults formerly in foster care with financial assistance, housing, employment, education, and other support services to promote their successful transition to adulthood.[83] However, due to inadequate funding, the percentage of youth ages 14 and older who received essential transition services through the Chafee Program decreased for all types of services between 2015 and 2018.[84] It is important to increase funding for this important program.

For transition-aged foster youth, schools are not just a place to learn reading, writing, and arithmetic. Schools are also a place to feel safe, develop healthy relationships, and find a level of stability and acceptance that they may not get at home. As the stakes are especially high for foster children, schools should do everything possible to minimize school transfers for foster youth (and in general). According to Kristin Myers, an assistant professor at the University of Northern Colorado and an expert in foster care and education for unhoused youth, school is the last best chance for many aging-out foster youth to get into college or find their vocation, and thus decrease their likelihood of poverty and homelessness as adults.[85]

One example of an effective nongovernmental program that helps transition-aged foster youth is the national nonprofit called Fostering Hope (https://iamfosteringhope.org), which offers a mentoring program composed of "cool uncles" and "cool aunts"—adult volunteers who serve as a positive role model in a foster youth's life. Mentoring programs loosely modeled off of Big Brothers Big Sisters can make a profound difference in the life of foster youth. Another compelling example comes from the University of Maryland, Baltimore, which initiated a partnership between a housing nonprofit and local social service agencies to provide two-bedroom units available exclusively for transitioning youths.[86] To be sure, with over a third of young adults aging out of the foster care system into homelessness by the time they are 26 years old, considerably more efforts must be made to house, train, and support this very vulnerable population.

The McKinney-Vento Homeless Assistance Act is the primary federal initiative to assist children and youth experiencing homelessness in schools across the country. Every year, federal dollars are distributed to states, who, in turn, distribute funds to local school districts to assist youth experiencing homelessness. The McKinney-Vento Act is designed to ensure that unhoused children and youth have equal access to the same free, appropriate public education, including preschool, as other children and youth. For instance, because unhoused students move from one school to another with frequency, a substantial portion of the federal McKinney-Vento money is spent on transportation so that students can continue in their current school. Other approved expenses include tutoring, before- and after-school mentoring, and other forms of academic support; school supplies; and specialized training and professional development for teachers and other school staffers. But because of budget limitations at the federal level, very good programs for unhoused students are left unfunded or grossly underfunded in many districts.[87] Substantially increasing federal McKinney-Vento funding for programs for unhoused school-age children is desperately needed.

Generating a longer list of ways to improve our educational system to benefit youth and families experiencing homelessness (and millions of other students) is beyond the scope of this book, unfortunately. But given how students experiencing homelessness face significant and unique barriers to earning an education, it is worth highlighting that the concept of homework—work to be done at home after the end of the school day—is anathema to many students experiencing homelessness. Returning from school to a cramped, doubled- or tripled-up apartment or homeless shelter, where internet and computer access may be limited, does not provide a safe, relaxed place to study. Schools and teachers should be able to make accommodations for students experiencing homelessness, with the same care and discretion that students facing specific learning disabilities often receive.

***

The path toward ending homelessness—perhaps the most intersectional issue of our time—requires addressing problems in a variety of closely interrelated systems. This can seem incredibly daunting at first.

But we must remember that each system is made up of people: social workers, nonprofit executives, local elected officials, law enforcement, teachers and principals, doctors and nurses, landlords, employers, judges and lawyers, therapists, taxpayers, homeowners, renters, voters, advocates, community members, and, of course, you. While none of us can singlehandedly end homelessness, we can each do our part to help the people we meet and improve the systems we are part of. Together, we can move our country forward on this human rights crisis of our time.

And as a first step, it all begins with how we show up for one another.

KEY TAKEAWAYS

Though homelessness is a multifaceted issue that requires multifaceted solutions, here are a few systems-level solutions that would make a great impact on reducing homelessness.

Housing: Increase the supply of affordable and transitional or temporary housing, decrease the cost of construction, allocate more time and resources into keeping people in their homes, legislate a right to shelter or housing, and invest in community development.

Physical, mental, and behavioral health: Expand health care programs that directly target the experience of homelessness, increase funding for low-income primary care clinics, utilize outreach teams that combine medical care with social services, increase use of diversion intervention programs, carefully develop involuntary treatment protocols and follow-on plans, and create more accessible and affordable substance use and mental health facilities.

Work and financial support: Create low-barrier and flexible work opportunities, increase the minimum wage to at least $15 an hour, create state programs to supplement federal benefits, provide a basic income to many individuals and families experiencing homelessness, and change the tax code to increase equity.

Criminal justice: Eliminate and otherwise stop enforcing the various ordinances and statutes that criminalize homelessness, reduce penalties for minor offenses, improve police training and accountability, invest more time and resources in discharge planning, and decrease fines and legal fees.

Youth development: Increase the age limit for aging out of foster care from 18 to 21, minimize school transfers for foster youth, promote homeless youth shelters and housing programs that center the needs of LGBTQ+ youth, and substantially increase the federal funding for McKinney-Vento to better provide programs for unhoused school-age children and youth.

13

Healing Our Humanity

When *We* Walked By

Kevin had arranged to meet Adam in the early afternoon at a well-trafficked street corner in the Castro, in front of a popular grocery store where Adam often panhandled. Kevin and Adam had been connected via text through a mutual acquaintance, who suggested that Adam would be an ideal person to talk with about Kevin's nascent storytelling project inviting his unhoused neighbors to record their experiences of life on the streets through wearable cameras. As Kevin walked the few blocks from the San Francisco MUNI metro station to the meeting spot, he instinctively reached his hand into his pants pocket and gripped his keys, positioning his car key between his thumb and forefinger as a makeshift weapon. Kevin worried that Adam might lunge at him, and that he might need to defend himself.

The irony was not lost on Kevin that day: here he was, meeting a person experiencing homelessness whom he shared a mutual connection with, who had generously offered to take time out of their day to listen to his half-baked idea for building empathy with people living on the streets, and he still could not get past his own preconceptions of "the homeless," formed through years of fear-mongering local news accounts, upsetting "I was followed/harassed/etc." horror stories on social media, and his own unchecked assumptions. "They" were untrustworthy, erratic, and dangerous, unable to control their actions due to mental illness, drug addiction, or both. Kevin had a beloved uncle who had lived on the streets for 30 years, but it did not matter: the harmful stereotypes that he eventually hoped to help others confront were once his very own.

***

In January 1986 Don had just started his job as the executive director of the Samaritan Ministry of Greater Washington, an Episcopal Church–based agency serving those in poverty and homelessness. Although he had worked in a church-related job more than 20 years earlier, he was brand new to the issue of homelessness. He was meeting a colleague for lunch in downtown Washington, DC, at a restaurant near a very large shelter that occupied an entire city block and was owned and run by the Community for Creative Non-Violence. Sitting in his car at a stoplight near the shelter, he was surprised at the number of men standing on the sidewalk, dressed in tattered clothes. Some had liquor bottles in their hand; others were staring off into space; one had a shopping cart filled to the brim with large trash bags. To Don, all of them looked really "down and out." Don quietly rolled up the window of his car, locked the doors, and whispered to himself, "What have I gotten myself into?" before driving off. Months later, after getting to know a number of men and women who were experiencing homelessness, Don reflected on that day driving to the restaurant, and wondered what he had been so afraid of.

***

Amanda was five when she first thought about the issue of homelessness. Amanda and her mom were sitting on a bench outside a Chick-fil-A in southern Georgia when a person experiencing homelessness came up to them: tall and slim, wearing a slightly offset denim baseball cap and sporting a white beard that faintly reminded her of Santa Claus. Like them, he sat on the other end of the bench eating his sandwich. He never once looked up at them, not even a glance in their direction, keeping his head low under the shade of his cap. Passersby smiled warmly at Amanda and her mom, but not at the man on the other end of the bench. They were three people eating waffle fries on a Saturday afternoon on a bench, yet the world only saw two of them: a kindergartener and her mom. For the man, the mellowness of Southern hospitality wasn't offered. He received no soft grins, no waves, no "how y'all doing todays." There was neither kindness nor acknowledgment of his presence. Amanda was outside because of a temper tantrum, a center-floor meltdown after being told she could not have both ice cream and a milkshake. He was outside because he had no other choice. Amanda remembers quickly glancing at the man on the other side of the bench, but just for a moment; as she would continue to do for many years hence, she quickly averted her eyes, glued her gaze to the floor, and quietly held her breath until he disappeared.

***

Andrijana always felt uncomfortable at intersections where a person experiencing homelessness would sit or stand, holding up some sign signaling their distress and a cup of change. Part of it was sheer sadness trickling over to her comfortable and safe life, but another part was a sense that she was an actor in a play she couldn't control—an overwhelming sense that she couldn't do anything. So it was easier to shove away the mental confusion and ignore their pleas for help.

Our stories aren't that different from anyone else's. We've wrestled with many of the common questions: What do you say to a person who is visibly experiencing homelessness? How do you start a conversation? Should you offer food? What if they decline? What if a person experiencing homelessness asks for money—should you give it? Do most people experiencing homelessness struggle with mental illness or a substance use disorder (or both)? Is homelessness a choice? Are most of our unhoused neighbors from the area? Why are there so many people experiencing homelessness in the first place? Is there anything we can actually do to help?

We did not write this book to condemn any group, reject our flawed but beloved country, or perpetuate false binaries between "us" and "them," whether between "the homeless" and "the housed" or some enlightened few as opposed to some uninformed many. This constant battle of right versus wrong and good versus evil leaves no room for human complexity, compassion, grace, or growth. The reality is that all of us, including the four of us coauthors, harbor some prejudice toward our neighbors experiencing homelessness, unwittingly or not. All of us, to some degree, are influenced by societal narratives that equate financial wealth and status to human worth.

This may not be our fault, but we believe it is our responsibility to see, acknowledge, unlearn, educate, and grow from, again and again. We believe the risk is not in sometimes being wrong on an incredibly multifaceted, intersectional issue like homelessness, but in not having the courage to be wrong, by not asking the hard questions of ourselves and each other, and listening to what we may hear. Questions like, What might it look like to respond to the homelessness crisis of today with humanity at the forefront?

To consider how we might respond to this crisis with a renewed sense of shared humanity in the future, we look first to a telling example from the past, when the homelessness crisis in San Francisco was briefly 25 times worse than it is today.[1]

In Times of Crisis

In the early morning hours of Wednesday, April 18, 1906, a 7.9 magnitude earthquake struck along the San Andreas Fault in Northern California, with the epicenter just two miles off the coast of San Francisco. The massive quake caused a conflagration that destroyed some 28,000 buildings in San Francisco, leveling more than 500 blocks in the city center. More than 3,000 people died, and about 80% of the city was destroyed. In the aftermath of the 1906 earthquake and fire, some 250,000 residents of San Francisco were displaced, establishing makeshift camps in park areas and in burnt-out ruins of buildings. For a short period of time, more than half of the city's 400,000 residents experienced homelessness.

In response, the city did not pass anti-camping ordinances. Law enforcement was not mobilized to raze tents and confiscate belongings. Local residents whose homes withstood the brunt of the disaster did not join together to form anti-survivor, not-in-my-backyard protests.

Instead, city officials and local residents rallied together to help. "As winter approached, the city built 5,300 small wooden cottages for those still in need of housing" while "the army housed 20,000 refugees in military-style tent camps."[2] Camps formed playgroups for kids and dining halls for individuals and families, which became the centers for social life. Tenants paid $2 a month toward the $50 price of their earthquake cottage, many assembled in Golden Gate Park. After paying off their new home, the owners were required to move their cottages out of the camp, leaving earthquake cottages scattered throughout San Francisco, in an early example of scattered site housing. In June 1908, just two years after one of the most devastating disasters in American history, the last camp closed; 250,000 unhoused survivors had been housed.

According to the historical accounts of many survivors, the aftermath of the 1906 earthquake and fire was a time of civic renewal and mutuality in San Francisco, as evidenced by the creation of emergency rezoning ordinances, outdoor soup kitchens, refugee camps and earthquake cottages as affordable housing, and emergency assistance and goodwill from countless volunteers. Overwhelmingly, survivors were embraced, not ostracized. Or to put it another way, survivors were able to discover a social home, in addition to physical housing.

Though far from universal, often short-lived, and with many painful counterexamples,[3] the overall public response to highly visible disasters in the United States tends to be along the lines of how people in San Francisco met their moment in 1906: an initial outpouring of support and sympathy for those displaced or otherwise affected. This is what sociologist Charles E. Fritz described in 1961 as the emergence of the "therapeutic community,"[4] or "the period of elevated social capital utilization and expansion that often is reported immediately after a natural disaster," as Kevin wrote in his previous book, *Natural Disasters as a Catalyst for Social Capital*. Within the therapeutic community, "helping is contagious; residents notice fellow residents helping and feel obliged to contribute" and "all attention is focused on the community's survival and recovery [. . .] 'we' takes precedence over 'me.'"[5] As psychologists Krys Kaniasty and Fran Norris succinctly put it, "The sudden, unambiguous, and visibly distressing nature of disasters frequently invokes high levels of unsolicited help and spontaneous goodwill."[6]

When people experience homelessness as a result of a natural disaster, we tend to blame external forces, not individual flaws. The immediate focus is (rightfully) on the pain and suffering caused by the natural hazard—the hurricane, the wildfire, the floodwaters— and the corresponding impact on people, not on any individual choices or behaviors that may seem ill-fated in hindsight: not evacuating in time, not purchasing adequate fire insurance, choosing to live in a flood-prone area, and so on. The media validates our feelings of charity and goodwill by showing heart-wrenching images and providing nonstop coverage from the ground: a child being saved, a person miraculously pulled from the rubble, a beloved family dog that somehow finds its way home. Storytelling of this sort encourages us to care and stay vigilant as to what is going on, and to connect with others regarding what we are seeing and experiencing together, further reinforcing our own comity and kindness. We are compelled to neither look away nor walk by.

Compassion, not condemnation, takes center stage. For why would we condemn? We tend to see ourselves in the people affected, recognizing them as victims, no more or less flawed than any of the rest of us as humans. We stand in solidarity with them, blurring the lines between us and them with phrases like "it could have been me," "but for the grace of God go I," and "we are all in this together," and with hashtags on social media like #ParadiseStrong, #SWFLStrong, and the like. In short, we imagine and articulate an alternate universe where "we" are "them."

The contrast to chronic homelessness in the United States could not be more stark. Unlike a highly visible natural disaster,[7] homelessness in the US can be thought of as a type of unnatural disaster. Most of us do not see or comprehend the broken systems and forgotten humanity that cause this type of predominantly human-made disaster. By some metrics, an abject lack of affordable housing and other failures in social service systems and in our shared humanity are far more pernicious than fires and floods and other naturally occurring hazards; they adversely affect tens of millions of housed and unhoused people in the United States each year, compared to an estimated 600,000 people who have lost their homes as a result of natural disasters between 1980 and 2020 in the US. Yet we see no flames to decry, no rising floodwaters to point to as the clear culprits for our modern calamity of homelessness and housing insecurity. Instead, we only see a particularly hard-hit subsection of unsheltered people experiencing homelessness, survivors of multiple broken systems and humanity's shortcomings. And sadly, our response is all too often "What did they do wrong?" or "What's wrong with them?"

As coauthors, we believe there is a better way. By treating our neighbors experiencing homelessness not as problems to be solved but as people to be loved, we have found that problems tend to get solved. While there are no fires to help put out, no sandbag walls to build, and no Red Cross blood drives to support, there are our neighbors, experiencing homelessness, whom we can either choose to walk by, metaphorically and literally, or whom we can choose to embrace. The choice is ours, as the problem is partly of our own making.

When we see "them" as part of "us"—people, not problems—we are significantly more likely to care enough to address structural, systems-level problems. If we love someone as our neighbor, if we imagine them as our own brother or sister, we are more likely to stand in solidarity with them in fighting for what they need: emergency rezoning ordinances, direct cash assistance, new housing construction, addiction treatment programs, employment opportunities that offer a living wage, eliminating anti-them ordinances. And so, by working to heal our humanity, we are much more likely to find ways to fix broken systems—the problem is no longer abstract or irrelevant, but personal. And as systems improve, we see positive outcomes—housing 250,000 disaster survivors in just over two years! two-thirds of unhoused basic income recipients secure housing!—which helps us further see *them* as part of *us*.

When humanity leads the way, system improvements follow, and as systems change for the better, people can live happier, healthier, more productive lives, which makes it even easier to recognize our common humanity in one another, and want to double down. It is a *virtuous* cycle, and it begins with us. By recognizing our neighbors experiencing homelessness more fully as fellow human beings, and acting accordingly, we can each play a tangible and invaluable role in helping end the ongoing national catastrophe that is homelessness in America. This is the focus for the remainder of this book, and the work we hope you will join us in going forward.

Taking Individual Action

Nurturing relationships

While many of us care about the issue of homelessness, surprisingly few of us personally know our unhoused neighbors as neighbors, friends, or as the mothers, fathers, sisters, brothers, sons, and daughters that they are. This leads to a disconnect between "us" and "them." We opened the introduction with this observation and now begin to bring this book to a close with the same, for many of the ways in which our humanity has fallen short on this issue stem from the simple fact that we do not know who "they" are. So now that you have spent many hours with us through these pages (thank you!), we invite you to commit an additional hour or two within the next 30 days to get to know one of your neighbors experiencing homelessness, and thus take an initial step toward helping to end relational poverty on the streets.

This could begin by saying hello to an unsheltered neighbor. Clean socks are one of the most requested items on the streets, and a terrific conversation starter: "Hi, would you like a pair of clean socks? How's your day going?" If the person seems open to sharing more, go with it. If not, please don't take it personally: a smile followed by "Alright, take care" is friendly enough. Use your discretion and common sense, engage people in well-trafficked public spaces during the daytime, go with a friend if their presence would help you feel more comfortable. If you feel uncomfortable, it is absolutely okay to continue on your way—no one expects you to talk to everyone. We might just suggest taking a moment afterward to reflect on why you felt uncomfortable: Was it due to fear, unfamiliarity, or something else? Remember: you do not need to be a hero or a saint on this issue. Connecting with our neighbors experiencing homelessness is about being more fully human with each other and ourselves.

If a neighbor experiencing homelessness seems open to connecting, consider asking if there is anything they need, including whether they might have any loved ones they would like to try to reconnect with through Miracle Messages. Family and friend reunifications are essential, can be lifesaving, and everyday volunteers can play a surprisingly vital role. As we mentioned earlier in this book, the majority of successful shelter exits in San Francisco occur as a result of family and friend reunifications.[8] While one-way bus ticket programs help thousands of individuals experiencing homelessness relocate each year to live with out-of-town relatives, these widely replicated programs have a mixed track record[9] and are more of a final step to reuniting people who are already in touch to live together, rather than a first step toward rebuilding relationships or locating long-lost loved ones. In all likelihood, you can play an important role in helping people experiencing homelessness in your community reconnect with their loved ones.

Volunteers and staff members at Miracle Messages have facilitated over 800 reunions since December 2014, delivering messages from individuals experiencing homelessness across the US and Canada to loved ones around the world (and increasingly, also *from* family members to their missing relatives who may be unhoused). These messages often begin with a simple "I love you," "I miss you," "I'm sorry," "I want you back in my life," "I'm still alive," and the like. As a volunteer with

Miracle Messages, you can help facilitate reunifications in three tangible ways: offering reunification services directly to people experiencing homelessness in your community, contacting local homeless service providers to ask if (and how) they currently help their clients reconnect with family members and friends (and if needed, mentioning Miracle Messages, which is free and available nationwide for nonprofit referral partners), or joining Miracle Messages' global community of "digital detectives," who make phone calls, write emails and letters, and conduct online searches to help locate loved ones, deliver messages, and reunite families. You can learn more on how to get involved by visiting www.miraclemessages.org, joining one of Miracle Messages' weekly volunteer orientations and trainings, or by referring a neighbor experiencing homelessness to Miracle Messages' easy-to-remember toll-free hotline, 1-800-MISS-YOU.

To be sure, loved one reunification is not a silver bullet for ending homelessness, and sometimes family is part of the problem, not part of the solution: "you know your relationships better than we do," as Miracle Messages' volunteers often say. And many of our neighbors experiencing homelessness have extensive histories of trauma, abuse, neglect, hurt, and disappointment that lead to a deep distrust of others, including well-intentioned volunteers doing outreach. But for the relative minority of individuals experiencing homelessness for whom reconnecting with a loved one might be of interest, family and friend reunification programs like Miracle Messages can play a critical role in helping them overcome digital literacy and access barriers, bureaucratic barriers, and most importantly of all, emotional barriers like shame, fear, and self-loathing.[10]

If striking up conversations on the street feels impractical or unsafe, and doing digital sleuthing is not your cup of tea, consider volunteering with a local meal service provider, homeless nonprofit, or faith-based outreach program in your community, ideally in a capacity that includes spending time directly with people experiencing homelessness.[11] Handing out warm meals to dozens of people is great; sitting down to share a meal with one person can be even better. Regardless, be mindful of falling into the savior complex, which we discussed in chapter 4 on paternalism. You will most likely learn and grow more from your initial conversations with your neighbor experiencing homelessness than they will. As Aboriginal activists said in the 1970s, "If you have come here to help me, you are wasting your time. But if you have come because your liberation is bound up with mine, then let us work together."[12]

Or would you prefer connecting with a person experiencing homelessness as a phone buddy? Consider volunteering with Miracle Friends. Hundreds of volunteers from around the world spend as little as 20–30 minutes a week having one-to-one phone calls and text exchanges with their unhoused friend, to offer general support and check-in. Over 100,000 conversation minutes have been logged by volunteers throughout the United States and Canada, as well as in Germany, India, the Philippines, Chile, Kenya, and elsewhere, who have been matched with people experiencing homelessness in San Francisco, Los Angeles, South Florida, and more.

AJ, who works in software in Bahrain and discovered Miracle Messages from someone on LinkedIn, is a volunteer with Miracle Friends but admitted he was unsure about it at first:

> "I was still apprehensive about the whole thing, how putting two people together could have any impact. But it was really transformational. People in two completely different places could become friends, and I truly consider Jaime a friend."

Jaime, a young man in Los Angeles who recently secured housing, said he felt the same way:

> "I didn't think much of it. Little by little, you know, you start building that bond. It was a good feeling. I mean, I was going through so much at the time. I didn't have a place. Literally living out of a suitcase. It made me feel hopeful. I remember a lot of times AJ would be like, 'Hey, don't give up. Stay focused. There's a light at the end of the tunnel.' He was right. [. . .] I'm really glad to always have AJ to talk to. And I can always text him when I feel like talking to someone. We'll spend like an hour talking about whatever it may be. He's really fun to talk to."[13]

You can learn more about Miracle Friends and sign up from anywhere in the world through the get involved page on Miracle Messages' website, www.miraclemessages.org.

Many other innovative homeless service providers enable some type of virtual interaction with people experiencing homelessness, even if it is asynchronous. Beam (https://beam.org), founded by Alex Stephany in 2017, is an award-winning social enterprise in the United Kingdom that helps homeless Londoners and refugees start new careers and find secure housing through crowdfunding campaigns. In addition to being able to donate to individuals experiencing homelessness like Michael, who dreams of becoming a security guard, you can also post a message of support wishing him luck, thanking him for sharing his story, and reminding him that "everyone is behind you." Samaritan, founded by Jonathan Kumar in 2016, is a social enterprise with a similar concept based out of Seattle, Washington. Samaritan (www.samaritan.city) is a support platform that works with health and human service providers across the country to link their unhoused patients to the social and financial capital they need to meet their housing, income, and health goals, providing incentives along the way and empowering a wider community of supporters to donate and offer notes of encouragement. HandUp (https://handup.org), founded by Rose Broome, Sammie Rayner, and Zac Witte in 2013, is a charitable giving platform predominantly for homelessness nonprofits, but it was previously focused on helping individuals experiencing homelessness crowdfund directly from donors and supporters.

It is also imperative that we recognize the importance of self-care for people wanting to make a difference. For example, Augsburg University has a whole plan for providing self-care for advocates, including sections called "Identifying Your Role and Practicing Self-Care," "Self-Care and Prevention of Burnout Among Activists," "Self-Care for Activists: Sustaining Your Most Valuable Resource," and "Activists, Don't Feel Guilty about Self-Care and Setting Boundaries."[14] Another good source for self-care assistance is Israa Nasir's "Balancing Self-Care and Social Activism." As she says, "When we witness or observe the trauma of others, we can experience the symptoms of trauma (emotionally and in our bodies)."[15] Her specific suggestions include: do a daily check-in on your emotional energy and create systems of support. Miracle Messages hosts regular "compassion calls" for volunteers, just to talk with and support one another in what comes up with their phone buddies or through their efforts to facilitate reunions. Nurturing our relationship with ourselves and with other advocates will enable us to better show up in relationships with our friends experiencing homelessness.

And finally, it is important to recognize that relational poverty is not something that only afflicts our neighbors experiencing homelessness. Loneliness is at epidemic levels in the United States today, adversely affecting our physical health and life expectancy, and having increased substantially during the COVID-19 pandemic.[16] A 2021 report from the Harvard Graduate School of Education suggests that 36% of all Americans—including 61% of young adults—feel "serious loneliness."[17] And many groups are highly stigmatized and discriminated against in our society, based on race, ethnic origin, gender identity, immigration status, physical and mental disabilities, language, religion, and more, whether or not they are experiencing homelessness.

While a detailed overview of all types of isolation and stigma are well beyond the scope of this book, it is important to recognize the widespread role of relational poverty in our wider society, including our own privileges and how we might be complicit in dehumanizing others. Therefore, in engaging in relationship-building work, we should avoid any sense of superiority in connecting deeper with our neighbors experiencing homelessness as neighbors. One tangible way to do this is by also elevating peer-based support models in our local community: organizations like Downtown Streets Team in Northern California and The Healing WELL in San Francisco empower people to chart a path to self-sufficiency through the dignity of work, therapy, and wellness programs, almost always in highly supportive peer-based settings. Even the presence of at least one nurturing relationship between two individuals experiencing homelessness can be life-sustaining: as Lainie poignantly described her special bond with her son Gabe, "We kept each other going. We talked about our plans, our hopes, and our dreams, you know? There were times where we did want to give up, but we just kept listening to each other."

Healthy social ties are critical for us as human beings: nurturing relationships create positive social norms, propelling us away from destructive habits. We want to live longer and be healthier so we can spend more time with the people we cherish. Supportive relationships bolster our immune, endocrine, and cardiovascular systems, and increase our life expectancy.[18] To be sure, we all need food, water, shelter, clothing, sleep, and access to hygiene to meet our basic physiological needs. But we also need love, trust, affection, belonging, and acceptance to be fully human, as Maslow's Hierarchy of Needs famously depicts.[19]

No one should go through homelessness. But as long as homelessness exists, we believe no one should go through homelessness alone—for who among us can get through life alone?

Shattering stigmas

Martin Luther King Jr. understood that the civil rights movement must take place in the court of public opinion, along with the courts of law. As Michelle Alexander writes in *The New Jim Crow*, King believed it was a "flawed public consensus—not merely flawed policy—that was at the root of racial oppression."[20] Long-standing narratives needed to be reexamined, new stories needed to be told, hearts and minds needed to be transformed. The same can be said today for the movement to end homelessness in the United States: it is a struggle for recognizing our common humanity with our neighbors experiencing homelessness as much as it is a struggle for more affordable housing. Indeed, one cannot be won without the other.

As the stigmas and stereotypes of homelessness are partly of our own creation, adoption, and perpetuation, we can also play a critical role in changing them, thereby helping eliminate the profound shame afflicting so many of our neighbors experiencing homelessness.

One of the simplest actions we can each take is to use person-first language in describing people experiencing homelessness as *people* experiencing homelessness. As we wrote in chapter 2, we believe that today's blanket descriptions of "the homeless" will one day appear as antiquated and offensive as labeling LGBTQ+ individuals "the homosexuals," as was done in a 1967 episode of the documentary television series *CBS Reports*.[21] Describing people experiencing homelessness as "the homeless" erases the incredible diversity of people and circumstances therein, affixes a permanent identity on what should be seen as an impermanent situation, and invites us to forget that we are talking about real human beings here—someone's mom, dad, brother, sister, son, or daughter.

If you would not describe someone as a "housed person" or a member of "the housed," it is probably best to avoid a meaningless monolith like "the homeless." We might suggest using a person-first term like person experiencing homelessness, a short but friendly unhoused neighbor, or the like—anything that better prioritizes their personhood. We find that simply choosing to use more thoughtful terminology ourselves prompts others to ask about it, which tends to lead to much-needed thoughtful conversations around this issue. In general, there is no need to patrol your friends' speech or social media posts: the best way to counter the bad is with the better. The only exception we suggest is when terms like "the homeless" are used by the media and influencers. Given their reach and role in public discourse, we believe journalists and thought leaders have an obligation to be a bit more respectful in how they describe our neighbors experiencing homelessness. And so, the next time you find a mention of "the homeless" in your local newspaper, television news station, or a popular social media post, consider reaching out to the journalist, editor, producer, or influencer, and asking (with compassion and respect, of course) why they chose not to use person-first language around homelessness. Feel free to blame *When We Walk By,* and while you are at it, perhaps ask them if they have read our book!

Another effective way to advance the "public consensus" around homelessness is to educate yourself (and others) about the facts and figures of who is actually experiencing homelessness, and to correct harmful and misleading stereotypes as they come up. For example, over 60% of Americans view the cause of homelessness as a variety of personal failings. In reality, homelessness is caused by many broken systems and failures in our humanity, with little to do with individual choices or behaviors—"housed" and "unhoused" people both make mistakes and are imperfect, so why should anyone experience homelessness?

As many as 85% of people incorrectly cite drug and alcohol use as major causes of homelessness. In reality, most studies show that around 33% of people experiencing homelessness have problems with alcohol or drugs, many of whom are self-medicating to diminish their pain, shame, and suffering. When we overlook these mitigating circumstances, we are falling into the attribution bias, or the tendency to ignore circumstances and perceive individual behaviors as immutable characteristics.

As many as 67% of people incorrectly cite mental illness and related mental disorders as major factors of homelessness. In reality, 20% to 25% of people experiencing homelessness suffer from some form of severe mental illness. And for those who are suffering from untreated mental health challenges, we should provide empathy, treatment, ongoing support resources, and connection, not disdain and rejection.

And hardly anyone chooses to "be homeless."

We all need to be mindful of the confirmation bias, or the tendency to extrapolate truths based on our own very limited direct experiences and perceptions. For example, how many people solely think of homelessness as what they can visibly see on the streets? In reality, less than 40% of the 582,462 people experiencing homelessness each night are unsheltered, using the HUD definition of homelessness. If we use the broader Department of Education definition, which includes children and families couchsurfing with others, and use our own approximation that as many as 6 million people experience homelessness each year in the US, the ratio of unsheltered homelessness is significantly less. So the next time you hear someone offhandedly describe "the homeless" as single unsheltered men, ask about the approximately 1 in 30 American children—2.5 million—who experience homelessness each year. "Family and child homelessness is a crisis and it is not getting the attention it deserves," said Ellen Bassuk, MD, the founder and former president of the National Center on Family Homelessness.[22]

Finally, all of us who use social media play a role in facilitating the spread of information online and determining what is trending at any given time. What you can do: follow and share social media accounts that shatter the stigma surrounding homelessness, such as Invisible People (https://invisiblepeople.tv), a nonprofit organization in the US that creates YouTube videos and unfiltered stories featuring the names and faces of real people experiencing homelessness. While watching one of these videos, consider how your assumptions and beliefs are either affirmed or unsettled by what you see. And remember the power of your own voice on this issue: write a post sharing a personal anecdote, picture, video, quote, or reflection from your own thoughts, experiences, and questions around homelessness. The more courageous you are in sharing your own learning on this issue—including any lessons or takeaways from this book—the more likely others will do the same. If you do post, please use the hashtag #WhenWeWalkBy, or get in touch with us through our website, www.whenwewalkby.com, so we might share it, too. In one way or another, we are all influencers and influenced; we each have the power to use our platforms and voices to help remake the public consensus around homelessness.

For Kevin, one of the most heartbreaking days at Miracle Messages was the *first time* he heard a person experiencing homelessness say "I can't, I feel dirty," after changing their mind about wanting to try to reconnect with a loved one. If each of us commits to a few of the actions discussed here to help reduce the stigmas around homelessness, we might just help someone experiencing homelessness not feel so ashamed or loathsome. That alone would make all of this worthwhile.

Radical hospitality, not exclusion

Have you ever visited someone else's home and felt touched by how warmly you were welcomed? Perhaps you were invited over for Thanksgiving dinner or a Friday evening Shabbat meal by a friend. You gladly accepted the invitation, but as you approach the front door, you start to feel a bit nervous, wondering if you will know anyone else, or if you will be judged for only bringing a bottle of wine you grabbed from the local convenience store before arriving. You consider turning around and heading home when the door swings open, and your friend enthusiastically greets you with a smile and hug. They hang your coat up, hand you a warm drink, and begin introducing you to everyone else. The host comes over to greet you and notices the bottle of wine in your hand. They exclaim, "Oh perfect, we needed one more red! Thank you!" before whisking it away to be opened and shared. After an evening of good food and laughter, the host insists that you take some leftovers and come back to visit again soon. You feel loved.

The contrast to how our society generally treats people experiencing homelessness en masse could not be more stark: herded like cattle into and out of shelters to abide by strict entry and exit times, waiting in endless lines to receive services with no guarantee of availability, terrified to reveal their housing situation to their coworkers and family for fear of rejection, and so on.

The most memorable cardboard sign that Kevin ever saw was held by a man experiencing homelessness who was sitting down on his backpack, with his head cast downward and his shoulders slumped forward. In simple block letters, the sign read "At least give me the finger." As coauthors who do not have lived experience of homelessness, we cannot imagine being so ignored by other people that we would actually prefer a middle finger in our faces as at least some form of acknowledgment that we exist. We hope that you cannot imagine it, either.

When it comes to homelessness, we each have a choice to make. We can choose to keep avoiding, excluding, and disregarding our neighbors experiencing homelessness, hoping they will just go away. Or we can choose to welcome, include, and embrace them as neighbors.

Ready to help? There is plenty to do, and most actions are straightforward: make eye contact, start a conversation, share a meal. Assemble and hand out basic hygiene kits with essentials, which might include any of the following: soap and shampoo, a toothbrush and toothpaste, dental floss, deodorant, bandages, sunscreen, lotion, lip balm, tissues, hand wipes, hand sanitizer, and feminine hygiene products like tampons and pads. Or consider hosting an assembly party through Simply the Basics (www.simplythebasics.org), a globally reaching hygiene bank that provides people with their most basic needs with dignity, and boasts hundreds of community partnerships. "What the vast food banks system did for food insecurity and awareness, Simply the Basics is doing for hygiene care," says their founder and CEO Meghan Freebeck.

Want to do more? Protest anti-homeless ordinances in your city (e.g., bans on public camping, sleeping, loitering, serving meals), and call your local city councilmembers to fight these inhumane, potentially unconstitutional laws. Vote for local candidates and platforms that promote affordable housing and denser zoning laws, not anti-homeless rhetoric and NIMBYism. Find examples of hostile architecture and design in your city (e.g., sectioned benches, sidewalk boulders, loud-speakers blaring music to prevent loitering), take pictures or videos, and share them on social media, using the hashtag #WhenWeWalkBy. We will collect some of the most memorable photos, insights, and stories from our readers, and share them at www.whenwewalkby.com.

Consider volunteering with a local nonprofit that provides essential services (meals, hygiene, health and wellness, clothing, social support, reunifications) and does so with love and compassion. One great example of this was LavaMae[x], a nonprofit founded by Doniece Sandoval in 2013 that taught and funded organizations around the world to bring mobile showers to people experiencing homelessness. The mobile showers that LavaMae[x] offered in San Francisco, Oakland, and Los Angeles were critical—sadly, LavaMae[x] ceased its programs and operations as of June 2023 due to "an unprecedented budget shortfall." Yet the ripple effect of incubating scores of local hygiene programs across the country continues, carrying on LavaMae[x]'s approach of Radical Hospitality, or "meeting people wherever they are with extraordinary care," which "helps restore dignity, rekindle optimism, and fuel a sense of opportunity."[23] Volunteer at a LavaMae[x]-esque mobile shower program in your area, such as the Happy Feet Clinic led by UCLA students, the Suitcase Clinic led by UC Berkeley students, and the Choose Love Foundation in South Florida founded by Gabby Cordell. Remember, it's not just what an organization does, but how they do it: Do they treat people experiencing homelessness as problems to be solved, or as people to be loved?

The unifying idea behind all of these initiatives is simple: let's embrace our neighbors experiencing homelessness as neighbors. While our judgmental brains (and local ordinances) may try to dehumanize and exclude them—going so far as to not even recognize a beloved member of our very own family in plain sight if they are dressed up to appear homeless (as we saw in the New York City Rescue Mission experiment from chapter 3) and scapegoating those whom we do see for major problems like street crime and open-air drug dealing—we can counter these exclusionary underpinnings by going out of our way to include, welcome, embrace, greet, listen to, speak with, and love our neighbors experiencing homelessness, every single day.

And remember, exclusion presumes unbelonging, but there is no Planet Homelessness from where our neighbors experiencing home-lessness emerged. Homelessness is a homegrown problem. Most of our unhoused neighbors were once our housed neighbors—and family members, classmates, and friends. It's long past time that we start treat-ing them as such.

Dignity and respect, not paternalism

Does anyone know what you and your family need better than you do? Of course not, and it would probably be offensive to suggest it. Yet society's approach to ending homelessness generally presumes that people experiencing homelessness cannot make good decisions for themselves and their loved ones, or at least that we as a society can make better decisions on their behalf.

Paternalism can be quite easy to identify when it is top-down: government agencies at all levels that regulate where people experi-encing homelessness and other low-income groups can live, whom they can cohabitate with, what they can eat, how they can spend their money, and what bureaucratic hoops they have to jump through to prove they are deserving and trustworthy; a news media that rein-forces harmful group stereotypes (especially toward minority groups) through typically blanket negative coverage of "the homeless" only interrupted by occasionally fawning over one person experiencing homelessness who does a good deed as *one of the good ones*;[24] civic groups, nonprofits, and city officials that display aggressive, don't-feed-the-pigeons-type signage to discourage residents from giving money to people panhandling,[25] despite mixed findings (at best) on the comparable downside of giving money to people panhandling. In a March 2013 survey of 146 self-identified panhandlers in San Francisco, 94% said they use some of the money for food, 44% use some of the money for drugs or alcohol, 82% are experiencing homelessness, 62% are disabled, 95% live in San Francisco, and just 3% said they don't want housing.[26]

But paternalism can be much harder to identify when we are directly complicit in it, or even the source of it. We must remember that homelessness is not a sign of incompetence, laziness, or any other negative trait; rather, surviving homelessness requires incredible resilience, motivation, and resourcefulness. We do not need to fix or punish our neighbors experiencing homelessness: progressive paternalism and punitive paternalism are both counterproductive. Instead, we can move past these broken-humanity models and launch ourselves on a journey toward real wisdom on this issue, by beginning with a simple, humble acknowledgment: "I know only one thing: that I know nothing," as Socrates famously said. Or as Jennifer, whom we met in chapter 8, shared at the end of a recent meeting of activists and thought leaders interested in changing public narratives around homelessness:

> "With all due respect, what I'm hearing here from everyone [. . .] is that people are offering 'seats at the table' when it's not their table! Please don't get into the savior complex mode and invite me to sit at your table. In fact, it's my table and I'm not asking for a seat. It was already and is always now my seat. I'm the one who experienced all this trauma and turmoil. I know what the problems are and what I need. I built it. There would be no table without me. I invite you to come to sit at my table and let's have a conversation."

We have found it invaluable to try to retain a beginner's mindset on this issue, taking time to get to know people experiencing homelessness, listening to their stories, and engaging together as neighbors: What are their challenges, frustrations, hopes, and dreams? This human-centered design approach cannot be done on a macro level, at least initially. We each need to spend time with individuals, one-on-one, who are currently or formerly experiencing homelessness. This is how each program of Miracle Messages started: with a conversation. As the Talmud wisely reminds us, "Whoever saves a single life [. . .] saved the whole world," including our own.[27]

We are grateful to you for reading this book, but we hope it is not a final step. We hope you will share what you learned (and continue to learn) with others, buy copies for your friends and family members, start a reading group, or add *When We Walk By* to your book club. But we also hope you will engage in similar conversations with people currently or formerly experiencing homelessness. Toward that end, we have created a Lived Experience Speakers Bureau, where you can request a speaker who has personally experienced homelessness (including a few individuals featured in this book) to share their story and participate in your book club, company lunch and learn, conference, or other gathering. Please visit www.whenwewalkby.com for details and to submit a speaker request, review reading guides, read and watch additional stories, explore other resources, and connect deeper.

Other effective ways to connect with people experiencing homelessness as friends, neighbors, and thought partners include signing up as a volunteer phone buddy with Miracle Friends for weekly calls and texts with an unhoused friend (the program is 100% virtual), joining online forums such as the r/almosthomeless, r/HomelessSurvival, and r/homeless Reddit groups, or volunteering at a local service provider.

Regardless of the channel, try to avoid making assumptions about the people you meet. It is crucial to start from a baseline of curiosity, rather than self-righteousness. And if you decide to offer food, socks, hygiene kits, or money to unsheltered individuals experiencing homelessness, and they decline to engage, please don't be disheartened. Remember, we don't know their story.

And finally, we encourage you to support basic income programs for people experiencing homelessness like the New Leaf Project, the Denver Basic Income Project, and Miracle Money. As we highlighted in chapter 4, in study after study and pilot after pilot, people experiencing homelessness have proven to be excellent stewards of their money. As the research shows, most funds are spent on housing, food, and other essentials like medications, transportation, child care, unexpected family emergencies, and savings. "They spent the money better than we could have spent it for them," as Kevin remarked after a majority of unhoused Miracle Money recipients were able to secure stable housing after six months of receiving $500 a month and having a phone buddy. Consider donating to basic income and cash transfer programs that invest directly in our neighbors experiencing homelessness.

When We Walk Together

Blaming homelessness on individuals, even if it is nonsense, is much more convenient than anything related to fixing broken systems or healing our humanity. Before long, after finishing this book, inevitably you will hear someone refer to homelessness as "a choice," or read a news article or social media post that implies that homelessness is caused by poor life decisions or character flaws. When this happens, we hope you will not walk by, so to speak, but instead engage in conversation, perhaps inviting them to read this book and rethink their assumptions.

Feel free to cite the multitudinous data we shared, including that one in three young adults (and three in five Black young adults[28]) who age out of the foster care system will experience homelessness by the time they are 26 years old;[29] that high rates of homelessness correspond to cities with high costs and low supplies of housing;[30] that 45% of individuals experiencing homelessness have at least one job[31] and another 40% cannot work as a result of disability;[32] that minority groups are disproportionately driven into homelessness, a result of racism and discrimination deeply embedded in many broken systems.[33] Or that the stories of Elizabeth, Jennifer, Rand, Gabe and Lainie, Ray, Timothy, Jeffrey, Tom, Ronnie, Joseph, Linda, Uncle Mark, and many others featured in this book matter.

Whatever the data or stories you may keep in your back pocket, or personal experiences you draw on, we hope that two of the main takeaways you share with others are that ending homelessness is our collective responsibility, and that our neighbors experiencing home-lessness are no different than you or me. They are us, and we are all in this together.

This is counter to the worship of "rugged individualism" that seems to be everywhere in our society—and is absolutely devastating for our neighbors experiencing homelessness. Recall Linda, whom we met in chapter 5, who received a letter in jail from her daughter, pleading with her to "come live with them." She knew how she would respond: she wouldn't. "I didn't want to go to them," Linda reflected. "I didn't want her or my family to see me in the condition that I was in. I didn't want to impose. I didn't think she should have to care for a mother who was lost." Linda didn't want to be a burden, since she felt like she was a failure, or at least failing. So she chose to live on the streets alone over the shame of appearing broken in front of her family.

Maybe if Arnold Schwarzenegger met Linda when she was at her lowest point, he could have reminded her that "I am not a self-made man. I got a lot of help." Or maybe, you can.

Actually, you don't need to swoop in as an action hero here. Quite the opposite, really. The next time you are at a dinner with your friends, giving a talk to an audience, trying to impress a recruiter or a date, just lead with vulnerability. Share at least one of the ways in which you rely on others every day. No self-made facade, no posturing, no pretending: describe the countless people who have helped you get to where you are, along with the poor choices you have made (and still occasionally make), the suffering you have endured, the family members you are estranged from, the things you regret, the ways in which you sometimes feel scared, lonely, resentful, and sad. Or simply examples in your own life when hard work and determination alone were not enough to get you through.

For despite the cliché, not every challenge can or should be neatly wrapped up in a bow of "what doesn't kill you makes you stronger."[34] Traumas are not just obstacles to overcome and later highlight as part of your sterling biography: they are traumas. Share yours, not as a medal on your jacket or as part of a dispiriting game of comparison but as a wound from a familiar war, one that your neighbors experiencing homelessness are almost certainly still facing: a grim health prognosis, emergency surgery, job loss and prolonged period of unemployment, eviction, wildfire that took nearly everything, domestic violence, addiction, poverty, childhood trauma, unfathomable death of a family member, debilitating injury, incarceration, falling out with a loved one, untreated clinical depression, isolation and loneliness, shame and self-loathing, and other hard human experiences.

For most of our readers and for us as coauthors, we have the immense privilege of being able to choose whether to hide or reveal these types of vulnerabilities, the raw, painful parts of our own stories. For most of our neighbors experiencing homelessness, this is not an option: they live it in the open, on the streets, in the cramped car, at the chaotic shelter, painfully raw. So we invite you to share openly. By choosing to diminish the myth around your own individual success story, you can help undercut the exceptionally harmful narrative of homelessness as an individual failure, and perhaps even chip away at our societal construct that the world revolves around individuals.

And finally, if you happen to be one of the tens of millions of Americans who have experienced homelessness or housing insecurity at some point in your life and are now relatively secure in your housing, job, finances, and relationships, the world especially needs to hear your story. Please open up if you feel it is safe to do so, even if it is scary at first: "I, too, experienced homelessness." You will be able to change hearts and minds by sharing your experiences, thereby personalizing this issue among your friends, family, colleagues, and social media followers—who now, through your strength and vulnerability, can name a friend, family member, colleague, and role model whom they know and love who has experienced homelessness. In doing so, you will also help your neighbors who are currently experiencing homelessness: raising your hand, waving it around a bit, answering a few questions, and saying "yup, that was me, 'they' are us."

And if you do, please include us in the conversation by using the hashtag #WhenWeWalkBy or by reaching out through our website www.whenwewalkby.com, so we can celebrate you, too.

When we think about the issue of homelessness, each of us would ideally be able to think of a person we love, as opposed to some nameless, faceless caricature. In a sense, we each need to find our own Uncle Mark: someone we love, whom we could never imagine walking by.

KEY TAKEAWAYS

Times of crisis reveal what's missing in today's response to homelessness: a deep human care that, rooted in relationships and a distinct "we" mentality, urgently seeks to help those who are suffering.

We begin to heal our humanity through relationships: by getting to know a person experiencing homelessness and listening to their story.

Healing our humanity must also encompass unpacking years of learned biases and stereotypes. Simple ways we can do this include using person-first language, questioning our assumptions with data and stories, and engaging in our communities and networks to help change the narrative around homelessness.

We should aim to extend radical hospitality to our neighbors experiencing homelessness. Simple actions, such as making eye contact or sharing a meal, and larger movements, such as successfully protesting anti-homeless ordinances or hostile architecture, are vital to creating a more inclusive society.

Redirecting paternalistic beliefs begins with the acknowledgment that we do not know what's best for someone whose shoes we have not walked in. Instead, we should approach issues around homelessness with curiosity, and engage with our unhoused neighbors with respect. Direct cash transfer programs are one highly effective and empowering way to invest in our neighbors experiencing homelessness.

Share your insights, takeaways, and stories from reading this book with your family, friends, neighbors, and colleagues on social media using the hashtag #WhenWeWalkBy. If you are part of a book club, social group, corporate team, or religious congregation, share this book and offer to host a conversation around homelessness. Consider inviting a speaker from our Lived Experience Speakers Bureau; details and speaker requests are available at www.whenwewalkby.com, along with reading guides, memorable stories and insights from our readers, and other resources. Suggest this book be added to your local library or class curriculum. If you are part of a book club, select *When We Walk By* and books from our recommended reading list (p. 241) to read and discuss. And if you include *When We Walk By* in your book club or class curriculum, want to share your lessons from reading this book, or would like to connect further, please get in touch with us at www.whenwewalkby.com.

Acknowledgments

IN NOVEMBER 2018, KEVIN FIRST proposed the idea to Don about writing a book together. Kevin works full-time leading the nonprofit Miracle Messages, and Don had more than enough projects keeping him busy. But the fanciful idea had staying power, and it turned into this book.

Over the past five years of collaboration—brainstorming, outlining, resting, researching, interviewing, writing, and rewriting, as well as plenty of laughing, some arguing, and conversing nearly every week—Kevin and Don have benefited from many thought partners along the way.

First of all, we would like to express our deep gratitude to Andrijana Bilbija and Amanda Banh, who started as student interns and turned into exceptional contributing authors due to their great minds, golden hearts, and total dedication to this project. This book would never have been written without their hard work and many invaluable contributions. Thank you both so much.

Nearly 20 interns in total have been involved in this project at varying points, most of them (including Amanda and Andrijana) recruited as undergraduates from Princeton University, Don's alma mater. Some helped with research; others wrote preliminary drafts of key sections. We are indebted to all of them for their wonderful efforts: Mckenna Brownell, Rebecca Cao, Sarah Drapkin, Julia Ilhardt, Katya Kopach, Violet Mamur, Maia Materman, Evelyn Moradian, Jennifer No, Jinn Park, Remy Reya, Jiyoun Roh, Claire Silberman, Grady Trexler, Ayame

Whitfield, and Hana Widerman. Each of you gave this project tremendous energy and life.

There are many other friends and colleagues who have offered their thoughtful feedback on early chapter drafts and outlines, including Paul Muniz, Sarah Hurwitz, Andrea Palmer, Michele Cantos, Katie Gee Salisbury, Martha Lawrence, William Sweeney, Louis Tse, Ji Hea Kim, and Myles Cohen. All four of us are deeply grateful for your sound guidance and wisdom.

We are particularly grateful to all our courageous interviewees: Elizabeth, Gabe and Lainie, Jennifer, Rand, Ray, Tom, Linda, and Johnny. And to those whose stories helped guide this project: Uncle Mark, Jeffrey, Ronnie, Joseph, Timothy, and many others. Your words and journeys underpin this entire book. Thank you so much for honoring us all with your stories.

Our publisher, North Atlantic Books, surpassed our lofty expectations. Shayna Keyles, Janelle Ludowise, Susan Bumps, Bevin Donahue, Julia Sadowski, Gabby Cazares-Lopez, Sariah Jimenez, and Drew Cavanaugh have been especially helpful throughout, offering terrific suggestions and support. We appreciate you and all of your colleagues at NAB for your skillful collaboration, and for believing in us.

The dedicated staff and global volunteer community at Miracle Messages have also been extremely gracious in helping us connect with our unhoused interviewees, offering us their time and energy, and showing us by example that we can each play a role in ending homelessness in America. Kevin could not ask for a better team, board, and supporters, including Colette Lay, Madeline Mazzocchi, Gabby Cordell, John Ma, Jenni Taylor, Nelly Stastny, Mark Askins, Rosalie Silva, Ashley Dockendorf, Jen McClure, Jim Olson, Melissa Gregory, Scott Layne, Kim Lynch, Julia Ip, Jessica Donig, Gloria Duffy, Darwyn Metzger, Barry Brown, Amanda Weitman, Ross Boucher, Kari and Philip Kaplan, Mark Donig, Natalie Oveyssi, Beth Attebery, Nathan Diaz, Brandon Salesberry, Andy Robbins, Adrian Schurr and team at Google.org, Justin Baldoni, Rich Havard, Steve Sarowitz and team at Wayfarer, Ben Henwood, Gisele Corletto, Amy Stein, Steve Quezada and team at the USC Suzanne Dworak-Peck School of Social Work, Katrina Van Gasse and team at AidKit, Craig Walker and team at Dialpad, and so many others. Thank you so much for inspiring us every day.

. Finally, Kevin and Don would like to express their deepest gratitude for their families and significant others. Kris Adler is the best brother Kevin could have ever asked for—I am so proud of you. Paul Adler, Kevin's dad, taught him that true masculinity is synonymous with emotional honesty and the courage to be vulnerable—I am so grateful for you. Joan Farrington, Kevin's mom, was the strongest and kindest person Kevin ever knew—I miss you everyday. Tajáh Tubbs, Kevin's wife and an emergency medicine physician, has offered invaluable insights, perspective, and prayer at critical moments in writing this book, and unconditional love to Kevin since they first met in the early months of the pandemic—you are the greatest blessing in my life, and I love you with all my heart. And Don's wife, Lynn, has reviewed many chapters and provided excellent feedback; she has also continued to be his support and inspiration throughout—thank you, Love.

Recommended Media

Books

Evicted by Matthew Desmond

The New Jim Crow by Michelle Alexander

No House to Call My Home: Love, Family, and Other Transgressions by Ryan Berg

Homelessness Is a Housing Problem by Gregg Colburn and Clayton Page Aldern

Golden Gates: The Housing Crisis and a Reckoning for the American Dream by Conor Dougherty

No Room of Her Own: Women's Stories of Homelessness, Life, Death & Resistance by Desiree Hellegers

Profit and Punishment: How America Criminalizes the Poor in the Name of Justice by Tony Messenger

Housing First: Ending Homelessness, Transforming Systems, and Changing Lives by Deborah Padgett, Benjamin Henwood, and Sam Tsemberis

Journeys Out of Homelessness: The Voices of Lived Experience by Jamie Rife and Donald Burnes

The Color of Law by Richard Rothstein

In the Midst of Plenty: Homelessness and What to Do about It by Marybeth Shinn and Jill Khadduri

No Way Home: The Crisis of Homelessness and How to Fix It with Intelligence and Humanity by Wayne Winegarden

Documentaries and Videos

The Invisible Class (screening requests available on www.theinvisible class.com/)

Lead Me Home (available on Netflix)

American Street Kid (available on YouTube)

Under the Bridge: The Criminalization of Homelessness (available on YouTube)

America's Hidden Homeless: Invisible People on the Streets (available on YouTube)

* * *

Explore the many TED and TEDx talks that touch on homelessness, including Kevin's "Don't Be a Stranger" (www.ted.com/talks/kevin_f _adler_don_t_be_a_stranger) and Don's "Ending Homelessness: Why Aren't We There Yet" (www.youtube.com/watch?v=SLEIPEzN40Y)

Notes

Preface

1 That is, until a high-level executive at GoPro emailed me threatening a cease and desist and potential legal action—gotta love corporate social responsibility—but that's a story for another time.

2 For what it's worth, not a single camera was lost or stolen by one of the homeless autobiographers, a question that I often received, rather tellingly. The only incident I am aware of was when one participant was attacked on the streets shortly after wearing the camera. He and I concluded that someone had spotted the camera around his chest and tried to steal it—a reminder of the significant dangers our unhoused neighbors face each day. Fortunately, he was fine. I discontinued the project shortly thereafter.

Introduction

1 Tanya de Sousa et al., "The 2022 Annual Homeless Assessment Report (AHAR) to Congress, Part 1: Point-in-Time Estimates of Homelessness," US Department of Housing and Urban Development, December 2022, www.huduser.gov/portal/sites/default/files/pdf/2022-AHAR-Part-1.pdf.

2 The PIT count is a one-night snapshot of sheltered and unsheltered people experiencing homelessness that occurs in January in cities across the United States, usually involving volunteers with clipboards canvassing neighborhoods to try to count and survey each person experiencing homelessness one by one.

3 "Homelessness in America: Overview of Data and Causes," National Law Center on Homelessness and Poverty, January 2015, https://homelesslaw.org/wp-content/uploads/2018/10/Homeless_Stats_Fact_Sheet.pdf.

4 A recent report from the metro Denver Continuum of Care suggests that the total number of different people experiencing homelessness over the course of a year, based on people accessing services and reported in the Homelessness Management Information System, is about five times the number reported in its PIT count. (Metro Denver Homelessness Initiative, "State of Homelessness: 2020 Report," 7)

5 "National Overview," National Center for Homelessness Education, https://profiles.nche.seiservices.com/consolidatedstateprofile.aspx.

6 Eric Gartland, "Hidden Housing Instability: 3.7 Million People Live in Doubled-Up Households," Center on Budget and Policy Priorities, September 6, 2022, www.cbpp.org/blog/hidden-housing-instability-37-million-people-live-in-doubled-up-households.

7 de Sousa et al., "2022 Annual Homeless Assessment Report."

8 "LGBTQ+ Youth Homelessness," National Network for Youth, 2022, https://nn4youth.org/lgbtq-homeless-youth/.

9 Jeff Olivet, "Inequity Is All Too Clear in Chicago," US Interagency Council on Homelessness Newsletter, December 8, 2022, www.usich.gov/news/inequity-is-all-too-clear-in-chicago-usich-visits-illinois; Jeff Olivet et al., "SPARC Phase One Study Findings," Center for Social Innovation, March 2018, https://c4innovates.com/wp-content/uploads/2019/03/SPARC-Phase-1-Findings-March-2018.pdf.

10 Bill Pitkin, "Homelessness Is a Housing and Racism Problem," Housing Matters: The Urban Institute, May 11, 2022, https://housingmatters.urban.org/articles/homelessness-housing-and-racism-problem.

11 "Report of the Economic Well-Being of U.S. Households," Board of Governors of the Federal Reserve System, 2022, www.federalreserve.gov/publications/2022-economic-well-being-of-us-households-in-2021-dealing-with-unexpected-expenses.htm.

12 Jeffrey Horne, "From Rags to Riches! (Everyone Got a Story to Tell)!" IMDbPro, November 25, 2014, www.imdb.com/list/ls071882028/.

13 Fannie Mae, "Homelessness in America: Americans' Perceptions, Attitudes and Knowledge," Gallup, November 2007, https://shnny.org/uploads/2007_Gallup_Poll.pdf.

14 "Poll Reveals Strong Bipartisan Support for Action on Housing Affordability," National Low Income Housing Coalition, September 20, 2021,
   https://nlihc.org/resource/poll-reveals-strong-bipartisan-support-action
   -housing-affordability.

15 "Public Opinion Polling on Housing Affordability and Policy in June/
   July 2021," Opportunity Starts at Home, 2021, www.opportunity
   home.org/wp-content/uploads/2021/09/Tarrance-NLIHC-Poll-Fact
   -Sheet.pdf.

16 Maxine Waters, "Preface: Out of Reach for Too Long—Why We Must
   Continue to Fight for Equity in Housing," in "Out of Reach: The High
   Cost of Housing," National Low Income Housing Coalition, July 28,
   2022, https://nlihc.org/sites/default/files/oor/2022/OOR_2022_Mini
   -Book.pdf.

17 See, for example, Gregg Colburn and Clayton Page Aldern, *Homelessness Is a Housing Problem: How Structural Factors Explain US Patterns*
   (Oakland: University of California Press, 2022).

18 Housing First is based on the notion that unhoused people need to
   get into housing before addressing other issues, such as substance
   addiction or mental illness. This is in marked contrast to the earlier continuum of care model that provided housing at the end of
   successful treatment of these other issues. Quoted in: Cynthia Grif-
   fith, "New Study Shows the Biggest Threat to Homeless People Is
   Your Misguided Opinion," Invisible People, July 8, 2022, http://bit
   .ly/3VlTnbl.

19 Chris Herring, "Complaint-Oriented Policing: Regulating Homelessness
   in Public Space," *American Sociological Review* 84, no. 5 (September 5,
   2019), https://doi.org/10.1177/0003122419872671.

20 See, for example, Thidarat Phoosit and Emily Fromke, "Loving
   Our Neighbors Experiencing Homelessness," Shared Justice, September 9, 2022, www.sharedjustice.org/most-recent/2022/9/9/loving
   -our-neighbors-experiencing-homelessness.

21 This critique of "we, as a society" is not meant to single out the family
   members and friends of people experiencing homelessness, who sometimes have to make the difficult decision to cut off a loved one. As
   Kevin and the Miracle Messages team say in their outreach, "Sometimes, family is part of the problem, not part of the solution." Abuse
   and trust violations can occur in either direction, regardless of housing
   status.

22 Christopher Herring, "Cruel Streets: Criminalizing Homelessness in San Francisco," PhD diss., University of California, Berkeley, 2020, https://escholarship.org/uc/item/39k7400g.

23 Jennifer Wolch and Michael Dear, *Malign Neglect: Homelessness in an American City* (San Francisco: Jossey-Bass, 1993).

24 Erika Bolstad, "Prompted by Pandemic, Some States Buy Hotels for the Homeless," Pew Charitable Trusts, December 4, 2020, www .pewtrusts.org/en/research-and-analysis/blogs/stateline/2020/12/04 /prompted-by-pandemic-some-states-buy-hotels-for-the-homeless.

25 Conversation with James Ginsburg, the director of a drug and alcohol treatment center for people experiencing homelessness in Colorado, February 12, 2021.

26 Julia Ip, Alison Peart, and Lei Nguyen, "Miracle Money Proof-of-Concept Program Evaluation," Miracle Messages, 2022, https:// static1.squarespace.com/static/5e98c388f5b32f0d7b5e23f3/t/61c d46348e186f78e90f59e9/1640842812353/Miracle+Money+ Program+Evaluation.pdf.

Chapter 1: Relational Poverty

1 This estimate is based on Kevin's conversations with over 1,000 individuals experiencing homelessness in the San Francisco Bay Area between 2013 and 2023 and corroborated by numerous homeless surveys, including "Santa Clara County Homeless Census and Survey: Comprehensive Report, 2019," Santa Clara County, 2019, https://osh .sccgov.org/sites/g/files/exjcpb671/files/2019%20SCC%20Homeless%20 Census%20and%20Survey%20Report.pdf, and the 2019 LAHSA Adult Demographic Survey, linked here: "Homelessness and Employment," Homelessness Policy Research Institute, August 2020, https:// socialinnovation.usc.edu/wp-content/uploads/2020/08/Homelessness -and-Employment.pdf.

2 Gregg Colburn and Clayton Page Aldern, *Homelessness Is a Housing Problem: How Structural Factors Explain U.S. Patterns* (Oakland: University of California Press, 2022), 51.

3 Stephen W. Hwang, Maritt J. Kirst, Shirley Chiu, George Tolomiczenko, Alex Kiss, Laura Cowan, and Wendy Levinson, "Multidimensional Social Support and the Health of Homeless Individuals," *Journal of Urban Health* 86, no. 5 (2009): 791–803.

4 A successful shelter exit happens when a client verifiably moves into stable housing, as opposed to returning to the streets or an unknown outcome through a denial of service, end of a time-limited stay, or client choice. The vast majority of reunifications occurred through the City's Homeward Bound one-way bus ticket program. See slide 13 at "Embarcadero SAFE Navigation Center," San Francisco Department of Homelessness and Supportive Housing, Community Meeting, April 3, 2019, www.rinconhillsf.org/wp-content/uploads/2019/04/SWL330-Community-presentation-4.3.19-FINAL.pdf.

5 "Housing First, 2021," Homeless Hub, www.homelesshub.ca/solutions/housing-accommodation-and-supports/housing-first.

6 Nels Anderson, *The Hobo: The Sociology of the Homeless Man* (Chicago: University of Chicago Press, 1923).

7 Robert Putnam, *Bowling Alone: The Collapse and Revival of American Community* (New York: Simon & Schuster, 2000).

8 Pierre Bourdieu, "The Forms of Capital," in *The Handbook for Theory and Research for the Sociology of Education,* ed. J. Richardson (Westport, CT: Greenwood, 1986), 243.

9 "Economic Well-Being of U.S. Households," Federal Reserve.

10 584,000 total people experiencing homelessness from 2020 Point-in Time survey, "Homeless Statistics by State," www.usich.gov/tools-for-action/2020-point-in-time-count/, 1 × 4.5 (shift from point-in time to annual) + 1,386,000 public school students experiencing homelessness in 2018–19 school year, "Key Findings of 2018–2019 Public School Data on Children and Youth Homelessness."

11 Matthew Desmond, "Disposable Ties and the Urban Poor," *American Journal of Sociology* 117, no. 5 (March 2012): 1295–1335, https://scholar.harvard.edu/files/mdesmond/files/desmond.disposableties.ajs_.pdf.

12 Mark S. Granovetter, "The Strength of Weak Ties," *American Journal of Sociology* 78, no. 6 (May 1973), https://snap.stanford.edu/class/cs224w-readings/granovetter73weakties.pdf.

13 Timothy Carney, *Alienated America: Why Some Places Thrive While Others Collapse* (New York: Harper Collins, 2019), 84–85; Claire Cain Miller, Josh Katz, Francesca Paris, and Aatish Bhatia, "Vast New Study Shows a Key to Reducing Poverty: More Friendships Between Rich and Poor," *New York Times,* August 1, 2022, https://www.nytimes.com/interactive/2022/08/01/upshot/rich-poor-friendships.html.

14 "Bonding social capital is within a group or community whereas bridging social capital is between social groups, social class, race, religion or other important sociodemographic or socioeconomic characteristics." (www .socialcapitalresearch.com/difference-bonding-bridging-social-capital/)

15 Raj Chetty, quoted in David Leonhardt, "'Friending Bias': A Large New Study Offers Clues about How Lower-Income Children Can Rise up the Economic Ladder," *New York Times*, August 1, 2022, www.nytimes .com/2022/08/01/briefing/economic-ladder-rich-poor-americans.html.

16 Julianne Holt-Lunstad, Timothy B. Smith, Mark Baker, Tyler Harris, and David Stephenson, "Loneliness and Social Isolation as Risk Factors for Mortality: A Meta-analytic Review," *Perspectives on Psychological Science* 10, no. 2 (2015): 227–37.

17 Margot Kushel, "Homelessness among Older Adults: An Emerging Crisis," *Generations* 44, no. 2 (2020): 1–7.

18 National Academies of Sciences, Engineering, and Medicine, *Social Isolation and Loneliness in Older Adults: Opportunities for the Health Care System* (Washington, DC: National Academies Press, 2020), https://doi.org/10.17226/25663.

19 Manfred E. Beutel, Eva M. Klein, Elmar Brähler, Iris Reiner, Claus Jünger, Matthias Michal, Jörg Wiltink et al., "Loneliness in the General Population: Prevalence, Determinants and Relations to Mental Health," *BMC Psychiatry* 17, no. 1 (2017): 1–7; National Academies, *Social Isolation and Loneliness*.

20 Laurie A. Theeke, "Loneliness: A Significant Stressor That Requires Intervention," Robert Wood Johnson Foundation, August 4, 2014, www.rwjf.org/en/blog/2014/08/loneliness_a_signif.html.

21 Matthieu Lambert, "Relational Poverty—The Main Root Cause of Homelessness," 2018, www.linkedin.com/pulse/relational-poverty-main -root-cause-homelessness-matthieu-lambert/.

22 Jeff Olivet is currently the director of the United States Interagency Council on Homelessness. Marc Dones is currently the CEO of the King County Regional Homelessness Authority.

23 Olivet et al., "SPARC Phase One Study Findings," 12. See also Desmond, "Disposable Ties and the Urban Poor."

24 Olivet et al., "SPARC Phase One Study Findings."

25 "Who Are the Missing Missing?," Outpost for Hope, 2019–2020, www.outpostforhope.org/the-missing-missing.

26 The Lifeline Assistance Phone gives struggling low-income Americans free cell phones, voice minutes, texting, and limited data usage. ("What Is the Obamaphone?," Obamaphone, www.obamaphone.com/what-is-the-obama-phone)

27 Katie Deighton, "'I Sleep Outside of Google to Use the Wifi': SXSW through the Eyes of Austin's Homeless," The Drum, March 19, 2019, www.thedrum.com/news/2019/03/19/i-sleep-outside-google-use-the-wifi-sxsw-through-the-eyes-austin-s-homeless.

28 "Individuals' Right under HIPAA to Access Their Health Information, 45 CFR §164.524," US Department of Health and Human Services, January 23, 2020, www.hhs.gov/hipaa/for-professionals/privacy/guidance/access/index.html.

Chapter 2: Stigma, Stereotypes, and Shame

1 Bruce G. Link and Jo C. Phelan, "Conceptualizing Stigma," *Annual Review of Sociology* 27 (2001): 363–85, www.jstor.org/stable/2678626.

2 Erving Goffman, quoted in B. G. Link and J. C. Phelan, "Conceptualizing Stigma," 367.

3 Arlie Russell Hochschild, *Strangers in Their Own Land: Anger and Mourning on the American Right* (New York: New Press, 2016), 5.

4 Hochschild, *Strangers in Their Own Land*, xi.

5 "Transgender Rights II: Last Week Tonight with John Oliver (HBO)," YouTube, October 16, 2002, www.youtube.com/watch?v=Ns8NvPPHX5Y.

6 de Sousa et al., "2022 Annual Homeless Assessment Report."

7 Stacey Mosel, "Substance Abuse and Homelessness: Statistics and Rehab Treatment," American Addiction Centers, September 14, 2022, https://americanaddictioncenters.org/rehab-guide/homeless.

8 It is worth noting that these percentages are based on the relatively narrow definition of homelessness used by HUD. A broader definition of homelessness (which we have preferred in this book, such as one that includes those who are doubled- or tripled-up with loved ones, for instance) would result in lower proportions here. "Mental Illness and Homelessness," National Coalition for the Homeless, July, 2009, www.nationalhomeless.org/factsheets/Mental_Illness.pdf. See also "Homelessness

and Mental Illness: A Challenge to Our Society," Brain and Behavior Research Foundation, November 19, 2019, www.bbrfoundation.org /blog/homelessness-and-mental-illness-challenge-our-society.

9   Saul McLeod, "Fundamental Attribution Error," Simply Psychology, 2018, www.simplypsychology.org/fundamental-attribution.html.

10 Romeo Vitelli, "Why Is Homelessness So Stigmatized?," *Psychology Today*, June 5, 2021, www.psychologytoday.com/us/blog/media -spotlight/202106/why-is-homelessness-so-stigmatized.

11 David Conrad and Lori Young, *Homelessness and Housing Security in U.S. Culture: How Popular Culture and News Depict an American Challenge* (Washington, DC: Center for Media and Social Impact, September 2019).

12 Very rarely is the journey from *rags-to-housed-but-still-barely-getting-by*, so to speak, which might make for a less inspiring story but would be a much more accurate representation.

13 Beth Breeze and Jon Dean, "Pictures of Me: User Views on Their Representation in Homelessness Fundraising Appeals," *International Journal of Nonprofit and Voluntary Sector Marketing* 17, no. 2 (2012): 134.

14 M. L. Schuster, *Homeless Voices: Stigma, Space, and Social Media* (Washington, DC: Rowman & Littlefield, 2022), 25.

15 Elizabeth C. Pinel, "Stigma Consciousness: The Psychological Legacy of Social Stereotypes," *Journal of Personality and Social Psychology* 76, no. 1 (1999): 114–28, https://pubmed.ncbi.nlm.nih .gov/9972557/.

16 A. Farina, J. Allen, and B. B. Saul, "The Role of the Stigmatized Person in Affecting Social Relationships," *Journal of Personality* 36, no. 2 (1968), https://pubmed.ncbi.nlm.nih.gov/4232450/; B. G. Link et al., "A Modified Labeling Theory Approach to Mental Disorders: An Empirical Assessment," *American Sociological Review* 54, no. 3 (1989): 400–23, www.jstor.org/stable/2095613; E. R. Wright, W. P. Gronfein, and T. J. Owens, "Deinstitutionalization, Social Rejection, and the Self-Esteem of Former Mental Patients," *Journal of Health and Social Behavior* 41, no. 1 (2000): 68–90, https://pubmed.ncbi.nlm.nih .gov/10750323/; B. G. Link et al., "Public Conceptions of Mental Illness," *American Journal of Public Health* 89, no. 9 (1999), 1328–33, https://pubmed.ncbi.nlm.nih.gov/10474548/; B. G. Link, "Mental Patient Status, Work, and Income: An Examination of the Effects of a Psychiatric Label," *American Sociological Review* 47, no. 2 (1982),

202–15, https://pubmed.ncbi.nlm.nih.gov/7091929/; B. G. Link, F. T. Cullen, J. Frank, and J. F. Wozniak, "The Social Rejection of Former Mental Patients: Understanding Why Labels Matter," *American Journal of Sociology* 92, no. 6 (1987), 1461–1500, https://psycnet.apa.org /doi/10.1086/228672; S. Rosenfeld, "Labeling Mental Illness: The Effects of Received Services and Perceived Stigma on Life Satisfaction," *American Sociological Review* 62, no. 4(1997): 660–72, www.jstor .org/stable/2657432.

17 Jeffrey Olivet et al., "Racial Inequity and Homelessness: Findings from the SPARC Study," *Annals of the American Academy of Political and Social Science* 693, no. 1 (January 2021): 82–100, https://doi .org/10.1177/0002716221991040; Erin Vinoski Thomas and Chloe Vercruysse, "Homelessness among Individuals with Disabilities: Influential Factors and Scalable Solutions," JPHMP Direct, 2019, https:// jphmpdirect.com/2019/07/24/homelessness-among-individuals -with-disabilities/; Brodie Fraser et al., "LGBTIQ+ Homelessness: A Review of the Literature," *International Journal of Environmental Research and Public Health* 16, no. 15 (July 2019): 2677, https://doi .org/10.3390/ijerph16152677.

18 Emily Meanwell, "Profaning the Past to Salvage the Present: The Symbolically Reconstructed Pasts of Homeless Shelter Residents," *Symbolic Interaction* 36, no. 4 (November 2013), https://doi.org /10.1002/symb.79.

19 Isabel Wilkerson, *Caste: The Origins of Our Discontents* (New York: Random House, 2021).

20 Michelle Obama, *Becoming* (New York: Viking, 2018).

21 It bears mentioning that access to basic hygiene and sanitation is unimaginably scarce on the streets as well, which compounds the feeling of uncleanliness experienced by many of our unhoused neighbors.

22 Barb, "A Caring Adult: Barb's Journey," in *Journeys out of Homelessness: The Voices of Lived Experience,* Jamie Rife and Donald W. Burnes (Boulder, CO: Lynne Rienner, 2019), 25–26.

23 Kerri Tobin and Joseph Murphy, "The New Demographics of Homelessness," in *Ending Homelessness*, 35–36.

24 Taylor Orth and Carl Bialik, "Who Do Americans Blame for Homelessness," YouGov America, May 17, 2022, https://today.yougov .com/topics/politics/articles-reports/2022/05/17/american-attitudes -on-homelessness-poll.

25 Outside in America Team, "Bussed Out: How America Moves Its Home-
    less," *Guardian*, December 20, 2017, www.theguardian.com/us-news
    /ng-interactive/2017/dec/20/bussed-out-america-moves-homeless
    -people-country-study; Joe Winner, "Miami Is Planning to Build a
    'Homeless Island,'" ESPN Southwest Florida, August 19, 2022, https://
    espnswfl.com/listicle/miami-is-planning-to-build-a-homeless-island/.

Chapter 3: Exclusion

1   Stephanie Yang, "Social Experiment Caught on Video Shows the
    Homeless Have Become So Invisible, People Wouldn't Even Notice
    If They Walked by Their Own Families" (press release), Cision PR
    Web, April 24, 2014, http://www.prweb.com/releases/makethem
    visible/04/prweb11790851.htm.

2   Susan T. Fiske et al., "A Model of (Often Mixed) Stereotype Content:
    Competence and Warmth Respectively Follow from Perceived Status
    and Competition," *Journal of Personality and Social Psychology* 82,
    no. 6 (June 2002): 878, https://pubmed.ncbi.nlm.nih.gov/12051578/.

3   Amy J. C. Cuddy et al., "Stereotype Content Model across Cultures:
    Towards Universal Similarities and Some Differences," *British Journal
    of Social Psychology* 48, no. 1 (March 2009): 1–33, https://pubmed
    .ncbi.nlm.nih.gov/19178758/.

4   Lasana T. Harris and Susan T. Fiske, "Dehumanizing the Lowest of the
    Low: Neuroimaging Responses to Extreme Out-Groups," *Psycholog-
    ical Science* 17, no. 10 (October 2006): 847–53, https://pubmed.ncbi
    .nlm.nih.gov/17100784/.

5   Humans dehumanize many groups beyond just people experiencing
    homelessness, including groups that often overlap with homelessness.
    This includes people of different races, ethnicities, religions, sexual ori-
    entations, gender identities, nationalities, immigration statuses, physical
    and mental disabilities, and more. By overlooking our common humanity
    anywhere, we are more likely to tolerate global inequity, war, severe laws
    and punishments. We hope our readers will extrapolate the importance of
    recognizing our common humanity outside of homelessness, too.

6   René Girard and Charles Taylor, "Complementary Engagements with
    the Crisis of Modernity," in *The Palgrave Handbook of Mimetic Theory
    and Religion*, ed. J. Alison and W. Palaver (New York: Palgrave Macmil-
    lan, 2017), 335–42, https://doi.org/10.1057/978-1-137-53825-3_44.

7   Girard and Taylor, "Complementary Engagements."

8   Mark Napier and Jonathan Marks, "How Closely Related Are People to Each Other?," *Discover*, www.discovermagazine.com/planet-earth /how-closely-related-are-people-to-each-other.

9   In a 2018 talk at Full Circle Fund's UNITE!, an event connecting San Francisco Bay Area nonprofits with local funders and volunteers, long-time homeless advocate and nonprofit leader Del Seymour memorably said, "Have a passion for the people that really are struggling out there, our brothers and sisters. There's no planet called homelessness, where these people came down in a rocket ship and dropped here. They're our cousins, man. They're our brothers, they're our sisters, they're our neighbors."

10 Fiona Macrae, "Microsoft Proves You ARE Just Six Degrees of Separation from Anyone in the World," *Daily Mail*, August 4, 2008, www.dailymail .co.uk/sciencetech/article-1041077/Microsoft-proves-ARE-just-degrees -separation-world.html.

11 Lars Backstrom, Paolo Boldi, Marco Rosa, Johan Ugander, and Sebastiano Vigna, "Four Degrees of Separation," in *Proceedings of the 4th Annual ACM Web Science Conference* (New York: ACM, 2012), 33–42.

12 "Homelessness in America: Overview of Data and Causes," National Law Center on Homelessness and Poverty, January 2015, https://home lesslaw.org/wp-content/uploads/2018/10/Homeless_Stats_Fact_Sheet .pdf; "Student Homelessness in America: School Years 2017–18 to 2019– 20," National Center for Homelessness Education, January 1, 2021, https://nche.ed.gov/wp-content/uploads/2021/12/Student-Homeless ness-in-America-2021.pdf; Eric Gartland, "Hidden Housing Instability: 3.7 Million People Live in Doubled-Up Households," Center on Budget and Policy Priorities, September 6, 2022, www.cbpp.org/blog/hidden -housing-instability-37-million-people-live-in-doubled-up-households.

13 This is different from asking, "How many of you know someone who has experienced homelessness?" Many of us know someone who experienced homelessness in the past, but few of us know someone (or at least are aware that we know someone) who is currently without a home.

14 Katherine Levine Einstein, David M. Glick, and Maxwell Palmer, *Neighborhood Defenders* (Cambridge: Cambridge University Press, 2020).

15 Chris Herring, "The New Logics of Homeless Seclusion: Homeless Encampments in America's West Coast Cities," *City and Community* 13, no. 4 (December 2014), https://doi.org/10.1111/cico.12086.

16 "Beloved Community Village Evaluation: Final Report, October 2020," University of Denver Graduate School of Social Work, Center for Housing and Homelessness Research, October 2020, 54.

17 Tatiana Flowers, Tamara Chuang, and Brammhi Balarajan, "Denverites Worried Crime Would Accompany Safe Outdoor Spaces. Data Shows the Opposite Happened," *Colorado Sun*, October 24, 2022, https://coloradosun.com/2022/10/24/safe-outdoor-space/.

18 A national group based in Denver, called the Mindset Shifters, is attempting to dig into these issues and find ways to change anti-homeless attitudes and behaviors.

19 "Homeless in Los Angeles County, California," Los Angeles Almanac, http://www.laalmanac.com/social/so14.php.

20 Inyoung Kang, "Where Does California's Homeless Population Come From?," *New York Times*, November 6, 2019, www.nytimes .com/2019/11/06/us/homeless-population.html.

21 Kang, "Where Does California's Homeless Population."

22 Winnie Hu, "'Hostile Architecture': How Public Spaces Keep the Public Out," *New York Times*, November 8, 2019, www.nytimes .com/2019/11/08/nyregion/hostile-architecture-nyc.html.

23 "First National Study of State Laws Criminalizing Homelessness Released," National Homelessness Law Center, December 1, 2021, https://homelesslaw.org/first-national-study-of-state-laws-criminalizing -homelessness-released/.

24 Eric Tars, "Criminalization of Homelessness," National Homelessness Law Center, https://nlihc.org/sites/default/files/AG-2021/06-08 _Criminalization-of-Homelessness.pdf.

25 George Parampathu, "Anti-homeless Laws May Violate California's Equal Protection Doctrine," SCOCAblog, March 6, 2022, http://scocablog.com /anti-homeless-laws-may-violate-californias-equal-protection-doctrine.

Chapter 4: Paternalism

1 Austin Schempp, "Homeless Runner Raises $10,000 at San Francisco Half Marathon," *Runners World*, July 28, 2014, www.runners world.com/news/a20803630/homeless-runner-raises-10-000-at-san -francisco-half-marathon/.

2 See the section on confirmation bias and attribution bias in chapter 2.

3   "Has a Homeless Person Ever Refused Food You've Offered Them? If So, Did They Provide an Explanation?," Quora, www.quora.com /Has-a-homeless-person-ever-refused-food-youve-offered-them-If-so -did-they-provide-an-explanation/answer/Tanja-Miranda-2.

4   Howard M. Fillit, "Paternalism," Science Direct, www.sciencedirect .com/topics/medicine-and-dentistry/paternalism.

5   Generally speaking, in-demand items for people experiencing home-lessness include money, socks, underwear, toiletries, feminine hygiene products, warm clothing, pet food, and baby supplies.

6   Iain De Jong, *The Book on Ending Homelessness* (Victoria, BC: Friesen, 2019), 27.

7   "Young Homeless Man Shares Real Truth about Sleeping Rough in Cardiff, Wales," Invisible People, June 12, 2018, www.youtube .com/watch?v=TRRbCzZH_HY&t=407s.

8   "Homeless Man Returns Expensive Engagement Ring Accidentally Dropped in Change Cup," Radar, February 13, 2013, https://radar online.com/exclusives/2013/02/homeless-man-returns-engagement -ring/; Meena Hart Duerson, "Homeless Man Who Returned Ring Gets over $175K in Donations," *Today*, March 5, 2013, www.today.com /news/homeless-man-who-returned-ring-gets-over-175k-donations -1C8695127.

9   "Homeless Man Returns Accidental Donation," Local 3 News, February 18, 2013, www.local3news.com/homeless-man-returns-accidental -donation/article_ba8e859c-95a0-5c69-8c7c-f42abff9198b.html.

10   Multiple news stories made note that Harris was raised by his reverend grandfather, as if his upbringing by a clergyman provided the missing context for why a person experiencing homelessness acted in such an upstanding way.

11   Duerson, "Homeless Man Gets $175K."

12   Travis L. Dixon, "A Dangerous Distortion of Our Families," Color of Change, January 2018, https://colorofchange.org/dangerousdistortion/.

13   Steve Berg, "The Disturbing Realities of Homelessness and Violence," National Alliance to End Homelessness, January 24, 2022, https:// endhomelessness.org/blog/the-disturbing-realities-of-homelessness -and-violence/.

14   "Homelessness Myths and Facts," Washington State Dept of Commerce, December 8, 2016, www.commerce.wa.gov/wp-content/uploads /2016/12/hau-chg-mythsfacts-12-8-2016.pdf.

15 "Our Impact," Foundations for Social Change, June 2022, https://for socialchange.org/impact.

16 "Taking Bold Action on Homelessness, Foundations for Social Change: New Leaf Project, 2021, 3, https://static1.squarespace .com/static/5f07a92f21d34b403c788e05/t/624f36ebfd37700ce13c0 06b/1649358579199/2021_FSC_Statement_of_Impact_w_Expansion +(Public).pdf; Adele Peters, "What Happened after These Unhoused People Got Monthly $500 Checks? Two-Thirds Have Homes," *Fast Company*, February 2, 2022, www.fastcompany.com/90717489 /what-happened-after-these-unhoused-people-got-monthly-500 -checks-two-thirds-have-homes.

17 Six years to the day that Kevin helped facilitate Miracle Messages' first reunion, helping Jeffrey reconnect with his family after 22 years apart; Jeffrey's story is featured in chapter 1.

18 Ip, Peart, and Nguyen, "Proof-of-Concept Program Evaluation."

19 "Cutting out the Middle Men," *Economist*, November 4, 2010, www .economist.com/britain/2010/11/04/cutting-out-the-middle-men.

20 C. Evashwick, "Creating the Continuum of Care," *Health Matrix* 7, no. 1 (Spring 1989), https://pubmed.ncbi.nlm.nih.gov/10293297/.

21 P. Holley, "Kansas Wants to Ban Welfare Recipients from Seeing Movies, Getting Tattoos," *Chicago Tribune*, April 6, 2015, www.chicagotribune .com/nation-world/chi-kansas-welfare-20150406-story.html.

22 Lindsay Drane Amaral, "Why Trump's New Food Stamp Rule Is about Cruelty, Not Responsibility," *Washington Post*, January 3, 2020, www.washingtonpost.com/outlook/2020/01/03/why-donald-trumps -new-food-stamp-rule is about-cruelty-not responsibility/.

23 Caitlin Dewey, "Trump Wants to Slash Food Stamps and Replace Them with a 'Blue Apron-Type Program,'" *Washington Post*, February 12, 2018, www.washingtonpost.com/news/wonk/wp/2018/02/12 /trump-wants-to-slash-food-stamps-and-replace-them-with-a-blue -apron-type-program/.

24 Rahim Kurwa, "The New Man in the House Rules: How the Regulation of Housing Vouchers Turns Personal Bonds into Eviction Liabilities," *Housing Policy Debate* 30, no. 6 (August 2020): 1–24, https:// doi.org/10.1080/10511482.2020.1778056.

25 Kurwa, "New Man in the House Rules," 13.

26 Kurwa.

27 Serena Rice, "Our Perceptions about the 'Unworthy Poor' Haven't Changed," Talk Poverty, August 20, 2015, https://talkpoverty .org/2015/08/20/unworthy-poor.

28 For the first time, according to the 2020 PIT survey, there were more unsheltered individuals than there were individuals in shelters or transitional housing.

29 Heather Knight, "The City's Panhandlers Tell Their Own Stories," *San Francisco Chronicle,* October 26, 2013, www.sfgate.com/bayarea/article /The-city-s-panhandlers-tell-their-own-stories-4929388.php.

30 Wayne Schutsky, "Effectiveness of Panhandling Signs Doubted," *Scottsdale Progress,* June 17, 2019, www.scottsdale.org/news/effectiveness -of-panhandling-signs-doubted/article_06791052-8ef4-11e9-b920 -6711c7fad1c9.html.

31 James Andreoni, Justin M. Rao, and Hannah Trachtman, "Avoiding the Ask: A Field Experiment on Altruism, Empathy, and Charitable Giving," *Journal of Political Economy* 125, no. 3 (June 2017), https:// doi.org/10.1086/691703.

Chapter 5: Individualism

1   Alissa Quart, "Can We Put an End to America's Most Dangerous Myth?," *New York Times*, March 9, 2023, www.nytimes.com/2023/03/09/opinion /art-of-dependence.html.

2   Arnold Schwarzenegger, "Commencement and Graduation: Arnold Schwarzenegger—'None of Us Can Make It Alone,' University of Houston—2017," Speakola, May 12, 2017, https://speakola.com/grad /arnold-schwarzenegger-houston-2017.

3   Schwarzenegger, quoted in Jatinder Singh, "Arnold Schwarzenegger—'I Am Not a Self-Made Man,'" Lighthouse International Community, www.lighthousecommunity.global/post/arnold-schwarzenegger-i-am -not-a-self-made-man.

4   "One Woman's Journey from Homeless to Harvard," *Talk of the Nation*, National Public Radio, September 9, 2010, www.npr.org /2010/09/09/129753532/one-womans-journey-from-homeless-to

-harvard; "Madness in the Streets: Mental Illness, Homelessness and Criminal Behavior," Best MSW Programs, www.bestmswprograms .com/mental-illness-homelessness-criminal-behavior/.

5   "The Drug War Invades Our Homes," Uprooting the Drug War, https:// uprootingthedrugwar.org/housing/; Michelle Alexander, *The New Jim Crow: Mass Incarceration in the Age of Colorblindness,* Tenth Anniversary Edition (New York: The New Press, 2020); Kim Hopper, Ezra Susser and Sarah Conover, "Economies of Makeshift: Deindustrialization and Homelessness in New York City," *Urban Anthropology and Studies of Cultural Systems and World Economic Development* 14, no. 1/3 (Spring-Summer-Fall 1985), https://eportfolios.macaulay.cuny.edu /goldwyn17/files/2017/01/Economies-of-Makeshift-Hooper.pdf. For a review of many of these factors, see Alice S. Baum and Donald W. Burnes, *A Nation in Denial: The Truth about Homelessness* (Boulder, CO: Westview, 1993).

6   Leroy Pelton, "Getting What We Deserve," *Humanist,* July–August 2006, 15.

7   Pelton, "Getting What We Deserve," 15.

8   Pelton, 15.

9   Pelton, 17.

10 E. Ann Carson, "Prisoners in 2018," US Department of Justice, Bureau of Justice Statistics, Bulletin, April 2020.

11 Meghan E. Irons, "Researchers Expected 'Outrageously High' Discrimination against Black Renters. What They Found Was Worse Than Imagined," *Boston Globe,* July 1, 2020, www.boston globe.com/2020/07/01/metro/Blacks-voucher-holders-face-egregious -housing-discrimination-study-says.

12 Marianne Bertrand and Sendhil Mullainathan, "Are Emily and Greg More Employable Than Lakisha and Jamal? A Field Experiment on Labor Market Discrimination," NBER Working Paper Series, July 2003, https://www.nber.org/system/files/working_papers/w9873/w9873.pdf; "Employers' Replies to Racial Names," *National Bureau of Economic Research: The Digest,* no. 9, September 2003, www.nber.org/digest /sep03/employers-replies-racial-names.

13 Bryan Stevenson, *Just Mercy: A Story of Justice and Redemption* (New York: Spiegel and Grau–Random House, 2005).

Chapter 6: Housing

1   Elizabeth Softky, "The Seeds of Kwanza," *Los Angeles Times*, December 26, 1996, www.latimes.com/archives/la-xpm-1996-12-26-fo-12588 -story.html.

2   Chris Glynn and Alexander Casey, "Homelessness Rises Faster When Rent Exceeds a Third of Income," Zillow, December 18, 2018, www .zillow.com/research/homelessness-rent-affordability-22247/.

3   Emily Badger, "Whatever Happened to the Starter Home?," *New York Times*, September 25, 2022, www.nytimes.com/2022/09/25/upshot /starter-home-prices.html.

4   Public housing is a form of housing in which the property is usually owned by a government authority, either central or local. This is different from the housing voucher program, in which subsidies are provided to renters in units owned by private landlords.

5   "Public Housing Statistics," IProperty Management, May 9, 2022, https://ipropertymanagement.com/research/public-housing-statistics.

6   "Housing in the Seventies," US Department of Housing and Urban Development, 1974, www.huduser.gov/Publications/pdf/HUD-968.pdf.

7   Alex F. Schwartz, quoted in "Public Housing History," National Low Income Housing Coalition, October 17, 2019, https://nlihc .org/resource/public-housing-history.

8   Alexander, *New Jim Crow*, 57.

9   "Report: The War on Drugs Meets Housing," Drug Policy Alliance, February 4, 2021, https://uprootingthedrugwar.org/wp-content/uploads /2021/02/uprooting_report_PDF_housing_02.04.21.pdf.

10 Matthew Desmond, *Evicted: Poverty and Profit in the American City* (New York: Crown, 2017), 59.

11 D. Finger, "Public Housing in New Orleans Post Katrina: The Struggle for Housing as a Human Right," *Review of Black Political Economy* 38, no. 4 (2011): 327–37.

12 "The Distribution of Major Tax Expenditures in the Individual Income Tax System," Congressional Budget Office, May 2013. See also "Policy Basics: Federal Tax Expenditures," Center on Budget and Policy Priorities, December 8, 2020, www.cbpp.org/research/federal-tax/federal -tax-expenditures.

13 "Out of Reach," National Low Income Housing Coalition, 2022, https://nlihc.org/oor.

14 Andrew Aurand et al., "The GAP: The Shortage of Affordable Homes," National Low Income Housing Coalition, March 2021, https://nlihc .org/gap.

15 "Los Angeles, CA Rental Market Trends," RentCafe, July 2022, www .rentcafe.com/average-rent-market-trends/us/calos-angeles/.

16 Andrew Aurand, "The State of Affordable Housing for Renters with the Lowest Incomes," National Low Income Housing Coalition, February 23, 2022, https://housingmatters.urban.org/research-summary /state-affordable-housing-renters-lowest-incomes.

17 Will Fischer, Sonya Acosta, and Erik Gartland, "More Housing Vouchers: Most Important Step to Help More People Afford Stable Homes," Center on Budget and Policy Priorities, May 13, 2021, www.cbpp .org/research/housing/more-housing-vouchers-most-important-step-to -help-more-people-afford-stable-homes.

18 "An Assessment of Adams County's Efforts to Address Homelessness," Burnes Center on Poverty and Homelessness, University of Denver, 2016, http://www.adcogov.org/sites/default/files/Adams%20 Homelessness%20Assessment.

19 Quart, "America's Most Dangerous Myth."

20 Ben Kesling, "Thousands of Housing Vouchers for Homeless Veterans Go Unused," *Wall Street Journal,* January 23, 2020, www.wsj.com /articles/thousands-of-housing-vouchers-for-homeless-veterans-go -unused-11579780812.

21 Grace Elletson, "More Than $500,000 in Housing Vouchers Unused since 2017," VTDigger, December 9, 2019, https://vtdigger.org/2019/12/09 /more-than-500000-in-housing-vouchers-unused-since-2017/.

22 In Don's interview with Brenda Mascarenas, head of the voucher program for the Adams County, Colorado, housing authority (Maiker Housing), she indicated that only about 10% of their housing voucher fund could be used for new renters; 90% was used to keep existing renters in their apartments. (Don's interview with Brenda Mascarenas, August 2, 2022)

23 Desmond, *Evicted*, 303.

24 In the 1930s, maps of every metropolitan area in the US were color-coded by the Home Owners Loan Corporation, and later by the Federal

Housing Administration (FHA) before the same system was adopted by the Veterans Administration. The codes indicated where it was "safe" to insure mortgages, and neighborhoods with predominantly Black populations were colored red to tell appraisers that those areas were too "risky" in which to insure mortgages. Scott Beyer, "How the Government Destroyed Black Neighborhoods," Catalyst, April 2, 2020, https://catalyst.independent.org/2020/04/02/how-the-u-s-government -destroyed-black-neighborhoods/; Matthew Desmond and Mustafa Emirbayer, "What Is Racial Domination?," W. E. B. Du Bois Institute for African and African American Research, Du Bois Review 6, no. 2 (2009): 208, https://scholar.harvard.edu/files/mdesmond/files/what_is _racial_domination.pdf; Richard Rothstein, The Color of Law (New York: Liveright, 2017).

25 Ira Katznelson, When Affirmative Action Was White (New York: W. W. Norton, 2006), 128.

26 PBS, "RACE—The Power of an Illusion: Uncle Sam Lends a Hand," California Newsreel, 2003, www.pbs.org/race/000_About/002_06 _a-godeeper.htm.

27 Dedrick Asante-Muhammad, Jamie Buell, and Joshua Devine, "60% Black Homeownership: A Radical Goal for Black Wealth Development," National Community Reinvestment Coalition, March 2, 2021, https://ncrc.org/60-black-homeownership-a-radical -goal-for-black-wealth-development/.

28 Sara Rankin, "Hiding Homelessness: The Transcarceration of Homelessness," California Law Review, January 28, 2020.

29 Rankin, "Hiding Homelessness."

30 Rankin.

31 "Ending Chronic Homelessness in 2017," US Interagency Council on Homelessness, 2017, www.usich.gov/resources/uploads/asset _library/Ending_Chronic_Homelessness_in_2017.pdf; Manola Secaira, "Supporting Homeless Individuals: How Much Do We Spend?," Crosscut, August 31, 2018, https://crosscut.com/2018/08/supporting-homeless -individuals-how-much-do-we-spend.

32 Dennis Culhane, Stephen Metraux, and Trevor Hadley, "Public Service Reductions Associated with Placement of Homeless Persons with Severe Mental Illness in Supportive Housing," Housing Policy Debate 13, no. 1 (January 1, 2002), https://shnny.org/uploads/The _Culhane_Report.pdf.

33 "Myths about Homelessness," *Calgary Homeless Foundation*, 2020, www.calgaryhomeless.com/discover-learn/learn-about-homelessness/homelessness-in-calgary/myths-about-homelessness/.

34 "Homelessness Makes You Sick," *Health Care for the Homeless*, www.hchmd.org/homelessness-makes-you-sick.

35 Anna Gorman and Harriet Blair Rowan, "The Homeless Are Dying in Record Numbers on the Streets of L.A.," Kaiser Health News, April 24, 2019, https://khn.org/news/the-homeless-are-dying-in-record-numbers-on-the-streets-of-l-a/.

36 Maureen Stanley, "1900–2000: Changes in Life Expectancy in the United States," Senior Living, July 5, 2022, www.seniorliving.org/history/1900-2000-changes-life-expectancy-united-states/.

37 Sami Adler, "How Much Would It Cost to End Homelessness in America?," Global Giving, March 1, 2021, www.globalgiving.org/learn/how-much-would-it-cost-to-end-homelessness-in-america/.

38 For instance, "the median time for securing approval to build in San Francisco is 627 days—which puts 50% of projects at risk of losing funding due to delays." Bilal Mahmoud, "87 Permits, 1,000 Days of Meetings and $500,000 in Fees: How Bureaucracy Fuels S.F.'s Housing Crisis," *San Francisco Chronicle*, March 11, 2023, www.sfchronicle.com/opinion/openforum/article/sf-housing-development-red-tape-17815725.php.

39 "Project Homekey," County of San Mateo, www.smcgov.org/project-homekey.

Chapter 7: Work, Wages, and Wealth

1 Eli Wolfe, "San Jose: The Second Most Expensive Place to Rent in the Country," San Jose Spotlight, July 14, 2021, https://sanjosespotlight.com/san-jose-the-second-most-expensive-place-to-rent-in-the-country/.

2 Katie Honan, "Homeless Shelter Residents Booed, Told to 'Get a Job' at Queens Protest," DNA Info, July 1, 2014, www.dnainfo.com/new-york/20140701/elmhurst/homeless-shelter-residents-booed-told-get-job-at-queens-protest/.

3 Bruce Meyer, Angela Wyse, Alexa Grunwaldt, Carla Medalia, and Derek Wu, "Learning about Homelessness Using Linked Survey and Administrative Data," Becker Friedman Institute at

the University of Chicago, June 23, 2021, https://bfi.uchicago.edu /insight/finding/learning-about-homelessness-using-linked-survey-and -administrative-data/.

4 Tobin and Murphy, "New Demographics of Homelessness," 35.

5 Smiljanic Stasha, "The State of Homelessness in the US—2022," Policy Advice, September 29, 2022, https://policyadvice.net/insurance /insights/homelessness-statistics/.

6 Tobin and Murphy, 35.

·7 "Homelessness and Employment," Homelessness Policy Research Institute, August, 2021, https://socialinnovation.usc.edu/wp-content /uploads/2020/08/Homelessness-and-Employment.pdf.

8 Lack of sleep, transportation challenges, lack of access to restrooms and laundry facilities, violence and trauma, belongings and sensitive documents getting lost or stolen, social stigma, and relational poverty, to name just a few.

9 "Overcoming Employment Barriers," National Alliance to End Homelessness, August 21, 2013, https://endhomelessness.org/resource/overcoming -employment-barriers/.

10 "How Much of the Cost of Living Is Covered by Minimum Wage?," Divvy, 2020, https://getdivvy.com/blog/minimum-wage-vs-living-wage/.

11 "CPI Inflation Calculator," US Bureau of Labor Statistics, https://data.bls .gov/cgi-bin/cpicalc.pl?cost1=1.60&year1=196811&year2=202302.

12 "After the longest period in history without an increase, the federal minimum wage today is worth 27% less than 13 years ago—and 40% less than in 1968." (Economic Policy Institute, July 20, 2022, www.epi.org /multimedia/after-the-longest-period-in-history-without-an-increase-the -federal-minimum-wage-today-is-worth-17-less-than-10-years-ago-and -31-less-than-in-1968/)

13 Economic Policy Institute, "Longest Period in History."

14 "How Increasing the Federal Minimum Wage Could Affect Employment and Family Income," Congressional Budget Office, August 18, 2022, www.cbo.gov/publication/55681.

15 "The Cost of Living," Divvy.

16 Kathryn J. Edin and H. Luke Shaefer, $2.00 a Day: Living on Almost Nothing in America (New York: Mariner Books, 2016), xvii.

17 "The State of Homelessness in America 2013," National Alliance to End Homelessness, https://b.3cdn.net/naeh/bb34a7e4cd84ee985c_3vm6r7 cjh.pdf.

18 Lawrence Mishel and Jori Kondra, "Wages for the Top 1% Skyrocketed 160% since 1979 While the Share of Wages for the Bottom 90% Shrunk," Economic Policy Institute, December 1, 2020, http://bit.ly /3NQYE8o.

19 Josh Bivens and Jori Kandra, "CEO Pay Has Skyrocketed 1,460% since 1978," Economic Policy Institute, October 4, 2022, http://bit .ly/3DWIq8Z.

20 Lawrence Mishel and Jori Kandra, "Wage Inequality Continued to Increase in 2020," Economic Policy Institute, December 13, 2021, www.epi.org/blog/wage-inequality-continued-to-increase-in-2020 -top-1-0-of-earners-see-wages-up-179-since-1979-while-share-of -wages-for-bottom-90-hits-new-low/.

21 Robert D. Putnam with Shaylyn Romney Garrett, *The Upswing: How America Came Together a Century Ago and How We Can Do It Again* (New York: Simon and Schuster Paperbacks, 2020), 40.

22 Marybeth Shinn and Jill Khadduri, *In the Midst of Plenty: Homelessness and What to Do About It* (Hoboken, NJ: Wiley Blackwell, 2020).

23 "Chart Book: Temporary Assistance for Needy Families (TANF) at 26," Center on Budget and Policy Priorities, August 4, 2022, www .cbpp.org/research/family-income-support/temporary-assistance -for-needy-families-tanf-at-26.

24 Gene Falk and Patrick A. Landers, "The Temporary Assistance for Needy Families (TANF) Block Grant: Responses to Frequently Asked Questions," Congressional Research Service, March 31, 2022, https:// sgp.fas.org/crs/misc/RL32760.pdf.

25 Or as an unconditional gift through a basic income pilot; more on that in chapter 12.

26 Robert Collinso, Ingrid Gould Ellen, and Jens Ludwig, "Low Income Housing Policy," National Bureau of Economic Research, April 2015, www.nber.org/papers/w21071.

27 Matthew Desmond, "How Homeownership Became the Engine of Inequality," *New York Times Magazine Section*, May 10, 2017, https://longform.org/posts/how-homeownership-became-the-engine -of-american-inequality.

28 Erica York, "Summary of the Latest Federal Income Tax Data, 2022 Update," Tax Foundation, January 20, 2022, http://bit.ly/3X2qgM7.

29 "The Distribution of Major Tax Expenditures in 2019," Congressional Budget Office, October 2021, www.cbo.gov/publication/57585.

30 Chuck Marr, Samantha Jacoby, Sam Washington, and George Fenton, "Asking Wealthiest Households to Pay Fairer Amount in Tax Would Help Fund a More Equitable Recovery," Center on Budget and Policy Priorities, April 22, 2021, www.cbpp.org/research/federal-tax/asking -wealthiest-households-to-pay-fairer-amount-in-tax-would-help -fund-a.

Chapter 8: Health Care

1   Molly MacDonald, "Having Cancer Should Not Make You Homeless," The ASCO Post, December 10, 2019, https://ascopost.com/issues /december-10-2019/having-cancer-should-not-make-you-homeless/.

2   Mario Sims et al., "Importance of Housing and Cardiovascular Health and Well-Being: A Scientific Statement from the American Heart Association," *Circulation* 13, no. 8 (July 15, 2020), https://doi.org/10.1161 /HCQ.0000000000000089.

3   Seena Fazel, John R. Geddes, and Margot Kushel, "The Health of Homeless People in High-Income Countries: Descriptive Epidemiology, Health Consequences, and Clinical and Policy Recommendations," *Lancet* 384, no. 9953 (2014): 1529–40, www.ncbi.nlm .nih.gov/pmc/articles/PMC4520328/.

4   J. Adams et al., "Hospitalized Younger: A Comparison of a National Sample of Homeless and Housed Inpatient Veterans," *Journal of Health Care for the Poor and Underserved* 18, no. 1 (2007): 173–84, https://doi.org/10.1353/hpu.2007.0000. See also Margot Kushel's work, https://profiles.ucsf.edu/margot.kushel.

5   Adams et al., "Hospitalized Younger"; "Healthy Aging in Action," National Prevention, Health Promotion, and Public Health Council, November, 2018, 46, www.cdc.gov/aging/pdf/healthy-aging-in -action508.pdf.

6   Fazel, Geddes, and Kushel, "Health of Homeless People."

7   "Building a Movement to End Homelessness: Remembering Those Lost to Homelessness," National Coalition for the Homeless, December 21, 2018, https://nationalhomeless.org/category/mortality/.

8   Eugene L. Birch and Christopher Silver, "One Hundred Years of City Planning's Enduring and Evolving Connections," *Journal of the American Planning Association* 75, no. 2 (March 28, 2009), https://doi .org/10.1080/01944360902777031.

9   Paul Muniz, "On the Relationship between Poverty Segregation and Homelessness in the American City and Suburb," *Socius* 7 (March 9, 2021), https://journals.sagepub.com/doi/full/10.1177/2378023121996871#bibr6-2378023121996871.

10 Janey Rountree, Nathan Hess, and Austin Lyke, "Health Conditions among Unsheltered Adults in the U.S.," California Policy Lab, October 2019, www.capolicylab.org/wp-content/uploads/2023/02/Health-Conditions-Among-Unsheltered-Adults-in-the-U.S..pdf.

11 Sarah E. Rowan et al., "Lower Prevalence of SARS-CoV-2 Infection among People Experiencing Homelessness Tested in Outdoor Encampments Compared with Overnight Shelters—Denver, Colorado, June–July, 2020," *Clinical Infectious Diseases* 75, no. 1 (January 18, 2022): e157–e164, https://pubmed.ncbi.nlm.nih.gov/35040947/.

12 "A Homeless Man's Story," in Alice S. Baum and Donald W. Burnes, *A Nation in Denial: The Truth about Homelessness* (Boulder, CO: Westview, 1993), 56–73.

13 Sarah Arnquist, "The Million Dollar (Homeless) Patient," USC Center for Health Journalism, https://centerforhealthjournalism.org/resources/lessons/million-dollar-homeless-patient. This story is much like "Million Dollar Murray"; see Malcolm Gladwell, "Million Dollar Murray: Why Problems Like Homelessness May Be Easier to Solve Than to Manage," *New Yorker*, February 5, 2006, 96.

14 Fazel et al. "Health of Homeless People."

15 Pauline Bartolone and Kaiser Health News, "Without This Housing, I'd Be Dead," California Public Radio, October 6, 2017, www.capradio.org/news/the-view-from-here/2017/10/06/place-and-privilege/without-this-housing-id-be-dead.

16 Andrew Franco, Jonathan Meldrum, and Christine Ngaruiya, "Identifying Homeless Population Needs in the Emergency Department Using Community-Based Participatory Research," *BMC Health Service Research* 21, no. 428 (2021), https://doi.org/10.1186/s12913-021-06426-z.

17 "Supportive Housing Reduces Homelessness-and Lowers Health Care Costs by Millions," Rand Corporation, June 27, 2018, www.rand.org/blog/rand-review/2018/06/supportive-housing-reduces-homelessness-and-lowers.html.

18 Rand, "Supportive Housing."

19 "New Survey Finds Large Number of People Skipping Necessary Medical Care Because of Cost," National Opinion Research Center, March 26, 2018, www.norc.org/NewsEventsPublications/PressReleases/Pages/survey-finds-large-number-of-people-skipping-necessary-medical-care-because-cost.aspx.

20 "Report on the Economic Well-Being of U.S. Households in 2021," Board of Governors of the Federal Reserve System, May 27, 2022, www.federalreserve.gov/publications/2022-economic-well-being-of-us-households-in-2021-executive-summary.htm.

21 "Hospital and Surgery Costs," Debt.org, October 12, 2021, www.debt.org/medical/hospital-surgery-costs/.

22 Bruce Y. Lee, "Most GoFundMe Campaigns for Medical Bills Fail, Less Than 12% Reach Goals," *Forbes,* February 5, 2022, www.forbes.com/sites/brucelee/2022/02/05/most-gofundme-campaigns-for-medical-bills-fail-less-than-12-reach-goals/.

23 Michelle Van Ryn et al., "The Impact of Racism on Clinician Cognition, Behavior, and Clinical Decision Making," *Du Bois Review* 8, no. 1 (April 15, 2011): 199–218, www.ncbi.nlm.nih.gov/pmc/articles/PMC3993983/.

24 "Diversity in Medicine: Facts and Figures 2019: Figure 18. Percentage of All Active Physicians by Race/Ethnicity," American Association of Medical Colleges, 2018, www.aamc.org/data-reports/workforce/interactive-data/figure-18-percentage-all-active-physicians-race/ethnicity-2018.

Chapter 9: Mental and Behavioral Health

1 "Mental Health Myths and Facts," MentalHealth.gov, www.mentalhealth.gov/basics/mental-health-myths-facts.

2 Tobin and Murphy, "New Demographics of Homelessness," 44.

3 Tobin and Murphy indicate earlier on that page that there are reports of considerable variation in estimates of mental illness among people experiencing homelessness, ranging from 20% to as high as 80%.

4 Ronald C. Kessler, Patricia Berglund, Olga Demler, Robert Jin, Kathleen R. Merikangas, and Ellen E. Walters, "Lifetime Prevalence and Age-of-Onset Distributions of DSM-IV Disorders in the National

Comorbidity Survey Replication," *Archives of General Psychiatry* 62, no. 6 (2005): 593–602.

5   Bridget F. Grant et al., "Epidemiology of DSM-5 Alcohol Use Disorder: Results from the National Epidemiologic Survey on Alcohol and Related Conditions III," *JAMA Psychiatry* 72, no. 8 (2015): 757–66.

6   Carol L. M. Caton, Carol Wilkins, and Jacquelyn Anderson, "People Who Experience Long-Term Homelessness: Characteristics and Interventions," *Toward Understanding Homelessness: The 2007 National Symposium* (vol. 4, p. 2), https://aspe.hhs.gov/reports/toward-under standing-homelessness-2007-national-symposium-homelessness -research-people-who-0.

7   Lauren R. Fryling, Peter Mazanec, and Robert M. Rodriguez, "Barriers to Homeless Persons Acquiring Health Insurance through the Affordable Care Act," *Journal of Emergency Medicine* 49, no. 5 (November 2015): 2, https://doi.org/10.1016/j.jemermed .2015.06.005.

8   Ehren Dohler, Peggy Bailey, Douglas Rice, and Hannah Katch, "Supportive Housing Helps Vulnerable People Live and Thrive in the Community," Center on Budget and Policy Priorities, May 31, 2016, www.cbpp.org/research/housing/supportive-housing-helps-vulnerable -people-live-and-thrive-in-the-community.

9   "Homeless Consumers with Chronic Mental Illness Have 32% Higher Health Costs Than Those in Supportive Housing," Open Minds, June 10, 2021, https://openminds.com/market-intelligence/news/those-with -chronic-illness-who-experienced-chronic-homelessness-have-a-28-7 -higher-average-health-cost-per-year-than-those-in-permanent-supportive -housing/.

10 E. Fuller Torrey, *American Psychosis: How the Federal Government Destroyed the Mental Illness Treatment System* (New York: Oxford University Press, 2014), 17.

11 Vic DiGravio, "The Last Bill JFK Signed—and the Mental Health Work Still Undone," WBUR, October 23, 2013, www.wbur.org/news /2013/10/23/community-mental-health-kennedy.

12 Torrey, *American Psychosis*, 117; Christopher G. Hudson, "Benchmarks for Needed Psychiatric Beds for the United States: A Test of a Predictive Analytics Model," *International Journal of Environmental Research and Public Health* 18, no. 22 (November 2021): 8, https:// doi.org/10.3390/ijerph182212205.

13 "Analytics Improving Behavioral Health: Trends in Psychiatric Inpatient Capacity, United States and Each State, 1970 to 2014," NRI, September 5, 2017, www.nri-inc.org/our-work/nri-reports/trends-in-psychiatric -inpatient-capacity-united-states-and-each-state-1970-to-2014/.

14 Torrey, *American Psychosis*, 130.

15 "Drug Treatment Beds for the Poor Are Disappearing in N.J.," NJ.com, June 6, 2016, www.nj.com/news/2016/06/drug_treatment _beds_for_the_poor_are_disappearing_in_nj.html.

16 NJ.com, "Drug Treatment Beds."

17 Torrey, *American Psychosis*, 102.

18 Susan Scutti, "ERs 'Flooded' with Mentally Ill Patients with No Place Else to Turn," CNN, January 4, 2019, www.cnn.com/2019/01/03 /health/er-mental-health-patients-eprise.

19 Torrey, *American Psychosis*, 123.

20 P. F. Mangano and G. Blasi, "Stuck on Skid Row: LA Should Do What Other Cities Are: Move the Homeless into Permanent Housing, and Stop Just Managing the Problem," *Los Angeles Times*, October 29, 2007, as referenced in Torrey, 124.

21 Mangano and Blasi, "Stuck on Skid Row."

22 Joseph P. Morrissey and Howard H. Goldman, "Care and Treatment of the Mentally Ill in the United States: Historical Developments and Reforms," *Annals of the American Academy of Political and Social Science* 484, no. 1 (1986): 12–27, https://doi.org/10.1177/000271628 6484001002. This appears to be the first use of the term.

23 Morrissey and Goldman, "Care and Treatment."

24 Torrey, *American Psychosis*, 117.

25 "Serious Mental Illness Prevalence in Jails and Prisons," Treatment Advocacy Center, September 2016, http://bit.ly/3Ek37Nw.

26 Tala Al-Rousan et al., "Inside the Nation's Largest Mental Health Institution: A Prevalence Study in a State Prison System," *BMC Public Health* 17, no. 1 (April 2017), 1, https://bmcpublichealth .biomedcentral.com/articles/10.1186/s12889-017-4257-0.

27 "National Guidelines for Behavioral Health Crisis Care: A Toolkit," US Department of Health and Human Services, Substance Abuse and Mental Health Service Administration, 2020, www.samhsa .gov/sites/default/files/national-guidelines-for-behavioral-health-crisis -care-02242020.pdf, 33.

28 E. Fuller Torrey, "How to Bring Sanity to Our Mental Health System," Heritage Foundation, December 19, 2011, www.heritage.org/health-care-reform/report/how-bring-sanity-our-mental-health-system.

29 Torrey, *American Psychosis*, 110.

30 Doris Fuller, H. Richard Lamb, Michael Biasotti, and John Snook, "Overlooked in the Undercounted," Treatment Advocacy Center, December 2015, www.treatmentadvocacycenter.org/storage/documents/overlooked-in-the-undercounted.pdf.

31 Fuller et al., "Overlooked in the Undercounted."

32 Torrey, *American Psychosis*, 108–13.

33 Torrey, 121–23.

34 Based on the HUD definition of the number of people experiencing homelessness on any given night.

35 Tobin and Murphy, "New Demographics of Homelessness," 44.

36 Travis P. Baggett et al., "Mortality among Homeless Adults in Boston: Shifts in Causes of Death over a 15-Year Period," *JAMA Internal Medicine* 173, no. 3 (2013): 189–95, www.ncbi.nlm.nih.gov/pmc/articles/PMC3713619/.

37 "Death Rate Maps and Graphs: Drug Overdose Deaths Remain High," Centers for Disease Control and Prevention, June 2, 2022, www.cdc.gov/drugoverdose/deaths/index.html.

38 Baggett et al., "Mortality among Homeless Adults in Boston."

39 An-Pyng Sun, "Helping Homeless Individuals with Co-occurring Disorders: The Four Components," *Social Work* 57, no. 1 (January 2012): 23–37, https://doi.org/10.1093/sw/swr008.

40 See Baum and Burnes, *Nation in Denial*.

41 "1 in 5 Incarcerated People Is Locked Up for a Drug Offense" (graphic), Prison Policy Initiative, 2022, www.prisonpolicy.org/graphs/pie2022_drugs.html.

42 "Criminal Justice DrugFacts," National Institute of Drug Addiction, National Institute of Health, June 2020, https://nida.nih.gov/publications/drugfacts/criminal-justice.

43 Bankole Johnson, *Addiction Medicine: Science and Practice*, 2nd ed. (New York: Elsevier, 2019), 899.

44 Suzanne Zerger et al., "Differential Experiences of Discrimination among Ethnoracially Diverse Persons Experiencing Mental Illness and

Homelessness," *BMC Psychiatry* 14, no. 1 (December 14, 2014), 353, https://bmclpsychiatry.biomedcentral.com/articles/10.1186/s12888-014 -0353-1.

45 Johann Hari et al., *Chasing the Scream: The First and Last Days of the War on Drugs* (New York: Bloomsbury, 2015).

Chapter 10: Criminal Justice

1 "Madness in the Streets: Mental Illness, Homelessness and Criminal Behavior," Best MSW Programs, www.bestmswprograms.com /mental-illness-homelessness-criminal-behavior/.

2 "Homelessness and the Criminal Justice System," Homeless Policy Research Institute, July 2020, https://socialinnovation.usc.edu/wp -content/uploads/2020/07/Criminal-Justice-Literature-Review -Draft-V7.pdf.

3 Sara Gillespie et al., "The First Step toward Breaking the Homelessness-Jail Cycle," Urban Institute, May 19, 2016, www.urban.org/urban-wire /first-step-toward-breaking-homelessness-jail-cycle.

4 "Five Charts That Explain the Homelessness-Jail Cycle—and How to Break It," Urban Institute, September 16, 2020, www.urban.org /features/five-charts-explain-homelessness-jail-cycle-and-how-break-it.

5 "Housing Not Handcuffs 2019: Ending the Criminalization of Homelessness in US Cities," National Law Center on Homelessness and Poverty, December 2019, https://homelesslaw.org/wp-content /uploads/2019/12/HOUSING-NOT-HANDCUFFS-2019-FINAL.pdf.

6 "'Criminalizing Kindness': US Woman Arrested for Feeding Homeless People Sues," *Guardian*, October 28, 2022, www.theguardian.com/us-news/2022 /oct/28/arizona-woman-arrested-homeless-people-criminalizing-kindess.

7 "Arrested Several Times for Feeding the Hungry, Champion of the Poor Arnold Abbott Dies at 94," CBS News, Miami, February 22, 2019, www .cbsnews.com/miami/news/arrested-several-times-for-feeding-the-hungry -champion-of-the-homeless-arnold-abbott-dies-at-94/; Bob Norman, "Police Charge 90-Year-Old Man, 2 Pastors with Feeding Homeless," Local 10.com, November 3, 2014, www.local10.com/news/2014/11/04 /police-charge-90-year-old-man-2-pastors-with-feeding-homeless/.

8 "Housing Not Handcuffs 2019," 9.

9   Tars, "Criminalization of Homelessness."

10 Robert Davis, "Federal Court Rules Homeless People Have Property Rights," Invisible People, September 14, 2021, https://invisiblepeople .tv/federal-court-rules-homeless-people-have-property-rights/.

11 *Martin v. City of Boise*, 920 F. 3d 584, no. 15-35845 (2019), https:// scholar.google.com/scholar_case?case=10872202325524770184.

12 Sara K. Rankin, "Punishing Homelessness," *New Criminal Law Review* 22, no. 1 (2019), https://digitalcommons.law.seattleu.edu/faculty/810.

13 Sara Rankin, "Hiding Homelessness: The Transcarceration of Homelessness," *California Law Review* 109, no. 2 (2021), 562, https://digital commons.law.seattleu.edu/faculty/835.

14 Bailey Gray, Doug Smith, and Allison Franklin, "Return to Nowhere: The Revolving Door Between Incarceration and Homelessness," One Size Fits All Report Series, Texas Criminal Justice Coalition, February 2019.

15 Tobin and Murphy, "New Demographics of Homelessness," 44.

16 Bruce Western, *Homeward: Life in the Year After Prison* (New York: Russell Sage Foundation, 2018).

17 Dale Chappell, "New York's Prison-to-Shelter Pipeline Is Poor Option for Parolees," Prison Legal News, November 6, 2018, www.prison legalnews.org/news/2018/nov/6/new-yorks-prison-shelter-pipeline-poor -option-parolees/.

18 Jeremy Travis and Bruce Western, "The Era of Punitive Excess," Brennan Center, April 13, 2021, www.brennancenter.org/our-work /analysis-opinion/era-punitive-excess.

19 Barbara Oudekerk and Danielle Kaeble, "Probation and Parole in the United States, 2019," US Department of Justice, Office of Justice Programs, Bureau of Justice Statistics, July 2021, https://bjs .ojp.gov/sites/g/files/xyckuh236/files/media/document/ppus19.pdf.

20 "Growth in Mass Incarceration," The Sentencing Project, 2022, www .sentencingproject.org/research/.

21 Lucius Couloute, "Nowhere to Go: Homelessness among Formerly Incarcerated People," Prison Policy Initiative, August 2018, http://bit .ly/3EkTy15.

22 Roger Przybylski, "Adult Sex Offender Recidivism," US Department of Justice, SMART, https://smart.ojp.gov/somapi/chapter-5-adult-sex -offender-recidivism.

23 Alexander, *New Jim Crow*, 94.

24 Couloute, "Nowhere to Go."

25 Alexander, *New Jim Crow*, 57.

26 Nazish Dholakia, "How the U.S. Criminalizes Homelessness," Vera Institute of Justice, January 1, 2022, www.forbes.com/sites /forbeseq/2022/01/01/how-the-us-criminalizes-homelessness/.

27 Jugal K. Patel, Tim Arango, Anjali Singhvi, and Jon Huang, "Black, Homeless and Burdened by L.A.'s Legacy of Racism," *New York Times*, December 22, 2019, www.nytimes.com/interactive/2019/12 /22/us/los-angeles-homeless-black-residents.html.

28 Robin Smyton, "How Racial Segregation and Policing Intersect in America," Tufts Now, June 17, 2020, https://now.tufts.edu/2020/06/17 /how-racial-segregation-and-policing-intersect-america.

29 Tobin and Murphy, "New Demographics of Homelessness," 44.

Chapter 11: Youth Development

1 de Sousa et al., "2022 Annual Homeless Assessment Report."

2 National Center on Homeless Education, "National Overview."

3 "Student Homelessness in America: School Years 2017–18 to 2019–20," National Center for Homelessness Education, https:// nche.ed.gov/wp-content/uploads/2021/12/Student-Homelessness -in-America-2021.pdf.

4 Matthew Morton, Amy Dworsky, and Gina Miranda Samuels, "Missed Opportunities: Youth Homelessness in America. National Estimates," Chapin Hall at the University of Chicago, 2017. https://voicesofyouthcount.org/brief/national-estimates-of-youth -homelessness/.

5 P. M. Sullivan and J. F. Knutson, "Maltreatment and Disabilities: A Population-Based Epidemiological Study," *Child Abuse and Neglect* 24, no. 10 (2000): 1257–73, https://doi.org/10.1016 /s0145-2134(00)00190-3; "Homelessness and Adverse Childhood Experiences: The Health and Behavioral Health Consequences of Childhood Trauma," National Healthcare for the Homeless Council and the Bassuk Center, February 2019, https://nhchc.org/wp-content /uploads/2019/08/aces-fact-sheet.pdf.

6   C. Martijn and L. Sharpe, "Pathways to Youth Homelessness," *Social Science & Medicine* 62, no. 1 (January 2006): 1–12, https://pubmed .ncbi.nlm.nih.gov/15985321/.

7   Diane Santa Maria et al., "Drug Use Patterns and Predictors among Homeless Youth: Results of an Ecological Momentary Assessment," *American Journal of Drug and Alcohol Abuse* 44, no. 5 (2018), https:// doi.org/10.1080/00952990.2017.1407328.

8   M. N. Gattis and A. Larson, "Perceived Racial, Sexual Identity, and Homeless Status Related Discrimination among Black Adolescents and Young Adults Experiencing Homelessness: Relations with Depressive Symptoms and Suicidality," *American Journal of Orthopsychiatry* 86, no. 1 (2016): 79–90, https://doi.org/10.1037/ort0000096.

9   Fantasy T. Lozada, Tennisha N. Riley, Evandra Catherine, Deon W. Brown, "Black Emotions Matter: Understanding the Impact of Racial Oppression on Black Youth's Emotional Development," *Journal of Research on Adolescence* 32, no. 1 (March 2022): 13–33, https://doi .org/10.1111/jora.12699.

10 "LGBTQ+ Youth Homelessness," National Network for Youth, https:// nn4youth.org/lgbtq-homeless-youth/.

11 Caitlin Ryan et al., "Family Rejection as Predictor of Negative Health Outcomes in White and Latino Lesbian, Gay, and Bisexual Young Adults," *Pediatrics* 123, no. 1 (2009): 346–52, https://doi .org/10.1542/peds.2007-3524.

12 M. N. Gattis, "An Ecological Systems Comparison between Homeless Sexual Minority Youths and Homeless Heterosexual Youths," *Journal of Social Service Research* 39, no. 1 (January 1, 2013): 38–49, www .ncbi.nlm.nih.gov/pmc/articles/PMC3653327/.

13 Brodie Fraser, Nevil Pierse, Elinor Chisholm, and Hera Cook, "LGBTIQ+ Homelessness: A Review of the Literature," *International Journal of Environmental Research and Public Health* 16, no. 15 (August 16, 2019), www.ncbi.nlm.nih.gov/pmc/articles/PMC6695950/.

14 Janny S. Li and Lianne A. Urada, "Cycle of Perpetual Vulnerability for Women Facing Homelessness near an Urban Library in a Major U.S. Metropolitan Area," *International Journal of Environmental Research and Public Health* 17, no. 16 (August 2020), www.ncbi.nlm.nih.gov /pmc/articles/PMC7459588/.

15 Todd Lloyd and Ruth White, "HUD Releases FUP-FSS Demonstration to Help At-Risk Young Adults Transition to Adulthood," CSH Guest Blog, January 25, 2016, www.csh.org/2016/01/csh-guest-blog/.

16 "Foster Youth and Homelessness: What Are the Risk Factors?," National Alliance to End Homelessness, March 17, 2015, https://endhomeless ness.org/blog/foster kids and-homelessness-what-are-the-risk-factors/.

17 Janelle Blanco, "What Is Foster Care? Definition, History and Facts," Study.com, https://bit.ly/3t5W9pg.

18 J. C. McMillen et al., "Prevalence of Psychiatric Disorders among Older Youths in the Foster Care System," *Journal of the American Academy of Child and Adolescent Psychiatry* 44, no. 1 (2005), 88–95, https://doi.org/10.1097/01.chi.0000145806.24274.d2.

19 "International Educational Attainment," National Center for Educational Statistics, May 2022, https://nces.ed.gov/programs/coe/indicator_cac.asp#:~:text=During%20this%20period%2C%20the%20OECD,percentage%20points%20to%2047%20percent; "Older Youth Housing, Financial Literacy and Other Supports," National Conference of State Legislatures, www.ncsl.org/research/human-services/supports-older-youth.

20 For examples, see Jamie Rife and Don Burnes, *Journeys out of Homelessness*.

21 L. Heybach and W. Winter, "Improving Educational Services for Foster Children: An Advocate's Guide," Law Project of the Chicago Coalition for the Homeless and the Legal Assistance Foundation of Chicago, 1999.

22 S. J. Altshuler, "A Reveille for School Social Workers: Children in Foster Care Need Our Help!" *Social Work in Education* 19, no. 2 (1997), 121–27, https://doi.org/10.1093/cs/19.2.121; A. Zetlin, E. MacLeod, and C. Kimm, "Beginning Teacher Challenges Instructing Students Who Are in Foster Care," *Remedial and Special Education* 33, no. 1 (2012), https://doi.org/10.1177/0741932510362506.

23 "Child Welfare and Foster Care Statistics," Annie E. Casey Foundation, September 26, 2022, www.aecf.org/blog/child-welfare-and-foster -care-statistics.

24 P. J. Pecora, R. C. Kessler, J. Williams, K. O'Brien, A. C. Downs, D. English, and K. Holmes, "Improving Family Foster Care: Findings from the Northwest Foster Care Alumni Study, Seattle, WA," Casey Family Programs, 2005.

25 Rife and Burnes, *Journeys out of Homelessness.*

26 A. O'Higgins, J. Sebba, and F. Gardner, "What Are the Factors Associated with Educational Achievement for Children in Kinship or Foster Care: A Systematic Review," *Children and Youth Services Review* 79 (2017): 198–220, https://doi.org/10.1016/j .childyouth.2017.06.004.

27 W. W. Blome, "What Happens to Foster Kids: Educational Experiences of a Random Sample of Foster Care Youth and a Matched Group of Non-Foster Care Youth," *Child and Adolescent Social Work Journal* 14 (1997): 41–53, https://link.springer.com/article /10.1023/A:1024592813809.

28 E. V. Clemens, H. M. Helm, K. Myers, C. Thomas, and M. Tis, "The Voices of Youth Formerly in Foster Care: Perspectives on Educational Attainment Gaps," *Children and Youth Services Review* 79 (2017): 65–77, https://doi.org/10.1016/j.childyouth.2017.06.003.

29 "Beyond Suspensions," US Commission on Civil Rights, July 23, 2019, www.usccr.gov/files/pubs/2019/07-23-Beyond-Suspensions.pdf.

30 Donna St. George, "Study Shows Wide Varieties in Discipline Methods among Very Similar Schools," *Washington Post*, July 19, 2011, http://www.washingtonpost.com/local/education/study-exposes -some-some-myths-about-school-discipline/2011/07/18/gIQAV0s ZMI_story.html.

31 "School or the Streets, Crime and America's Dropout Crisis," Fight Crime: Invest in Kids, December 2016, https://alabamapartnershipfor children.org/wp-content/uploads/2016/12/School-or-the-Streets-Crime -and-Americas-Dropout-Crisis.pdf.

32 "International Educational Attainment," National Center for Educational Statistics.

33 Tobin and Murphy, "Demographics of Homelessness," 36.

34 "Civil Rights Data Collection: Data Snapshot (School Discipline)," US Department of Education, Office for Civil Rights, March 21, 2014, https://www2.ed.gov/about/offices/list/ocr/docs/crdc-discipline -snapshot.pdf.

35 German Lopez, "Black Kids Are Way More Likely to Be Punished in School Than White Kids, Study Finds," Vox, April 5, 2018, www.vox .com/identities/2018/4/5/17199810/school-discipline-race-racism-gao.

36 "Street Outreach Program Data Collection Project Final Report," Administration on Children, Youth and Families, Families and Youth Service Bureau, April 2016.

37 Chris Nelson, quoted in "Homelessness 101: Who, What, When, Where," Boulder Beat, August 23, 2022, https://boulderbeat.news /2022/08/23/homelessness-101-who-what-when-where/.

Chapter 12: Fixing Broken Systems

1 Trisha Thadani, "SF Has an Unprecedented $1.1 Billion to Spend on Homelessness. The Pressure Is On to Make a Difference," *San Francisco Chronicle*, July 15, 2021, www.sfchronicle.com/bayarea/article/S-F-has -an-unprecedented-1-1-billion-to-spend-16318448.php.

2 Adam Brinkley, "UN Report Calls Bay Area Homeless Crisis Human Rights Violation," Curbed San Francisco, October 26, 2018, https:// sf.curbed.com/2018/10/26/18028576/united-nations-rapporteur -homeless-farha-human-rights-violantion.

3 Brinkley, "Bay Area Homeless Crisis Human Rights Violation."

4 Megan Kelly, "Stevenson Counsels 'Proximity' to the Marginalized," The Heights for a Greater Boston College, October 14, 2019, www .bcheights.com/2019/10/14/stevenson-counsels-proximity-others/.

5 Fischer, Acosta, and Gartland, "More Housing Vouchers."

6 Amy Eskind, "These 3-D Printed Homes Cost Thousands Less and Are Being Built for the Homeless in Texas," *People*, December 13, 2019, https://people.com/human-interest/3d-printed-homes-for-homeless -community-first-village-austin/.

7 Tom Scalisi, "How Much Does It Cost to Build an Apartment Complex in 2022?," Levelset, July 28, 2022, www.levelset.com/blog/cost-to -build-an-apartment-complex/. Scalisi says the average cost per square foot in a large apartment complex across the US is $398. For an 800 sq ft apartment, that's slightly more than $300,000.

8 Lucas Marshall, "Container Craze: Are Shipping Container Houses Actually Cheaper?," One Key, November 3, 2021, https://onekey resources.milwaukeetool.com/en/are-shipping-container-homes -cheaper.

9   Krista Evans, "Tackling Homelessness with Tiny Houses: An Inventory of Tiny House Villages in the United States," *Professional Geographer* 72, no. 3 (2022): 360–70, https://doi.org/10:1080/00330124.2020.1744170.

10 "Oakland Calls Tuff Sheds a Success; First Village Removed as Lease Ends," KTVU Fox 2, January 29, 2019, www.ktvu.com/news/oakland-calls-tuff-sheds-a-success-first-village-removed-as-lease-ends.

11 See "Models and Best Practices: Community Land Trusts (CLTs)," Community-Wealth.org, https://community-wealth.org/strategies/panel/clts/models.html.

12 Solomon Greene and Jorge González-Hermoso, "How Communities Are Rethinking Zoning to Improve Housing Affordability and Access to Opportunity," Urban Institute, June 12, 2019, www.urban.org/urban-wire/how-communities-are-rethinking-zoning-improve-housing-affordability-and-access-opportunity.

13 Greene and González-Hermoso, "Rethinking Zoning."

14 M. Nolan Gray, "The Housing Revolution Is Coming," *Atlantic*, October 5, 2022, www.theatlantic.com/ideas/archive/2022/10/california-accessory-dwelling-units-legalization-yimby/671648/.

15 Eskind, "These 3-D Printed Homes."

16 "3D Printed Houses: What Are Their Pros and Cons?," OmniFab, 2022, www.omnifab.ph/blog/3d-printed-houses-what-are-their-pros-and-cons/.

17 "Public Housing Statistics," IProperty Management, May 9, 2022, https://ipropertymanagement.com/research/public-housing-statistics.

18 "Fiscal Year 2021 Budget in Brief," US Department of Housing and Urban Development, 2020, www.hud.gov/sites/dfiles/CFO/documents/BudgetinBrief_2020-02_06_Online.pdf.

19 "US: Budget Cuts Put Public Housing Tenants at Risk," Human Rights Watch, September 27, 2022, www.hrw.org/news/2022/09/27/us-budget-cuts-put-public-housing-tenants-risk.

20 Waters, "Out of Reach for Too Long."

21 "Low Income Housing Tax Credit (LIHTC)," US Department of Housing and Urban Development, www.huduser.gov/portal/datasets/lihtc.html.

22 "Social Networks and Getting a Job," Mark Granovetter, Stanford Center on Poverty and Inequality, YouTube, November 16, 2016, www.youtube.com/watch?v=g3bBajcR5fE.

23 "Scattered Site Permanent Supportive Housing as an Effective Solution to End Homelessness," Orange County United Way, https://unitedtoend homelessness.org/blog/scattered-site-permanent-supportive-housing -as-an-effective-solution-to-end-homelessness/.

24 James Hogan, "Scattered-Site Housing: Characteristics and Consequences," US Department of Housing and Urban Development, September 1996, www.huduser.gov/publications/pdf/scattered_site _housing.pdf.

25 Safe Parking LA, https://safeparkingla.org.

26 Jessica Guynn, "'Hidden Homeless Crisis': After Losing Jobs and Homes, More People Are Living in Cars and RVs and It's Getting Worse," *USA Today*, February 15, 2021, www.usatoday.com/story/money/2021/02 /12/covid-unemployment-layoffs-foreclosure-eviction-homeless-car -rv/6713901002/.

27 "Housing First," Canadian Observatory on Homelessness, 2021, www .homelesshub.ca/solutions/housing-accommodation-and-supports /housing-first.

28 Clayton Call and William Marble, "Where Self-Interest Trumps Ideology: Liberal Homeowners and Local Opposition to Housing Development," *Journal of Politics* 83, no. 4 (October 2021), https://doi .org/10.1086/711717.

29 Matthew Desmond, *Poverty, by America* (New York: Crown, 2023), 115.

30 Conor Dougherty, *Golden Gates: The Housing Crisis and a Reckoning for the American Dream* (New York: Penguin Books, 2021).

31 "San Francisco Homeless Count and Survey," Applied Survey Research, https://hsh.sfgov.org/wp-content/uploads/2022/08/2022-PIT-Count -Report-San-Francisco-Updated-8.19.22.pdf.

32 Shinn and Khadduri, *In the Midst of Plenty*, 130.

33 Shinn and Khadduri, 126.

34 Don's interview with Cathy Blair, a landlord recruiter for the city of Aurora, Colorado, November 23, 2022.

35 "Segregation Still Blights the Lives of African Americans," *Economist*, July 9, 2020, www.economist.com/briefing/2020/07/09/segregation-still -blights-the-lives-of-african-americans.

36 Christine Smith, "Why Economists Don't Like the Mortgage Interest Deduction," Open Vault Blog by the Federal Reserve Bank of St. Louis, May 8, 2018, www.stlouisfed.org/open-vault/2018/may/why-economists -dont-like-mortgage-interest-deduction.

37 "Leading Lobbying Spenders in the United States in 2021," Statista, www .statista.com/statistics/257344/top-lobbying-spenders-in-the-us/#:~: text=In%202021%2C%20the%20top%20lobbying,of%2066 .41%20million%20U.S.%20dollars.

38 Chuck Marr et al., "Year-End Tax Policy Priority: Expand the Child Tax Credit for the 19 Million Children Who Receive Less Than the Full Credit," Center for Budget and Policy Priorities, November 15, 2022, http://www.cbpp.org/research/federal-tax/year-end-tax-policy-priority -expand-the-child-tax-credit-for-the-19-million.

39 "The Child Tax Credit," The White House, www.whitehouse.gov/child -tax-credit/.

40 Claire Zippel, "9 in 10 Families with Low Incomes Are Using Child Tax Credits to Pay for Necessities, Education," Center on Budget and Policy Priorities, October 21, 2021, https://cbpp.org/blog/9-in-10-families-with -low-incomes-are-using-child-tax-credits-to-pay-for-necessities-education.

41 "The Callahan Legacy: Callahan v. Carey and the Legal Right to Shelter," Coalition for the Homeless, www.coalitionforthehomeless .org/our-programs/advocacy/legal-victories/the-callahan-legacy-callahan -v-carey-and-the-legal-right-to-shelter/.

42 Bridget Read, "'It Was Imperfect by Definition,'" Curbed New York, September 27, 2022, www.curbed.com/2022/09/right-to-shelter-interview -robert-hayes.html.

43 "Universal Declaration of Human Rights," United Nations, December 10, 1948.

44 "State of the Union Message to Congress: January 11, 1944," Franklin D. Roosevelt Presidential Library and Museum, http://www.fdrlibrary .marist.edu/archives/address_text.html.

45 Eric Tars, "Housing as a Human Right," National Homelessness Law Center, January 6, 2021, https://nlihc.org/sites/default/files/AG -2021/01-06_Housing-Human-Right.pdf.

46 "Model Emergency Housing Legislation," Open Society Foundations, December 8, 2020, www.justiceinitiative.org/publications/model -emergency-housing-legislation-protecting-the-right-to-housing-during -covid-19.

47 "Supreme Court Lets Martin v. Boise Stand: Homeless Persons Cannot Be Punished for Sleeping in Absence of Alternatives," National Homeless Law Center, December 16, 2019, https://homelesslaw .org/supreme-court-martin-v-boise/.

48 Ben Adam Climer and Brenton Gicker, "CAHOOTS: A Model for Prehospital Mental Health Crisis Intervention," *Psychiatric Times* 38, no. 1 (2021), www.psychiatrictimes.com/view/cahoots -model-prehospital-mental-health-crisis-intervention.

49 "Why Do Landlords Reject Vouchers, and What Can Be Done?," Affordable Housing Online News, July 15, 2019, https://affordable housingonline.com/blog/landlords-reject-vouchers-can-done/.

50 "The Clean Slate Initiative," 2023, https://www.cleanslateinitiative.org /states.

51 "Three Years into Denver's Innovative Social Impact Bond Program, Independent Report Points to Continued Success," Denver Mayor's Office, November 12, 2019, www.denvergov.org/content /denvergov/en/mayors-office/newsroom/2019/three-years-into-denver -s-innovative-social-impact-bond-program-.html.

52 Since Don is based in Denver, several of the examples derive from his experience there. These are not necessarily "best practices," but they seem to him to have some merit.

53 For starters, we suggest *The Color of Law* by Richard Rothstein, *Evicted* by Matthew Desmond, *Race for Profit* by Keeanga-Yamahtta Taylor, and *The New Jim Crow* by Michelle Alexander.

54 Katznelson, *When Affirmative Action Was White*, 162–70.

55 Rothstein, *Color of Law*, 207.

56 Ta-Nehisi Coates, "The Case for Reparations," *Atlantic*, June 2014, www .theatlantic.com/magazine/archive/2014/06/the-case-for-reparations /361631/; Rothstein, *Color of Law*, 237–38.

57 Tobin and Murphy, "Demographics of Homelessness," 35.

58 Comment in the thread "Why Some Homeless People Choose to Shiver Instead of Shelter," Reddit, November 18, 2022, www.reddit.com/r /homeless/comments/yyuxcu/why_some_homeless_people_choose_to _shiver_instead/.

59 "How Is Poverty Measured in the US?," ATD Fourth World, 2019, https://atdfourthworld-usa.org/map-blog/2019/04/08/poverty-line -how-is-poverty-measured-in-the-u-s.

60 Consumer Expenditures 2021," US Bureau of Labor Statistics, September 8, 2022, www.bls.gov/news.release/cesan.nr0.htm.

61 Diana Pearce, "Inflation, High Costs, and Making Ends Meet," Center for Women's Welfare, University of Washington School of Social Work, https://selfsufficiencystandard.org/blog_articles/inflation-high-costs-and-making-ends-meet/.

62 Or as an unconditional gift through a basic income pilot; more on that below.

63 "New Leaf Project," Foundations for Social Change, https://forsocialchange.org/new-leaf-project-overview.

64 Rebecca Tauber, "City Council Approves $2 Million for the Denver Basic Income Project," Denverite, September 12, 2022, https://denverite.com/2022/09/12/city-council-approves-2-million-for-the-denver-basic-income-project/.

65 Sharon Chin, "JA: Nonprofit Donates Basic Income to 100 People Experiencing Homelessness," CBS News Bay Area, March 1, 2023, www.cbsnews.com/sanfrancisco/news/ja-nonprofit-donates-basic-income-to-100-people-experiencing-homelessness.

66 "What Is the Street Crisis Response Team?," City of San Francisco, https://sf.gov/street-crisis-response-team.

67 Or as Los Angeles Mayor Karen Bass said while campaigning in 2022: "We have to stop allowing individuals to essentially kill themselves on the street." Her comments were made in support of Governor Gavin Newsom's CARE Court plan, which allows a third party, such as a family member, to seek court-ordered intervention on behalf of an individual suffering from severe mental illness. See Conan Nolan, "LA Mayoral Candidates Bass, Caruso Back 'CARE Court' Plan," NBC Los Angeles, April 24, 2022, www.nbclosangeles.com/news/local/la-mayoral-candidates-bass-caruso-back-care-court-plan/2877457.

68 "Navigating the Involuntary Hold Process," County of Orange (California) Health Care Agency, www.ochealthinfo.com/sites/hca/files/import/data/files/39874.pdf.

69 Maya Kaufman, "Democratic Mayors Lead Course Correction on Psychiatric Commitments," Politico, March 1, 2023, www.politico.com/news/2023/03/01/democratic-mayors-lead-course-correction-on-psychiatric-commitments-00084387.

70 Katherine Drabiak MD, "The Ethical Dilemmas behind Plans for Involuntary Treatment to Target Homelessness, Mental Illness and Addiction," USF College of Public Health News, February 10, 2023, https://hscweb3.hsc.usf.edu/health/publichealth/news/the-ethical -dilemmas-behind-plans-for-involuntary-treatment-to-target -homelessness-mental-illness-and-addiction.

71 Christina Pazzanese, "N.Y. Plan to Involuntarily Treat Mentally Ill Homeless? Not Entirely Outrageous," *Harvard Gazette*, December 8, 2022, https://news.harvard.edu/gazette/story/2022/12/n-y-plan-to -involuntarily-treat-mentally-ill-homeless-not-entirely-outrageous.

72 Ken Kraybill and Suzanne Zerger, "Providing Treatment for Homeless People with Substance Use Disorders: Case Studies of Six Programs," National Health Care for the Homeless Council, 2003, i, https://nhchc .org/wp-content/uploads/2019/08/CA05RCaseStudies-FINAL5.pdf.

73 J. Steven Lamberti, "Preventing Criminal Recidivism through Mental Health—Criminal Justice Collaboration," *Psychiatric Services* 67, no. 11 (July 15, 2016): 1206–12, www.ncbi.nlm.nih.gov/pmc/articles /PMC7280932/.

74 De Jong, 21.

75 "Placer Selected for Whole Person Care Pilot Program to Help Most Vulnerable Residents," County of Placer (California), November 7, 2016, www.placer.ca.gov/1246/Whole-Person-Care-pilot-program.

76 "Criminal Justice DrugFacts," National Institute of Drug Addiction.

77 "Drunk Driving Fatality Statistics," Responsibility.org, www .responsibility.org/alcohol-statistics/drunk-driving-statistics/drunk -driving-fatality-statistics/.

78 Ironically, at some basic level, homeless advocates, retail business owners, law enforcement, and local residents all want the same thing, albeit for different reasons: fewer unsheltered people on the streets. It is unfortunate then that the various sides of the "homeless sweeps" debate often end up in opposing factions rather than putting their differences aside to work together toward a shared goal, which we would argue is not achieved for anyone by police enforcement of encampment sweeps.

79 Herbert Ouche, "Decriminalization of Homelessness: The Impact of Martin v. City of Boise on the Relationship between the Police and People Experiencing Homelessness in Portland, Oregon," PhD diss.,

Northeastern University, 2022, https://repository.library.northeastern
.edu/files/neu:4f18k925w.

80 Tony Messenger, *Profit and Punishment: How America Criminalizes
the Poor in the Name of Justice* (New York: St. Martin's, 2021).

81 "Extension of Foster Care Beyond Age 18," Child Welfare Information
Gateway, www.childwelfare.gov/pubpdfs/extensionfc.pdf.

82 Katie K. Lockwood, Susan Friedman, and Cindy W. Christian, "Permanency and the Foster Care System," *Current Problems in Pediat-
ric and Adolescent Health Care* 45, no. 10 (October 2015), https://
doi.org/10.1016/j.cppeds.2015.08.005; "Aging Out of Foster Care,"
ThruProject, www.thruproject.org/words-from-a-mentor/.

83 "Helping Youth Transition to Adulthood: Guidance for Foster Parents," Child Welfare Information Gateway, 2018, www.childwelfare
.gov/pubPDFs/youth_transition.pdf.

84 "Child Welfare and Foster Care Statistics," Annie E. Casey Foundation, May 16, 2022, www.aecf.org/blog/child-welfare-and-foster
-care-statistics.

85 Interview with Kristin Myers.

86 "Building Partnerships to Support Stable Housing for Child Welfare-
Involved Families and Youth," Children's Bureau at the US Department
of Health and Human Services, November 2018, www.childwelfare
.gov/pubPDFs/bulletins_housing.pdf.

87 Don was on a review panel for proposals for McKinney-Vento funding at the Colorado Department of Education in 2019. Due to severe
budget constraints, only about a third of the proposals were funded.

Chapter 13: Healing Our Humanity

1 Of course, there are major differences between chronic homelessness
caused by a mix of broken systems, relational brokenness, and bad luck,
and episodic homelessness caused by fires, earthquakes, floods, and other
disasters. The latter can lead to the former, however, and we believe that
the variation in how people conjure their humanity (or not) in one situation compared to the other is incredibly instructive and worth considering.

2 "1906 Earthquake: Refugee Camps," National Park Service, February 28, 2015, https://home.nps.gov/prsf/learn/historyculture/1906
-earthquake-relief-efforts-living-accommodations.htm.

3 For example, in the immediate aftermath of Hurricane Katrina in
   2005, many people were left to die in some of the poorest parishes of
   New Orleans, which are overwhelmingly Black. In the US territory of
   Puerto Rico, the slow response to help in the aftermath of Hurricane
   Maria in 2017 resulted in the longest electricity blackout in US history,
   and it has led to thousands of deaths since, due to the persistent lack
   of permanent shelter and power. Although there is a marked difference
   between the response of the government and the general public, we are
   more than capable of looking away in others' hour of need. In general,
   disasters tend to unearth what was already fragile or broken in society,
   revealing who is most vulnerable and which systems are failing.

4 C. E. Fritz, "Disaster," in *Contemporary Social Problems*, ed. R. K.
   Merton, and R. A. Nisbet (New York: Harcourt, Brace and World,
   1961), 651–94.

5 Kevin F. Adler, *Natural Disasters as a Catalyst for Social Capital: A
   Study of the 500-Year Flood in Cedar Rapids, Iowa* (Lanham, MD:
   University Press of America, 2015), 64.

6 Krys Kaniasty and Fran Norris, "In Search of Altruistic Community:
   Patterns of Social Support Mobilization Following Hurricane Hugo,"
   American Journal of Community Psychology, 23, no. 4 (1995): 447–
   77, https://doi.org/10.1007/bf02506964.

7 Technically, the term *natural disaster* is a misnomer. Disasters occur at
   the confluence of natural hazards *and* human vulnerabilities—not all
   naturally occurring forces are inherently disastrous in their effect on
   humans. And with anthropogenic (or human caused) global warming
   leading to much greater frequency and severity of naturally occurring
   forces in the first place, the difference between "natural" and "unnatural" disasters should be considered less of a clear binary, and more of a
   blurred spectrum.

8 "Embarcadero SAFE Navigation Center," San Francisco Department
   of Homelessness and Supportive Housing, Community Meeting, April
   3, 2019, slide 13, www.rinconhillsf.org/wp-content/uploads/2019/04
   /SWL330-Community-presentation-4.3.19-FINAL.pdf.

9 In the past, Homeward Bound–type programs routinely bussed people
   out of state with little to no regard for whether they actually had
   somewhere safe to stay at their destination, a cruel and unproduc-
   tive practice that critics rightly described as "Greyhound Therapy."
   But today, with diligent case workers and more proper oversight
   in place, these city-run programs tend to play an important role in

ending homelessness for a segment of people. See "Bussed Out: How America Moves Its Homeless," *Guardian*, December 20, 2017, www.theguardian.com/us-news/ng-interactive/2017/dec/20/bussed-out-america-moves-homeless-people-country-study.

10 Other effective reunification programs include West Coast Care in Los Angeles (www.westcoastcare.org) and Problem Solving Interventions by the Department of Homelessness and Supportive Housing in San Francisco (https://hsh.sfgov.org/services/the-homelessness-response-system/problem-solving/problem-solving-interventions). These and other reunion programs play a critical role for individuals experiencing homelessness in their direct service areas. Miracle Messages, in addition to being the nonprofit that Kevin founded, is available nationwide.

11 As just two examples in San Francisco: The Healing WELL offers classes in mindfulness, poetry, yoga, self-defense, and more for people experiencing homelessness in the Tenderloin neighborhood (www.healingwellsf.org), while A Meal with Dignity assembles fresh and nutritious bagged lunches to distribute to unhoused neighbors—and offers a toolkit teaching others how to do the same (www.amealwithdignity.org).

12 This quote is frequently attributed to Lilla Watson, who was part of an Aboriginal activist group that used the statement, but Watson is not comfortable being credited with it. See Mz. Many Names, "Attributing Words," November 3, 2008, http://unnecessaryevils.blogspot.com/2008/11/attributing-words.html.

13 "Miracle Friends: Jaime and AJ," YouTube, December 5, 2022, https://youtu.be/YAWfBBmiP3E.

14 "Self-Care for Activists," Augsburg University, www.augsburg.edu/cwc/self-help/self-care-for-activists/.

15 Israa Nasir, "Balancing Self-Care and Social Activism," www.israanasir.com/articles/activism-selfcare.

16 See John Leland, "How Loneliness Is Damaging Our Health," *New York Times*, April 20, 2022, www.nytimes.com/2022/04/20/nyregion/loneliness-epidemic.html; U.S. Department of Health and Human Services, "New Surgeon General Advisory Raises Alarm about the Devastating Impact of the Epidemic of Loneliness and Isolation in the United States," May 3, 2023, https://www.hhs.gov/about/news/2023/05/03/new-surgeon-general-advisory-raises-alarm-about-devastating-impact-epidemic-loneliness-isolation-united-states.html.

17 Richard Weissbourd, Milena Batanova, Virginia Lovison, and Eric Torres, "Loneliness in America: How the Pandemic Has Deepened an Epidemic of Loneliness and What We Can Do about It," Harvard Graduate School of Education, February 2021, https://mcc .gse.harvard.edu/reports/loneliness-in-america.

18 Debra Umberson and Jennifer Karaz Montez, "Social Relationships and Health: A Flashpoint for Health Policy," *Journal of Health and Social Behavior* 51, no. S1 (2010): 57, https://doi.org /10.1177/0022146510383501.

19 Saul McLeod, "Maslow's Hierarchy of Needs," Simply Psychology, April 4, 2022, www.simplypsychology.org/maslow.html.

20 Alexander, *New Jim Crow*, 290.

21 Oliver, "Transgender Rights II"; Steve Hartman, "A Look at CBS News' 1967 Documentary: The Homosexuals," CBS News, June 26, 2015, www.cbsnews.com/news/how-far-weve-come-since-the-1967 -homosexuals-documentary/.

22 Ellen Bassuk, "Child Homelessness: A Growing Crisis," US Department of Health and Human Services, Substance Abuse and Mental Health Services Administration (SAMHSA), www.samhsa.gov/homelessness-programs -resources/hpr-resources/child-homelessness-growing-crisis.

23 "Who We Are," LavaMae[x], https://lavamaex.org/who-we-are.

24 Duerson, "Homeless Man Gets $175K"

25 For example: In Scottsdale, Arizona, "It's OK to say no. Give instead to agencies that help those in need"; in Fort Lauderdale, Florida, a big red "X" over clipart of a hand holding a cup with change dropping into it, followed by the warning "Don't contribute to the problem. Contribute to the solution instead," followed by a link to the city website; or a nearly identical sign in Fitchburg and Leominster, Massachusetts, but with the clipart replaced by an actual photo of a person panhandling.

26 Knight, "Panhandlers Tell Their Own Stories."

27 Dan Moskovitz, "Save One Life, Save the Entire World (Including Yourself)," Religious Action Center of Reform Judaism, May 24, 2019, https://rac.org/blog/save-one-life-save-entire-world-including -yourself.

28 "Foster Youth and Homelessness: What Are the Risk Factors?," National Alliance to End Homelessness, March 17, 2015, https://endhomelessness .org/blog/foster-kids-and-homelessness-what-are-the-risk-factors/.

29 "Foster Youth and Homelessness," National Alliance.

30 Andrew Khouri, "High Cost of Housing Drives up Homeless Rates, UCLA Study Indicates," *Los Angeles Times*, June 13, 2018, www .latimes.com/business/la-fi-ucla-anderson-forecast-20180613-story.html.

31 Tobin and Murphy, "New Demographics of Homelessness," 35.

32 Smiljanic Stasha, "The State of Homelessness in the US—2022," Policy Advice, September 29, 2022, https://policyadvice.net/insurance/insights /homelessness-statistics/.

33 de Sousa et al., "2022 Annual Homeless Assessment Report."

34 This aphorism is from the 19th century philosopher Friedrich Nietzsche, who glorified the idea of an *Übermensch*, or super-human, who achieves greatness and overcomes the need for God by transcending their feeble humanity.

Index

Community Solutions, 176
compassion fatigue, 74
confirmation bias, 37, 224
connection
    addiction and, 141
    degrees of separation and, 52
    on genetic level, 52
    necessity of, for survival, 24–27
    power of, 11–14, 221–222
Cordell, Gabby, 227
COVID-19 pandemic, 11–12, 24,
    101, 121, 182, 221
Craig, Daniel, 4
Crouse, Joan M., 79
Culhane, Dennis, 99

D

Dear, Michael, 11
degrees of separation, 52
dehumanization, 51, 72, 200
deinstitutionalization, 133, 142
De Jong, Iain, 65, 199
Denver Day Works, 190, 191
Denver Social Impact Bond
    project, 184
Desmond, Matthew, 26, 113,
    177–178
DignityMoves, 176
Dones, Marc, 29
Downtown Streets Team,
    190–191, 221
Drabiak, Katherine, 197
drug addiction, 37, 131, 137–141,
    197–200

E

Economic Policy Institute, 108
Edin, Kathryn, 108
emergency department (ED) visits,
    122–124, 128, 134
Empowerment Plan, 191
evictions, 180
exclusion, 49–59, 225–226

F

Facebook, 52
Fair Chance ordinances, 183–184
Fair Housing Act of 1968, 91, 95
Farha, Leilani, 167–168
Federal Poverty Level, formulation
    of, 191–192
Felix, Robert, 133
Fillit, Howard M., 64
Fiske, Susan, 50
foster care, 157–159, 162–163,
    203–205, 207, 231
Foster Care Independence Act of
    1999, 204
Fostering Hope, 204
Foundations for Social Change, 68
Freebeck, Meghan, 227
Fritz, Charles E., 213

G

Girard, René, 51
Goffman, Erving, 36
Goodness Village, 175–176
Gordon, Daanika, 150
Grammer, Kelsey, 4

H

HandUp, 220
Happy Feet Clinic, 227
Hari, Johann, 141
Harris, Billy Ray, 66–67, 84
Harris, Lasana, 50
Harris, Robin, 66
Harvey, Steve, 4
Hayes, Robert, 182
The Healing WELL, 221
health care, 119–128, 195–196, 206.
    See also mental illness; substance
    abuse
Health Insurance Portability and
    Accountability Act (HIPAA), 29
Herring, Chris, 9–10, 54

About the Authors

Kevin F. Adler is an award-winning social entrepreneur, nonprofit leader, and author. Since 2014, he has served as the founder and CEO of Miracle Messages, a nonprofit organization dedicated to helping people experiencing homelessness rebuild their social support systems and financial security, primarily through family reunification services, a phone buddy program, and direct cash transfers, including one of the first basic income pilots for unhoused individuals in the United States. Kevin's pioneering work on homelessness and relational poverty has been featured in the *New York Times*, *Washington Post*, *PBS NewsHour*, and in his TED Talk.

Kevin is also the author of *Natural Disasters as a Catalyst for Social Capital*, a book that explores how shared traumas can unite or divide communities. He has been honored as a Presidential Leadership Scholar, TED Resident, and Rotary Ambassadorial Scholar, for which he served one year in Oaxaca, Mexico. He received his MPhil in sociology from the University of Cambridge and his BA in politics from Occidental College. Kevin lives in the Bay Area with his wife, Tajáh. Motivated by his late mother's work teaching at underserved adult schools and nursing homes, and his late uncle's 30 years living on and off the streets,

Kevin believes in a future where everyone is recognized as invaluable and interconnected.

Learn more at kevinfadler.com or follow him @kevinfadler.

* * *

PHOTO CREDIT: LYNN K. BURNES

Don Burnes and his wife, Lynn, are the cofounders of the Burnes Institute for Poverty Research at the Colorado Center on Law and Policy, where he also served as a member of their board of directors, as a senior adviser to the Institute and to the Center. Previously, Don helped create the Burnes Center on Poverty and Homelessness at the University of Denver Graduate School of Social Work, where he also served as an adjunct faculty member and a scholar-in-residence. A local philanthropist concerned with the issues of homelessness and housing, he served on the State Interagency Advisory Group on Homelessness for Governor John Hickenlooper and served in a similar position for Governor Bill Ritter. He has been a member of Denver's Road Home Advisory Commission and the Colorado Housing and Homelessness Funders Collaborative.

Don has also been an executive director for various nonprofits, a historian, a researcher and educational policy consultant for the US Congress, a prolific writer, a philanthropic consultant, and active student of and policy analyst around issues of homelessness and poverty for over 35 years. He is the coauthor with Alice Baum of *A Nation in Denial: The Truth about Homelessness*, and is the coeditor of and a contributing author to *Ending Homelessness: Why We Haven't, How We Can*. His third book, *Journeys out of Homelessness: The Voices of Lived Experience*, was published in October 2019. In addition, Don has written numerous articles about homelessness and has made a variety of presentations, including a TEDx Talk, about the topic. He received his BA from Princeton, his MAT from Washington University in St. Louis, and his PhD in the politics of education from Columbia University.

* * *

Amanda Banh is a first-generation low-income woman of color who recently graduated with a BS in molecular biology from Princeton University. She is the proud daughter of Chinese-Vietnamese immigrants, whose history as the "hidden homeless"—couchsurfers and wage-laborers—in both their native land and in the US inspires her work. Her writing attempts to convey the complex nuances surrounding the issue of homelessness, which finds itself in the intersections of identity: of race, gender, language, and nationality. It is with these intimate stories of simultaneous hardship and resilience that she hopes to record the voices far too often left unheard and silenced by society.

* * *

Andrijana Bilbija graduated with a BS in psychology from Princeton University before beginning her role as program manager, now program consultant, at Housing and Neighborhood Development Services Inc. (HANDS), based in Orange, New Jersey. At HANDS, she designs and implements creative solutions to help uplift historically marginalized and underserved communities. As an immigrant from Bosnia and Herzegovina, she is driven to ensure all members of our collective American community are seen, valued, and served with dignity. In her spare time, Andrijana loves to cook, read, and write poetry.

About North Atlantic Books

North Atlantic Books (NAB) is an independent, nonprofit publisher committed to a bold exploration of the relationships between mind, body, spirit, and nature. Founded in 1974, NAB aims to nurture a holistic view of the arts, sciences, humanities, and healing. To make a donation or to learn more about our books, authors, events, and newsletter, please visit www.northatlanticbooks.com.